The New Dynamic Public Finance

Toulouse Lectures in Economics
Patrick Rey, Series Editor

Auctions: Theory and Practice,
Paul Klemperer

The New Dynamic Public Finance,
Narayana R. Kocherlakota

The series Toulouse Lectures in Economics is an annual joint project of Princeton University Press and the Institut d'Économie Industrielle of the University of Toulouse. The volumes are based on lectures presented over a week at the University of Toulouse by leading international researchers.

We invite scholars we admire and whom we want to hear discuss in depth their current research both during the lectures and through the week they will spend with us enjoying the Toulouse hospitality. Reflecting the broad range of interests of the Institute the lectures will call on microeconomists, macroeconomists, and econometricians both theoretical and applied. Behind this diversity the reader will find a constant intellectual rigor and attention to the real-world consequences of economic theories.

The IDEI is very grateful to the City of Toulouse and National Economic Research Associates, who kindly cover some of the local expenses incurred in the organization of the lectures for this series; neither of these institutions has any role in the selection of authors or themes for the series.

The New Dynamic Public Finance

Narayana R. Kocherlakota

Princeton University Press

Princeton and Oxford

Published by Princeton University Press,
41 William Street, Princeton, New Jersey 08540

In the United Kingdom: Princeton University Press,
6 Oxford Street, Woodstock, Oxfordshire OX20 1TW

Library of Congress Cataloging-in-Publication Data

Kocherlakota, Narayana Rao, 1963–
The new dynamic public finance / Narayana R. Kocherlakota.
  p. cm. – (Toulouse lectures in economics)
Includes bibliographical references and index.
ISBN 978-0-691-13915-9 (alk. paper)
1. Fiscal policy–Mathematical models.
2. Taxation–Mathematical models.
3. Finance, Public–Mathematical models. I. Title.
HJ192.5.K63 2010
336.001′5195–dc22   2009052297

British Library Cataloging-in-Publication Data is available

This book has been composed in LucidaBright using $\TeX$
Typeset and copyedited by T&T Productions Ltd, London

Printed on acid-free paper. ∞
press.princeton.edu

Printed in the United States of America

10 9 8 7 6 5 4 3 2 1

Contents

Preface

This book is based on the Sixth Toulouse Lectures in Economics that I gave at the Toulouse School of Economics on March 17-19, 2008. Being invited to give the lectures, and presenting them, were highlights of my professional career. I thank the faculty at the Toulouse School for their thoughtful comments and lavish hospitality.

The resulting book is designed to be used in an advanced Ph.D. course (second year or beyond) in either macroeconomics or public finance. For example, I covered the material in chapters 3-6 in a special nine-hour summer course at the University of Oslo in June 2008. (The students on the course were an outstanding group of European Ph.D. students and assistant professors. All had completed at least two years Ph.D. course work in macroeconomics and/or public finance.) For those who are so inclined, it would certainly be possible to teach chapters 3, 6, and 7 in one self-contained unit. These chapters have little if any treatment of taxes, and focus instead on properties of Pareto optimal allocations in dynamic settings with private information.

I owe thanks to a lot of people for their help. I have presented this material at many seminars and conferences over the years, and I thank the attendees for their comments and feedback. Some of the best young talent in our profession has worked on the new dynamic public finance during the course of this decade, and my own work owes a large debt to my interactions with them. In this vein, I've learned a great deal from Stefania Albanesi, Emmanuel Farhi, Marek Kapicka, Chris Sleet, Sevin Yeltekin, and Ivan Werning. I am especially indebted to my coauthors, Marco Bassetto, Mikhail Golosov, Borys Grochulski, and Aleh Tsyvinski. I have been talking to my colleague Chris Phelan about dynamic resource allocation and private information since we were in grad school together over twenty years ago. Those conversations have been fundamental to my understanding of the new dynamic public finance—and, indeed, to my understanding of all of economics.

Kenichi Fukushima, Futoshi Narita, Machiko Narita, Ctirad Slavik, and Hakki Yazici gave close readings of the contents and helped correct many lingering errors (although probably not all!). Two anonymous reviewers also gave useful comments. Richard Baggaley and Kimberley Johnson of Princeton University Press were very helpful during the entire process. Jon Wainwright of T&T Productions Ltd provided excellent copy editing.

Finally, my wife Barbara McCutcheon has provided emotional support and a continual flow of economic insight throughout the writing of this book. I dedicate it to her.

The New Dynamic Public Finance

1

Introduction

The goal of this book is to figure out at least some characteristics of the best possible tax system. This problem is a difficult one even to pose. The amount of tax that a typical citizen pays is a function of many economic variables. A far from exhaustive list includes labor earnings, interest income, dividend income, consumption, and money-holdings (via inflation). The dependence of collected taxes on these variables may be quite complicated. Moreover, taxes depend on asset incomes and asset holdings, and these represent the outcomes of decisions about how much wealth to transfer from one period to another. The problem of designing a good tax system that includes asset income taxes is intrinsically a *dynamic* one.

At the end of the 1990s, most of the research on optimal taxation in multiperiod settings was being done by macroeconomists (as opposed to specialists in public finance). Following an approach pioneered by Chamley (1986), the research made some rather strong assumptions: it restricted taxes to be linear and (generally) assumed all agents are identical. The resulting research program is extremely tractable. Unfortunately, it is also deeply flawed. Its key economic trade-off is that the government would like to make the taxes nonlinear but cannot. This basic tension is really irrelevant in the actual design of taxes, because governments *can* (and do) use nonlinear taxes.

In response to this conceptual problem, the *new dynamic public finance*[1] (NDPF) thinks about how to design optimal taxes using the fundamentally different approach pioneered by Mirrlees (1971). The NDPF explicitly allows taxes to be nonlinear and allows for heterogeneity among people in the economy. The heterogeneity comes from a rather natural source. People's labor earnings depend on their choices of labor inputs (how hard or how long to work). Increasing the size of this input causes them disutility, but generates more labor income. As Mirrlees (1971) originally did, the NDPF presumes that people differ in their *skills*, that is, in how much labor input they need to generate a given level of labor income. By way of extension to Mirrlees's baseline analysis, the NDPF allows for the possibility that these skills evolve over time stochastically (so that people may gain or lose skills over time in a surprising fashion).[2]

In the NDPF, the government commits itself *ex ante* to a tax schedule that maximizes a (possibly weighted) average of agents' utilities. The only restriction on this

----

[1] I believe that I can take full credit for the name "new dynamic public finance." In July 2004, I gave a plenary talk at a conference in Florence organized by the Society for Economic Dynamics. I knew that I wanted to choose a title for the talk that would generate attendance and also signal that I wanted to discuss an agenda broader than that suggested by my own individual papers. I chose the deliberately catchy "The new dynamic public finance." The title beautifully served its main, presentation-specific, purposes. I'm more surprised that it has continued to stick as a way to describe the literature—but it has. For example, Golosov et al. (2006) refer to the literature in exactly this way.

[2] In an early contribution, Eaton and Rosen (1980) discuss the structure of optimal linear taxes on earnings given this kind of skill risk.

schedule is that taxes can only depend on incomes, and not directly on people's skills. This restriction immediately translates into the main trade-off that the government faces when designing its optimal tax schedule. On the one hand, the benevolent government wants to provide insurance. People can turn out to be high skilled or low skilled at the beginning of their lives or over the course of their lives. The government would like to insure them against this skill risk. This force leads the government to favor high taxes on income. On the other hand, the government would like to motivate the high-skilled people to produce more income than the low-skilled people. This force leads the government to favor low taxes. The government's problem is to figure out how to resolve this tension in various dates and states.

I have made no explicit mention of private information in describing the NDPF. However, the government's inability to condition taxes directly on skills ends up implying that it has to treat agents as being privately informed about their productivities. It follows that the optimal tax problem in the NDPF is isomorphic to a dynamic contracting problem between a risk-neutral principal and a risk-averse agent who is privately informed about productivities. There is a large literature on such dynamic principal–agent problems (including work by Rogerson (1985), Spear and Srivastava (1987), Green (1987), and Atkeson and Lucas (1995)), and the NDPF exploits its technical insights in many ways.

In the remainder of this introduction, I discuss the scope of the book. I lay out four main lessons of the new dynamic public finance. Finally, I describe the structure of the book.

1.1 Scope

This book is *normative*. It is interesting and important
to figure out why we have the taxes that we have, but
this book does not seek to answer that question. Instead, it tries to figure out what taxes we *should* have.
It follows that the actual specification of taxes is irrelevant for the purposes of this book, except to in-
dicate the range of taxation possibilities available to
the government. Here's an analogy that might be helpful. The existence of agricultural subsidies and tar-
iffs means that the government has the ability to levy
these taxes. But the existence of these taxes does *not*
mean that economists are wrong to recommend their
elimination. In the same vein, if taxes recommended
by the NDPF differ from the taxes that are actually
used, there is no logical reason to conclude that there
is something wrong with the NDPF.

This argument does not imply that normative economics in general or the NDPF in particular is disconnected from reality. The ultimate goal of the NDPF is to
provide relatively precise recommendations as to what
taxes should be. These recommendations will depend
on a host of model parameters, and we will need to
use data to obtain these parameters. As yet, the NDPF
has not made much progress in obtaining good measures of the necessary inputs. This book reflects this
weakness, but in chapter 7 I provide some ideas about
how more progress can be made.

The normative focus means that I am not going to
discuss two recent and related literatures. One such
literature is on time-consistency. (More technically,
it focuses on the structure of sequential equilibrium
taxes when governments choose those taxes period-
ically.) The other literature is on dynamic political

economy. (It focuses on the structure of sequential equilibrium outcomes when taxes are determined by periodic voting.) These literatures examine the properties of equilibrium outcomes of particular dynamic games. Hence, they are trying to model the *actual* behavior of governments. They are not normative in nature and so lie outside the scope of this book.

1.2 Lessons

As the remainder of this book shows, we have learned a great deal in a short time from the NDPF. However, I think that there are four particularly important lessons that are worth emphasizing. The first three require preferences to exhibit separability between consumption and leisure. The last does not.

1.2.1 Lesson 1: Optimality of Asset Income Taxes

The first lesson concerns the design of optimal asset income taxes.[3] It is valid regardless of the data-generation process for skills. Consider a risk-averse person at date t who faces skill risk at date $(t + 1)$. Under an optimal tax system, the person's shadow interest rate from period t to period $(t + 1)$ must be less

---

[3] What does "optimal" mean? Throughout this book, the weights in the government's objective are restricted to be independent of agents' skill realizations. Technically, this restriction means that we are focusing on properties of *ex ante* Pareto optimal tax systems, in which the government's redistributional motives are based on attributes other than skills themselves.

However, the four lessons described in this section are also valid if the weights are allowed to depend on agents' skills at birth (but not on future skill realizations). Technically, we can say that the results also characterize interim Pareto optimal tax systems, in which the government may redistribute based on agents' initial skills.

than the market interest rate. This result immediately implies that an optimal tax system must confront such a person with a nonzero asset income tax that deters him from saving.

Intuitively, when preferences are separable between consumption and leisure, leisure is a normal good. Normality of leisure means that agents with a large amount of accumulated wealth in period $(t + 1)$ are harder to motivate in that period. Hence, on the margin, good tax systems deter wealth accumulation from period t to period $(t + 1)$ to provide people with better incentives to work in the latter period.

This result was originally derived by Diamond and Mirrlees (1978) in the context of a model of endogenous retirement. However, Diamond and Mirrlees restricted attention to a specific data-generation process for skills (a two-point Markov chain with an absorbing state). The contribution of the NDPF (and specifically of Golosov et al. (2003)) is to show that Diamond and Mirrlees's finding applies to *all* data-generation processes for skills, and can in fact be extended to models in which skills are endogenous.[4]

1.2.2   Lesson 2: An Optimal Asset Income Tax System

The first lesson implies that any optimal tax system features nonzero asset income taxes. The second lesson is about the structure of these nonzero asset income taxes, and is best divided into two parts. The first part is that in many settings, the optimal tax on a person's asset income in period $(t + 1)$ must be a nontrivial function of his labor income in period $(t + 1)$.

---

[4] The proof of the result is based on the elegant approach taken by Rogerson (1985) in a two-period context.

People's decisions about asset holdings in period t depend on their labor input plans in period $(t + 1)$, and optimal asset income taxes must take this intertemporal connection into account. (This conclusion was originally reached in work by Albanesi and Sleet (2006) and Golosov and Tsyvinski (2006).)

The second part of this lesson is that there is an optimal tax system in which taxes are linear functions of asset income in every period. In this system, given the information available at period t, period $(t + 1)$ asset income taxes are negative for people with surprisingly high labor income in period $(t + 1)$ and positive for people with surprisingly low labor income. The cross-sectional average asset income tax rate, and total asset income tax revenue, is always zero regardless of the aggregate state of the world. Thus, the tax system deters investment not through the level of asset income taxes, but through the positive covariance of these taxes with skill realizations. (This conclusion was originally reached in work by Kocherlakota (2005).)

1.2.3 Lesson 3: Optimal Bequest Taxes and Intergenerational Transmission

Some of the most exciting work in the NDPF concerns the optimal taxation of bequests (see, in particular, Phelan 2006; Farhi and Werning 2007). There are two main results. The first has nothing to do with incentives: even if parents are altruistic, in most Pareto optimal tax systems, optimal bequest taxes are negative. The intuition is simple. In any Pareto optimum in which society puts positive weight on all people, society cares about a child in two ways: through its ancestors and directly as a person. It follows that society always puts more weight on a given child than its ancestors do, and so society wants to subsidize parent–child transfers.

The second result is a characterization of a particular optimal bequest tax system and *is* connected to incentives and insurance. If parents are altruistic, it is optimal for a persons's after-tax outcomes to depend on his/her parents' labor earnings. This dependence is a good way to motivate parents to work hard. On the other hand, society does want to insure children somewhat against their parents' outcomes. As a result, it is optimal to subsidize bequests at a higher rate for poor parents than for rich parents.

1.2.4 Lesson 4: Individual Ricardian Equivalence and Social Security

In the NDPF, a person's labor income taxes at a given date are allowed to be a function of one's full history of labor earnings. This kind of generality mimics the flexibility that governments actually enjoy. For example, in the United States, social security transfers are a function of the full history of one's labor earnings.

The fourth lesson is that, with this degree of flexibility, optimality considerations only pin down the present value of labor income taxes as a function of a person's labor earnings. Thus, if a person owes $10,000 in taxes at age 25, the government could collect half of that at age 60 (with appropriate interest charges) without affecting individual decisions at all. This indeterminacy is essentially an individual-level version of Ricardian equivalence. (See Bassetto and Kocherlakota (2004) for a discussion.)

The government can exploit this indeterminacy to simplify the structure of labor income taxes. In particular, there is an optimal tax system in which the government imposes a flat tax on labor earnings while people are working, and then bases post-retirement social security transfers on the full history of labor earnings. Intuitively, all that matters for incentives and insurance is the dependence of the *present value* of labor income taxes on the history of labor incomes. Any required dependence can be fully encoded into the structure of post-retirement transfers, as long as agents can borrow against these transfers. (This argument is explained more fully in Grochulski and Kocherlakota (2008).)

1.3 Structure

The remainder of the book is divided into six chapters. The second chapter of the book concerns the Ramsey (that is, linear tax) approach to dynamic optimal taxation. The chapter derives the classic Chamley (1986) result concerning long-run capital income taxes. The chapter also contains a discussion of the limitations of the Ramsey approach and motivates the alternative Mirrleesian approach that informs the rest of the book.

As discussed above, the NDPF is closely linked to the problem of optimal resource allocation in dynamic economies with private information. Chapter 3 provides an analysis of such problems, including a discussion of the "reciprocal" Euler equation and the long-run properties of optimal allocations. Relative to other treatments, its novelty is that it allows for general specifications of data-generation processes for individual skills. This generality rules out the recursive approaches used by, among others, Atkeson and Lucas (1992). Instead, I employ classical perturbation methods similar to Rogerson (1985). These methods are both more general and (I believe) more intuitive.

In chapter 4, I develop the implications of the NDPF for macroeconomists. I set up a canonical optimal nonlinear taxation problem in a dynamic economy with heterogeneous agents. I show how, in terms of quantities, the solution to this problem is the same as the solution to the private information allocation problem in chapter 3. I use this connection to derive general properties of optimal taxes, and discuss the properties of a particular optimal tax system.

Chapter 5 extends the analysis to bequest taxes. Mathematically, the chapter is similar to the previous one. However, the results differ in important ways, because the societal objective puts more weight on descendants than parents do. This difference affects both the sign of bequest taxes and their dependence on the income levels of parents.

The analysis in these chapters 2–5 is entirely qualitative.[5] In chapter 6, I set forth recursive methods that in principle allow one to find approximate solutions to the basic nonlinear taxation problem when skills follow a Markov chain. This literature is an old one (dating back at least twenty years), but progress has been slow: much remains to be done. I then solve for optimal taxes in a simple numerical example. The example is purely illustrative, but it is nonetheless suggestive.

In chapter 7, I discuss possible paths for future research. This chapter is probably the most important but it is also necessarily the most speculative.

I should add a final warning about notation. In terms of their economic lessons, the various chapters are certainly cumulative. However, the chapters use rather distinct models to derive these lessons. For

---

[5] The material in chapters 3–5 extends and builds upon my survey of similar material in Kocherlakota (2006).

this reason, I have made no attempt to ensure that the notation is consistent *across* chapters, although it is consistent *within* chapters.

References

Albanesi, S., and C. Sleet. 2006. Dynamic optimal taxation with private information. *Review of Economic Studies* 73:1–30.

Atkeson, A., and R. E. Lucas, Jr. 1992. On efficient distribution with private information. *Review of Economic Studies* 59:427–53.

———. 1995. Efficiency and equality in a simple model of efficient unemployment insurance. *Journal of Economic Theory* 66:64–88.

Bassetto, M., and N. Kocherlakota. 2004. On the irrelevance of government debt when taxes are distortionary. *Journal of Monetary Economics* 51:299–304.

Chamley, C. 1986. Optimal taxation of capital income in general equilibrium with infinite lives. *Econometrica* 54:607–22.

Diamond, P., and J. A. Mirrlees. 1978. A model of social insurance with variable retirement. *Journal of Public Economics* 10:295–336.

Eaton, J., and H. Rosen. 1980. Taxation, human capital, and uncertainty. *American Economic Review* 70:705–15.

Farhi, E., and I. Werning. 2007. Inequality and social discounting. *Journal of Political Economy* 115:365–402.

Golosov, M., and A. Tsyvinski. 2006. Designing optimal disability insurance: a case for asset testing. *Journal of Political Economy* 114:257–79.

Golosov, M., N. Kocherlakota, and A. Tsyvinski. 2003. Optimal indirect and capital taxation. *Review of Economic Studies* 70:569–87.

Golosov, M., A. Tsyvinski, and I. Werning. 2006. New dynamic public finance: a user's guide. In *NBER Macroeconomics Annual 2006*, Volume 21 (ed. D. Acemoglu, K. Rogoff, and M. Woodford).

Green, E. 1987. Lending and the smoothing of uninsurable income. In *Contractual Arrangements for Intertemporal Trade* (ed. E. C. Prescott and N. Wallace). University of Minnesota Press.

Grochulski, B., and N. Kocherlakota. 2008. Nonseparable preferences and optimal social security systems. Working Paper, University of Minnesota.

Kocherlakota, N. 2005. Zero expected wealth taxes: a Mirrlees approach to dynamic optimal taxation. *Econometrica* 73:1587–621.

——. 2006. Advances in dynamic optimal taxation. In *Advances in Economics and Econometrics: Theory and Applications, Ninth World Congress*, Volume I (ed. R. Blundell, W. K. Newey, and T. Persson). Cambridge University Press.

Mirrlees, J. 1971. An exploration in the theory of optimum income taxation. *Review of Economic Studies* 38:175–208.

Rogerson, W. 1985. Repeated moral hazard. *Econometrica* 53:69–76.

Spear, S., and S. Srivastava. 1987. On repeated moral hazard with discounting. *Review of Economic Studies* 54: 599–617.

2
The Ramsey Approach and Its Problems

The Ramsey approach was the dominant approach to dynamic optimal taxation (and, indeed, for discussions of much of macroeconomic policy) in the late twentieth century. The approach begins with the premise that taxes are distorting. It captures this distortion in the simplest possible fashion by assuming that all taxes are linear functions of current variables. It then chooses those tax rates to optimize social welfare (measured in some fashion). As we shall see, the Ramsey approach is remarkably tractable, which is one of its main attractions.

In this chapter, I show how the Ramsey approach can be used to answer a fundamental question: how should a government time *capital income taxes* so as to minimize their distortionary impact? The analysis hews closely to that presented in Chamley (1986) and surveyed by Chari and Kehoe (1999). I then discuss a major weakness of the Ramsey approach, and sketch the alternative method that we will pursue in this book.

2.1   A Simple Model of Government Finance

Consider a model economy with an infinite number of periods, and a large number (a unit measure) of identical agents. The agents all have preferences of the form

$$\sum_{t=1}^{\infty} \beta^{t-1}[u(c_t) - v(l_t)], \quad 0 < \beta < 1,$$

where c_t is consumption at date t and l_t is labor at date t. I assume that u', $-u''$, v', and v'' exist and are positive. I also assume that $\lim_{c \to 0} u'(c) = \infty$ and $\lim_{l \to 0} v'(l) = 0$.

All agents are initially endowed with K_1 units of capital. Capital goods depreciate at rate δ. The agents have a technology that converts period t consumption goods one-for-one into period $(t + 1)$ capital goods, and vice versa. There are a large number of competitive firms with production functions that convert k units of capital and l units of labor into y units of consumption goods:

$$y = F(k, l),$$

where the function F is homogeneous of degree 1 and concave. I assume that $F_k, F_l > 0$, and

$$\lim_{k \to 0} F_k(k, l^*) = \lim_{l \to 0} F_l(k^*, l) = \infty \quad \text{for all } (k^*, l^*).$$

There is a government that can convert private consumption goods one-for-one into public goods. The government is required to create G_t units of public goods in period t. Note that G_t may be a nontrivial function of t.

The government needs to raise funds to generate its public goods. It does so in three possible ways: borrowing and lending, levying linear taxes on labor income, and levying linear taxes on capital income. Let τ_{lt} represent the period t tax rate on labor income and τ_{kt} represent the period t tax rate on capital income.

Define w_t to be the relative price of period t labor in terms of period t consumption, and r_t to be the relative price of period t capital usage in terms of period t consumption. Let q_t be the price of period t consumption in terms of a numeraire (this is basically the price of a t period zero-coupon bond). Then, given (τ_k, τ_l), we can define an equilibrium to be a specification of quantities (c^*, k^*, l^*) and prices (w, r, q) such that agents optimize:

$$(c^*, k^*, l^*) \in \arg \max_{(c,k,l)} \sum_{t=1}^{\infty} \beta^{t-1} \{u(c_t) - v(l_t)\} \quad (2.1)$$

$$\text{s.t.} \ \sum_{t=1}^{\infty} q_t [c_t + k_{t+1}]$$

$$\leqslant \sum_{t=1}^{\infty} q_t \{w_t l_t (1 - \tau_{lt})$$
$$+ r_t k_t (1 - \tau_{kt}) + (1 - \delta) k_t\},$$

$$c_t, l_t, k_t \geqslant 0 \quad \text{for all } t,$$

$$k_1 \leqslant K_1;$$

firms optimize:

$$\text{for all } t, (k_t^*, l_t^*) \in \arg \max_{k,l} F(k, l) - r_t k - w_t l; \quad (2.2)$$

and markets clear for all t:

$$c_t + k_{t+1} + G_t = F(k_t, l_t) + (1 - \delta) k_t. \quad (2.3)$$

(Note that depreciation is not tax-deductible, but the main results do not depend on this assumption.)

We do not explicitly impose a government budget constraint in equilibrium. However, it is straightforward to prove that, by Walras's law, any equilibrium allocation satisfies an intertemporal government budget constraint of the form:

$$\sum_{t=1}^{\infty} \{\tau_{lt} w_t l_t q_t + \tau_{kt} r_t k_t q_t\} = \sum_{t=1}^{\infty} q_t G_t. \qquad (2.4)$$

The government budget constraint (2.4) is not satisfied, and there is no equilibrium, for most specifications of (G, τ). For example, if the tax rates $(\tau_{kt}, \tau_{lt})_{t=1}^{T}$ equal zero at all dates, then there is no equilibrium for any positive specification of G.

2.2 The Dynamic Ramsey Taxation Problem: Setup

The government's goal in this economy is to choose tax rate sequences (τ_k, τ_l) so as to minimize the distortions associated with taxation. We assume that the government is able to commit to this choice at the beginning of period 1. This problem of choosing linear tax rates to raise sufficient revenue to fund a given level of expenditures is often called a *Ramsey taxation* problem.

Formally, we define $E(\tau_k, \tau_l)$ to be the set of equilibrium allocations, given tax rates (τ_k, τ_l). Then, we can formulate the government's problem as

$$\max_{(c,k,l,\tau_k,\tau_l)} \sum_{t=1}^{\infty} \beta^{t-1} \{u(c_t) - v(l_t)\}$$
$$\text{s.t. } (c, k, l) \in E(\tau_k, \tau_l). \quad (2.5)$$

This simple problem does implicitly make one nontrivial assumption. It assumes that if there are multiple equilibria given (τ_k, τ_l), then the government can choose which of these equilibria actually occurs. In this nonmonetary representative agent economy, this assumption typically is not problematic (because $E(\tau_k, \tau_l)$ is generally a singleton or empty).

This formulation of the government's problem is elegant but not useful. The following proposition allows us to convert the single abstract constraint into a system of usable equality constraints.

Proposition 2.1. *A strictly positive allocation* (c, k, l) *lies in* $E(\tau_k, \tau_l)$ *for some tax sequence* (τ_k, τ_l) *in which* $\tau_{k1} = \tau_{k1}^*$ *if and only if*

$$k_1 = K_1, \tag{2.6}$$

$$c_t + k_{t+1} + G_t = F(k_t, l_t) + (1 - \delta)k_t \quad \text{for all } t, \tag{2.7}$$

$$\sum_{t=1}^{\infty} \beta^{t-1}[u'(c_t)c_t - v'(l_t)l_t]$$
$$= K_1[1 - \delta + F_k(K_1, l_1)(1 - \tau_{k1}^*)]u'(c_1) > 0. \tag{2.8}$$

Proof. See the technical notes at the end of the chapter. □

Constraints (2.6) and (2.7) are feasibility constraints that describe how technological considerations shape what is achievable. The final constraint (2.8) is usually termed an *implementability* constraint and is a consequence of the government's only being able to use linear taxes. We derive the implementability constraint by replacing the after-tax prices in the agent's budget constraint with marginal rates of substitution. Arbitrarily nonlinear taxes allow the government to eliminate the connection between its tax revenues and the agent's marginal rates of substitution. But this connection cannot be removed if the government can only use linear taxes. The content of the proposition is that the implementability constraint exactly captures the impact of the restriction that taxes have to be linear.

Note that we have substituted out all tax rates except τ_{k1}^* in (2.8). Varying other tax rates induces a nontrivial response in quantities, and so we can replace those tax rates with the affected quantities. In contrast, period 1 capital is inelastically supplied (as long as its price is positive). Hence, it is not possible to eliminate τ_{k1}^* in the same fashion.

Using proposition 2.1, and assuming that the government's optimal choice of taxes generates a positive equilibrium allocation, we can convert the government's choice problem into

$$\max_{(c,k,l,\tau_{k1})} \sum_{t=1}^{\infty} \beta^{t-1}\{u(c_t) - v(l_t)\}$$

$$\text{s.t.} \sum_{t=1}^{\infty} \beta^{t-1}[u'(c_t)c_t - v'(l_t)l_t]$$

$$= K_1[1 - \delta + F_k(K_1, l_1)(1 - \tau_{k1})]u'(c_1),$$
$$(2.9)$$

$$c_t + k_{t+1} + G_t = F(k_t, l_t) + (1 - \delta)k_t \quad \text{for all } t,$$
$$k_1 = K_1,$$
$$c_t, k_{t+1}, l_t \geqslant 0 \quad \text{for all } t.$$

This problem is often termed the *primal problem*, because the government directly chooses quantities (and period 1 capital taxes) instead of choosing tax rates and thereby indirectly influencing quantities.

Governments ultimately choose tax rates, not quantities. Fortunately, once we solve the primal problem, it is straightforward to calculate the implied tax rates from the quantities. In equilibrium, firm and individual optimization imply that

$$F_l(k_t, l_t) = w_t, \qquad (2.10)$$
$$F_k(k_t, l_t) = r_t, \qquad (2.11)$$
$$u'(c_t)w_t(1 - \tau_{lt}) = v'(l_t), \quad (2.12)$$
$$\beta u'(c_{t+1})(1 - \delta + r_{t+1}(1 - \tau_{k,t+1})) = u'(c_t). \quad (2.13)$$

Hence, if $(c^*, k^*, l^*, \tau_{k1}^*)$ solves the primal problem, then the implied tax rates are

$$\tau_{lt} = 1 - \frac{v'(l_t^*)}{u'(c_t^*)F_l(k_t^*, l_t^*)}, \qquad (2.14)$$

$$\tau_{k,t+1} = 1 - \frac{(u'(c_t^*)/\beta u'(c_{t+1}^*)) - 1 + \delta}{F_k(k_{t+1}^*, l_{t+1}^*)} \qquad (2.15)$$

for $t \geqslant 1$.

2.3 The Dynamic Ramsey Taxation Problem: Solution

The solution to the dynamic Ramsey taxation problem hinges critically on how much revenue the government can raise using period 1 capital income taxes τ_{k1}. To see this, suppose we drop the implementability constraint from the primal problem. Removing a constraint in this way serves to enlarge the constraint set, and so we can think of this problem as being a *relaxed Ramsey problem*.

Proposition 2.2. *Let* $(c^{\mathrm{RP}}, l^{\mathrm{RP}}, k^{\mathrm{RP}})$ *be a solution to the relaxed Ramsey problem. Suppose*

$$\sum_{t=1}^{\infty} \beta^{t-1} \frac{u'(c_t^{\mathrm{RP}})G_t}{u'(c_1^{\mathrm{RP}})} < (1 - \delta + F_k(K_1, l_1^{\mathrm{RP}}))K_1.$$

Then, the optimal tax rates in a solution to the Ramsey problem are

$$\tau_{lt} = 0 \quad for \ t \geqslant 1,$$
$$\tau_{k,t+1} = 0 \quad for \ t \geqslant 1,$$
$$\tau_{k1} = \frac{\sum_{t=1}^{\infty} \beta^{t-1} u'(c_t^{\text{RP}}) G_t}{F_k(K_1, l_1^{\text{RP}}) K_1 u'(c_1^{\text{RP}})}.$$

Proof. See the technical notes at the end of the chapter.   □

The premise of this proposition is that the period 1 value of the capital stock is larger than the present value of the stream of government purchases. Under this assumption, the proposition demonstrates that it is optimal to fund government purchases using only the taxes on first period capital taxes. Intuitively, agents can make no decisions to influence the amount of period 1 capital in the economy, beyond discarding the capital entirely. Hence, as long the tax rate is not sufficiently high to induce the agents to discard their capital, any taxes on this factor are purely nondistortionary.

Proposition 2.2 contradicts the whole starting point of the Ramsey approach that taxes are necessarily distorting. To get around proposition 2.2, most analyses of the dynamic Ramsey problem assume that the government cannot adjust τ_{k1}. (Equivalently, they assume that τ_{k1} is bounded above by some small number.) Once one does so, it is no longer possible to fund all expenditures using nondistorting taxes. The policy analyst then faces a real trade-off about how to set taxes over time.

Intuitively, since both taxes are distortionary, it seems that societies should end up using both capital income taxes and labor income taxes. This intuition turns out to be wrong. Indeed, if the utility function u is of the power form, so that $u'(c) = c^{-\gamma}$, we get the remarkable result that capital income tax rates should be zero in any period $t > 2$.

Proposition 2.3. *Suppose $u'(c) = c^{-\gamma}$ for $\gamma > 0$ and (c^*, k^*, l^*) solves the primal problem, given $\tau_{k1} = 0$. Then, for $t \geqslant 2$,*

$$c_t^{*-\gamma} = \beta c_{t+1}^{*-\gamma}(1 - \delta + F_{k,t+1}(k_{t+1}^*, l_{t+1}^*)).$$

Suppose, using (2.15), we define the period $(t + 1)$ capital income tax rate to be

$$\tau_{k,t+1}^* = 1 - \frac{(u'(c_t^*)/\beta u'(c_{t+1}^*)) - 1 + \delta}{F_k(k_{t+1}^*, l_{t+1}^*)}.$$

Then $\tau_{k,t+1}^* = 0$ for any $t \geqslant 2$.

Proof. The first-order necessary condition for c_t^*, for $t \geqslant 2$, is given by

$$\beta^{t-1} c_t^{*-\gamma} = \beta^{t-1} c_t^{*-\gamma} \mu - \gamma \beta^{t-1} c_t^{*-\gamma} \mu + \lambda_t,$$

where μ is the Lagrange multiplier on the implementability constraint and λ_t is the multiplier on the period t resource constraint. Hence, for $t \geqslant 2$,

$$\frac{\lambda_{t+1}}{\lambda_t} = \frac{\beta c_{t+1}^{*-\gamma}}{c_t^{*-\gamma}}.$$

It follows that, for $t \geqslant 2$,

$$(1 - \delta + F_k(k_{t+1}^*, l_{t+1}^*)) = c_t^{*-\gamma} \beta^{-1} c_{t+1}^{*\gamma}$$

and plugging into the formula for capital tax rates proves the proposition. $\qquad\square$

Levying a positive tax on capital income means that future consumption goods are being taxed at a higher rate than current consumption goods. In general, optimal goods taxes depend on the good's income and price elasticities. But when $u'(c) = c^{-\gamma}$, consumption at different dates has the same income and price (that is, interest rate) elasticities. Hence, the tax rate on consumption at different dates should be the same, which means that the capital income tax rate needs to be zero.

This logic applies to capital income taxes in period 3 and thereafter. Period 1 consumption is different, because it enters the right-hand side of the implementability constraint (2.8). This difference implies that it is optimal to have a tax on period 2 capital income. Intuitively, the government is using this period 2 tax as an imperfect way to tax period 1 capital income.

For more general utility functions, the Ramsey approach generates an important, surprisingly robust, result: capital income taxes should be zero in the long run.

Proposition 2.4. *Suppose that a positive allocation* (c^*, k^*, l^*) *solves the primal problem, given* $\tau_{k1} = 0$. *Suppose too that the sequence* $(c_t^*, l_t^*, k_t^*)_{t=1}^{\infty}$ *converges to a positive limit. If we define*

$$\tau_{k,t+1}^* = 1 - \frac{(u'(c_t^*)/\beta u'(c_{t+1}^*)) - 1 + \delta}{F_k(k_{t+1}^*, l_{t+1}^*)}$$

to be the implied capital income tax rate in period $(t + 1)$, *then*

$$\lim_{t \to \infty} \tau_{k,t+1}^* = 0.$$

Proof. Let λ_t be the multiplier on the period t feasibility constraint, and μ be the multiplier on the implementability constraint. The first-order necessary conditions (FONCs) with respect to c_t and k_{t+1} are

$$\beta^{t-1} u'(c_t^*) = \beta^{t-1} u'(c_t^*)\mu + \beta^{t-1} u''(c_t^*) c_t^* \mu + \lambda_t,$$
$$\lambda_t = \lambda_{t+1}(1 - \delta + F_k(k_{t+1}^*, l_{t+1}^*)).$$

By assumption, c_t converges as t goes to infinity. It follows from the consumption FONC that $\lambda_t \beta^{1-t}$ converges as t goes to infinity. Plugging this result into the second FONC, we get

$$\lim_{t \to \infty} \beta(1 - \delta + F_k(k_{t+1}, l_{t+1})) = 1$$

and so

$$\lim \tau_{k,t+1}^* = 1 - \frac{\beta^{-1} - 1 + \delta}{\beta^{-1} - 1 + \delta} = 0.$$

$\square$

The intuition for this proposition is related to the logic underlying proposition 2.3. Again, a positive capital income tax at date t means that the government is essentially taxing consumption in period $(t + 1)$ at a higher rate than consumption in period t. The key to this proposition is that this difference in tax rates cumulates exponentially over time. Hence, if the government imposes a long-run positive capital income tax, then it is essentially taxing consumption at date $(t + s)$ at a rate *infinitely* higher than consumption at date t as s and t get large. Such an extreme level of distortion is suboptimal.

2.4 Problems with the Ramsey Approach

The Ramsey approach delivers a sharp answer to the question of optimal capital income taxation in a deterministic infinite-horizon representative agent economy. The answer (for the long run) is startlingly robust across different formulations of preferences and technology. In this section, I consider applications of the Ramsey approach to other questions and settings. We see that the Ramsey approach is disturbingly non-robust. In particular, the set of possible tax instruments makes a big difference in the answers to various optimal tax questions.

2.4.1 Overlapping Generations Economies

In deriving the zero capital income tax results, we used a model economy in which all agents are infinitely lived. Suppose we instead use an overlapping-generations framework in which agents are finitely lived. In such a model, there really is a host of Ramsey problems, indexed by how the government weights different generations. Do the zero tax results apply to the solutions to these problems? Erosa and Gervais (2002) and Garriga (2003) show that the answer to this question depends on the set of tax systems available to the government.

Suppose first that the government can impose different labor income tax rates, at a given point in time, on *differently aged* people. With age-dependent taxes, if the marginal utility of consumption $u'(c) = c^{-\gamma}$, capital income taxes should equal zero (in period 2 and thereafter) in the solutions to any of these Ramsey problems. The intuition behind the result is basically the same as in proposition 2.3.

Now suppose that the government is required to set the labor income tax rate to be the same for all people in a given period, regardless of their ages. In this case, the structure of the optimal tax depends on how the planner weights different generations. If the planner weights future generations sufficiently highly, then even in the long run, the solution to the Ramsey problem must feature shrinking life-cycle consumption. If labor income tax rates could be made age dependent, the government could achieve this goal by using labor income taxes that grow as people get older. Without this ability, the government is forced to use positive capital income taxes as an imperfect substitute. (In a similar vein, if the government discounts future generations' utilities at a sufficiently high rate, the government might set capital income taxes to be negative.)

2.4.2 Monetary Policy

The question of how to time capital income taxes is a classic one in *fiscal* policy. In the context of monetary economics, the nominal interest rate set by the Federal Reserve is essentially a tax on the liquidity services provided by money. It is possible to use the same optimal taxation tools to address how the Fed should set this tax. In this vein, Correia et al. (2008) apply the Ramsey approach in a class of sticky-price models. They find that the target interest rate should always be zero. Intuitively, money is an intermediate input, not a final good. It is a basic principle of public finance that taxing intermediate goods generates a double distortion (one each in production and consumption) that is best avoided by only taxing final goods.

Schmitt-Grohe and Uribe (2004) use the Ramsey approach in the *same* class of models to figure out the optimal response of monetary policy to aggregate shocks. They obtain a very different answer. They find that the target interest rate should typically be positive and should also vary in response to aggregate shocks. The reason behind the difference in answers is a subtle one. In sticky-price models, firms necessarily have market power and so earn profits. These profits are essentially like the returns to a fixed factor, and the government would like to tax them at a high rate. There are many ways to accomplish this task effectively: taxes on profits, consumption, or dividends. Correia et al. assume that the government can tax consumption, and that this tax rate can fluctuate with the state of the economy. In contrast, Schmitt-Grohe and Uribe rule out taxes on dividends, consumption, and profits. The government still has the same desire to tax away profits, but now has no direct instrument to use. Because market activity is liquidity intensive, it is optimal for the government to use the tax on liquidity services—the interest rate—as an imperfect way to tax firm profits.

2.4.3   Another Way to Proceed: The Mirrlees Approach

These are but two examples of a general problem with the Ramsey approach: the answers depend critically on the set of possible instruments. Indeed, we saw this problem even in the infinite horizon capital income tax problem. In that setting, proposition 2.2 underscores that the optimal tax on labor income depends on the upper bound on first period capital income taxes. This general lack of robustness is due to a fundamental limitation of the Ramsey approach: it takes the set of possible tax instruments as given. We need to *endogenize* the government's set of possible taxes in some fashion.

We can begin this process with the following simple question: why don't governments use lump-sum taxes? For example, suppose the government simply requires each adult to pay $30,000 or face jail-time. Such a plan would lead to an efficient allocation of resources, because it does not distort any adult's margins.

But this approach has a major problem: not everyone can produce $30,000 of income. According to this plan, any such person should be jailed. Such an outcome seems suboptimal, from both an *ex ante* and an *ex post* perspective. This consideration suggests a different rule. First, figure out how much income each person can produce. Then, levy a lump-sum tax on them according to that earning capacity.

This plan creates a new problem: how do we figure out their earning capacity without creating some kind of distortion? For example, suppose the government taxes everyone $30,000 who earns over $50,000, and taxes everyone zero who earns less than $50,000. There will be many people who will choose to earn $49,999. The government could instead try something based on initial conditions. For example, it might prescribe that all college graduates should pay $40,000 per year, while those who fail to graduate college should pay only $10,000 per year. Such a plan would help insulate the less fortunate against a high tax burden. However, it creates a disincentive for people to actually finish college.

This discussion illustrates the premise of the Mirrlees (1971) approach to optimal taxation. It is difficult or impossible to figure out each person's earning capacity using some separate measure of ability. If we cannot condition taxes on ability directly, then taxes are necessarily distorting. The optimal tax problem is about trading the level of these distortions off against government objectives (like public goods expenditures or redistribution). Mirrlees applied this insight to thinking about optimal taxation in a static setting. In what follows, we extend his analysis to dynamic taxation.

2.5 Summary

In this chapter, I have used the Ramsey approach to derive two distinct results about capital income tax rates. First, if $u'(c) = c^{-\gamma}$, then it is optimal to set capital taxes so that there is no distortion on capital accumulation decisions. Second, in the long run, for more general utility functions, it is optimal for capital income taxes to converge to zero.

I then argued that the Ramsey approach has fundamental flaws, and suggested using a generalization of Mirrlees's approach instead. In the remainder of the book, we take this path. Chapter 4 shows that once we do so, we reach different conclusions about optimal taxes.

2.6 Technical Notes

In this subsection, I provide proofs of propositions 2.1 and 2.2.

2.6.1 Proof of Proposition 2.1

I begin by proving the necessity of the three conditions. Suppose a positive sequence $(c, k, l) \in E(\tau_k, \tau_l)$

for some tax sequence (τ_k, τ_l) in which $\tau_{k1} = \tau_{k1}^*$. Let (w, r, q) be the associated wages, rental rates, and bond prices. Since $k_1 > 0$, it must be true that $(1 - \delta) + r_1(1 - \tau_{k1}^*) > 0$, and so it is individually optimal for agents to set $k_1 = K_1$. Market clearing implies that

$$c_t + k_{t+1} + G_t = F(k_t, l_t) + (1 - \delta)k_t \quad \text{for all } t. \quad (2.16)$$

The agents' utility functions are increasing in c_t and decreasing in l_t, and so the budget constraint holds with equality:

$$\sum_{t=1}^{\infty} q_t[c_t - w_t l_t(1 - \tau_{lt})]$$

$$= \sum_{t=1}^{\infty} q_t\{r_t k_t(1 - \tau_{kt}) + (1 - \delta)k_t - k_{t+1}\}. \quad (2.17)$$

The agents' first-order necessary conditions with respect to (l_t, c_t, k_{t+1}) imply that

$$w_t(1 - \tau_{lt})u'(c_t) = v'(l_t), \quad t \geq 1, \quad (2.18)$$

$$\frac{\beta^{t-1}u'(c_t)}{u'(c_1)} = \frac{q_t}{q_1}, \quad t \geq 1, \quad (2.19)$$

$$q_t = [1 - \delta + r_t(1 - \tau_{k,t+1})]q_{t+1}, \quad t \geq 1. \quad (2.20)$$

We can substitute these first-order necessary conditions into the budget constraint to obtain

$$\sum_{t=1}^{\infty} \beta^{t-1}[u'(c_t)c_t - v'(l_t)l_t]$$

$$= u'(c_1)[1 - \delta + r_1(1 - \tau_{k1}^*)]K_1. \quad (2.21)$$

The firm's first-order condition in the period 1 capital rental market implies that $r_1 = F_k(K_1, l_1)$, which completes the proof of necessity.

I now turn to the proof of sufficiency. Suppose (c, k, l) is positive and there exists

$$\tau_{k1}^* < \frac{1 - \delta}{F_k(K_1, l_1)} + 1$$

such that

$$k_1 = K_1, \tag{2.22}$$

$$c_t + k_{t+1} + G_t = F(k_t, l_t) + (1 - \delta)k_t \quad \text{for all } t, \tag{2.23}$$

$$\sum_{t=1}^{\infty} \beta^{t-1}[u'(c_t)c_t - v'(l_t)l_t]$$

$$= K_1[1 - \delta + F_k(K_1, l_1)(1 - \tau_{k1}^*)]u'(c_1). \tag{2.24}$$

As in equations (2.10)–(2.15), define

$$r_t = F_k(k_t, l_t), \tag{2.25}$$

$$w_t = F_l(k_t, l_t), \tag{2.26}$$

$$q_t = \beta^{t-1}u'(c_t), \tag{2.27}$$

$$\tau_{k,t+1} = 1 - \frac{(u'(c_t)/\beta u'(c_{t+1})) - 1 + \delta}{F_k(k_{t+1}, l_{t+1})}, \tag{2.28}$$

$$\tau_{lt} = 1 - \frac{v'(l_t)}{u'(c_t)F_l(k_t, l_t)}. \tag{2.29}$$

It is clear that (c, k, l) satisfies market-clearing. The definition of (w, r) also ensures that (k, l) are optimal choices for the firm given (w, r). It remains only to verify that (c, k, l) is optimal for the agent, given $(w, r, q, \tau_k, \tau_l)$. If (c, k, l) satisfies the agent's FOCs and budget constraint, then (c, k, l) is optimal. The FOCs are

$$\beta^{t-1}u'(c_t) = q_t\lambda, \tag{2.30}$$

$$q_t = q_{t+1}(1 - \delta + r_{t+1}(1 - \tau_{k,t+1})), \tag{2.31}$$

$$\beta^{t-1}v'(l_t) = q_tw_t\lambda(1 - \tau_{lt}). \tag{2.32}$$

If we set $\lambda = 1$, it is clear that these FOCs are satisfied. The budget constraint is given by

$$\sum_{t=1}^{\infty} q_t[c_t + k_{t+1}]$$
$$= \sum_{t=1}^{\infty} q_t[\{w_t l_t(1 - \tau_{lt}) + r_t k_t(1 - \tau_{kt})\}$$
$$+ (1 - \delta)k_t]. \quad (2.33)$$

The definition of (q, r) implies that

$$q_t[(1 - \delta) + r_t(1 - \tau_{kt})]k_t = q_{t-1}k_t,$$

and so we need only verify that

$$\sum_{t=1}^{\infty} q_t c_t = \sum_{t=1}^{\infty} q_t w_t l_t(1 - \tau_{lt})$$
$$+ q_1(1 - \delta + F_k(K_1, l_1)(1 - \tau_{k1}^*))K_1. \quad (2.34)$$

But if we substitute q_t in for $\beta^{t-1} u'(c_t)$ and $w_t(1 - \tau_{lt})q_t$ in for $\beta^{t-1} v'(l_t)$, then (2.34) is implied by the implementability constraint (2.24).

Note that the proof of sufficiency works because there are no restrictions on (τ_k, τ_l). Suppose, for example, that the government has to use a constant labor income tax rate over time. There is no guarantee that the labor income tax rates in (2.29) will satisfy this additional restriction.

2.6.2 Proof of Proposition 2.2

The proposition's hypothesis is that

$$\sum_{t=1}^{\infty} \beta^{t-1} u'(c_t^{RP})G_t < u'(c_1^{RP})(1 - \delta + F_k(K_1, l_1^{RP}))K_1.$$
$$(2.35)$$

We can rewrite the LHS of (2.35) as

$$\sum_{t=1}^{\infty} \beta^{t-1} u'(c_t^{RP})$$
$$\times [F(k_t^{RP}, l_t^{RP}) - k_{t+1}^{RP} + k_t^{RP}(1-\delta) - c_t^{RP}]$$
$$= \sum_{t=1}^{\infty} \beta^{t-1} u'(c_t^{RP})$$
$$\times [F_k(k_t^{RP}, l_t^{RP})k_t^{RP} + F_l(k_t^{RP}, l_t^{RP})l_t^{RP}$$
$$- k_{t+1}^{RP} + k_t^{RP}(1-\delta) - c_t^{RP}]$$
$$= \sum_{t=1}^{\infty} \beta^{t-1} u'(c_t^{RP})[F_l(k_t^{RP}, l_t^{RP})l_t^{RP} - c_t^{RP}]$$
$$+ u'(c_1^{RP})[F_k(K_1, l_1^{RP}) + (1-\delta)]K_1. \quad (2.36)$$

We can conclude that (2.35) implies that

$$\sum_{t=1}^{\infty} \beta^{t-1}[u'(c_t^{RP})c_t - v'(l_t^{RP})l_t] > 0.$$

Then, we can find a positive value of τ_{k1}^{RP} (possibly larger than 1) such that

$$u'(c_1^{RP})(1 - \delta + (1 - \tau_{k1}^{RP})F_k(K_1, l_1^{RP}))K_1$$
$$= \sum_{t=1}^{\infty} \beta^{t-1}[u'(c_t^{RP})c_t^{RP} - v'(l_t^{RP})l_t^{RP}]. \quad (2.37)$$

We know that

$$(c^{RP}, k^{RP}, l^{RP}, \tau_{k1}^{RP})$$

is a solution to the relaxed problem. But

$$(c^{RP}, k^{RP}, l^{RP}, \tau_{k1}^{RP})$$

satisfies the (tighter) constraints of the dynamic Ramsey problem itself, and so it solves the dynamic Ramsey taxation problem.

We can rewrite our formula for τ_{k1}^{RP} as follows:

$$u'(c_1^{RP})(1 - \delta + (1 - \tau_{k1}^{RP})F_k(K_1, l_1^{RP}))K_1$$

$$= - \sum_{t=1}^{\infty} \beta^{t-1} u'(c_t^{RP}) G_t$$

$$+ u'(c_1^{RP})[F_k(K_1, l_1) + (1 - \delta)]K_1 \qquad (2.38)$$

and so

$$\sum_{t=1}^{\infty} \beta^{t-1} u'(c_t^{RP}) G_t = u'(c_1^{RP}) \tau_{k1}^{RP} F_k(K_1, l_1^{RP}) K_1,$$

which proves the proposition.

References

Chamley, C. 1986. Optimal taxation of capital income in general equilibrium with infinite lives. *Econometrica* 54:607–22.

Chari, V. V., and P. Kehoe. 1999. Optimal fiscal and monetary policy. In *Handbook of Macroeconomics* (ed. J. Taylor and M. Woodford). New York: Elsevier.

Correia, I., J.-P. Nicolini, and P. Teles. 2008. Optimal fiscal and monetary policy: equivalence results. *Journal of Political Economy* 168:141–70.

Erosa, A., and M. Gervais. 2002. Optimal taxation in life-cycle economies. *Journal of Economic Theory* 105:338–69.

Garriga, C. 2003. Optimal fiscal policy in overlapping-generations economies. Working Paper, Florida State University.

Mirrlees, J. 1971. An exploration in the theory of optimum income taxation. *Review of Economic Studies* 38:175–208.

Schmitt-Grohe, S., and M. Uribe. 2004. Optimal fiscal and monetary policy under sticky prices. *Journal of Economic Theory* 114:198–230.

3

Basics of Dynamic Social Contracting

The Mirrleesian approach to optimal taxation is based on the premise that people differ in their abilities to produce, but taxes cannot be directly conditioned on those abilities. This premise implies that, from the point of the view of the tax system, people are *privately informed* about their skills. Since the goal of this book is to extend the Mirrleesian approach to dynamic economies, we have to understand properties of desirable allocations of resources in dynamic economies in which people are privately informed.

In this chapter, I take up this task. I consider a class of economies with a large number of agents. Agents' skills can evolve over time. The law of evolution of skills is commonly known, but the realization of an agent's skills at each date is known only to him. The existence of private information means that not all feasible allocations can actually be achieved by such societies. I use the Revelation Principle to provide a simple but complete mathematical characterization of the set of achievable allocations.

The main theorem in this chapter is a partial characterization of the behavior of consumption in a Pareto optimal allocation.[1] It shows that the reciprocal of an individual's period t marginal utility of consumption (MU_t) satisfies the restriction

$$\frac{1}{MU_t} = \beta^{-1} R^{-1} E_t \frac{1}{MU_{t+1}},$$

where β is the individual's discount factor and R^{-1} is society's discount factor. This *reciprocal Euler equation* was originally derived by Diamond and Mirrlees (1978) and Rogerson (1985) for special cases. Following Golosov et al. (2003), I derive the reciprocal Euler equation for a general class of models. In particular, the restriction is valid regardless of the law of motion of skills. I show how the reciprocal Euler equation can be used to reach general and significant conclusions about the intertemporal evolution of the distribution of consumption.

At this stage, I say nothing about taxes. I seek only to understand some basic properties of Pareto optimal *allocations* or quantities. In the following chapter, I discuss how we can use those features of Pareto optimal allocations to reach conclusions about taxes.

3.1 Class of Environments

In this section, I describe a class of economic *environments*. An environment is a specification only of preferences, technology, and information. I view these attributes of a society as being immutable, so that the government cannot affect them via policies. Once we

---

[1] I use the term Pareto optimal to mean "relative to all allocations achievable given the existence of private information." Other researchers may use the term "constrained Pareto optimal" for this concept.

know preferences, information, and technology, the problem of institutional design is to fill in the other details of agent interaction in such a way as to achieve desirable outcomes.

The environments last for T periods, where T is finite. The population of agents is sufficiently large that we can think of the economy as having a unit measure of agents. People are indexed by a parameter ω in the finite set Ω. A fraction $\pi_\Omega(\omega)$ of the population have parameter ω, and $\pi_\Omega(\omega) > 0$ for all ω in Ω. As will become clear, this parameter ω does not affect preferences, technology, or information. Instead, the parameter represents *ex ante* societal redistributional motives.

All people have the same preferences. They maximize the expected value of

$$\sum_{t=1}^{T} \beta^{t-1}[u(c_t) - v(l_t)], \quad 0 < \beta < 1. \qquad (3.1)$$

Here, c_t is consumption in period t and l_t is effort in period t. I require u', v', $-u''$, and v'' to all be positive. Hence, utility is an increasing and concave function of consumption, and a decreasing and convex function of effort.

Agents are distinguished by *skills*. At date t, an agent with skill θ_t who exerts effort l_t generates $y_t = \theta_t l_t$ units of consumption as output. I assume that y_t is observable. However, both l_t and θ_t are privately known to the agent. Thus, it is impossible to know if an agent who generates little output does so because he exerts little effort or because he has low skills.

Skills evolve over time in the following stochastic fashion. Let Θ be a finite set, and π_Θ be a probability density function over Θ^T. At the beginning of period 1,

Nature draws a skill vector θ^T for each agent from Θ^T according to π_Θ. The vector θ^T represents the agent's lifetime sequence of skills. These draws are independently and identically distributed (i.i.d.) across agents, and are independent of ω (so that all agents, regardless of their ωs, have the same π_Θ). At date t, an agent privately learns the realization of θ_t. Thus, at date t, an agent knows his history θ^t, but does not know future realizations of his skills.

If there were a small number of agents, then the cross-sectional distribution of skill realizations in the population would be random. (For example, with some probability, all agents could be highly skilled, or all could be low skilled.) In contrast, I have described a model in which there is a large population—in fact, a unit measure—and the draws of θ^T are i.i.d. across agents. With such a large population, a law of large numbers holds,[2] and so the fraction of agents who have skill history θ^T is given by π_Θ. (In later chapters, I extend the analysis to allow for publicly observable aggregate shocks.)

I am flexible about the specification of π_Θ. This flexibility means that I am being wholly agnostic about the time series behavior of θ_t. For example, suppose $T = 2$ and $\Theta = \{\theta_H, \theta_L\}$. If $\pi_\Theta(\theta_i, \theta_j) = 1/4$ for all i, j in $\{H, L\}$, then θ_t is i.i.d. over time. If $\pi_\Theta(\theta_i, \theta_j) = 3/8$ if $i = j$ and $\pi_\Theta(\theta_i, \theta_j) = 1/8$ if $i \neq j$, then θ_t is autocorrelated over time.

An allocation in this setting specifies the amount of output y produced by each agent and the amount of consumption consumed by each agent, as a function

---

[2] The mathematics underlying this bald assertion is deep and beyond the scope of this book. See Sun (2006) for a useful discussion.

of the date, the history θ^t, and ω. Let

$$D = \{\theta^T \mid \pi_\Theta(\theta^T) > 0\}.$$

Then, an allocation (c, y) is a mapping such that

$$c : \Omega \times D \to R_+^T, \tag{3.2}$$

$$y : \Omega \times D \to [0, \bar{y}]^T, \tag{3.3}$$

$$(c_t, y_t) \text{ is } (\omega, \theta^t)\text{-measurable.} \tag{3.4}$$

The last restriction requires that (c_t, y_t) depends only on (ω, θ^t), and not on future realizations of θ. Note that I restrict output to be bounded from above by $\bar{y}$. This upper bound makes the set of feasible allocations compact and thereby ensures the existence of optimal allocations.

To simplify notation, I assume for now that the economy is a small open one, with gross interest rate $R > 1$. (I relax this assumption in later chapters.) Hence, I define an allocation (c, y) to be *feasible* if

$$\sum_{\omega \in \Omega} \sum_{\theta^T \in \Theta^T} \sum_{t=1}^{T} R^{-t} \pi_\Omega(\omega) \pi_\Theta(\theta^T)$$

$$\times \{c_t(\omega, \theta^T) - y_t(\omega, \theta^T)\} \leqslant 0. \tag{3.5}$$

This restriction says that the present value of per-capita consumption is no larger than the present value of per-capita output.

The class of environments is highly general in some respects. In particular, I impose no restrictions on the evolution of θ. This agnosticism is desirable, because there is still considerable dispute about the time series behavior of individual wages. On the other hand, I require preferences to be additively separable between consumption and labor, and over time.

This assumption ensures that the marginal rate of substitution between consumption at different dates is publicly known. This property of preferences plays an important role in what follows.

3.2 Incentive-Compatibility

The inequality (3.5) describes the set of allocations that are achievable, given the limits imposed by technology. But because some information is private, not all feasible allocations are actually achievable in this environment. Suppose, for example, that $T = 1$, Ω is a singleton, and $\Theta = \{\theta, \theta'\}$. Consider a feasible allocation such that

$$c_1(\theta) = c_1(\theta') \quad \text{and} \quad y_1(\theta) > y_1(\theta').$$

In this allocation, type θ agents produce more output, but consume the same, as type θ' agents. However, the type θ agents cannot be identified as such. They can always choose to act like the type θ' agents and produce the low amount of output. This allocation may be *physically feasible*, but it is nonetheless *impossible* to achieve. Society simply has no way to get some agents to produce more output without giving those agents more consumption.

This little example captures the basic restrictions that private information imposes in an economy. If skills are publicly observable, then society can require highly skilled people to act in a certain way. However, if skills are private information, agents can always pretend to have skills other than the ones that they actually have. If the agent is to produce and consume according to the dictates of the allocation, it must be true that agents don't want to mimic another skill type, and get that skill type's allocation of (c, y).

We can use this insight to model the impact of private information more systematically. As specified earlier, let $D = \{\theta^T \mid \pi_\Theta(\theta^T) > 0\}$ be the set of lifetime skill sequences that can occur with positive probability. Define a *mimicking strategy* σ to be any mapping from $D \to D$ such that σ_t is θ^t-measurable. By using a mimicking strategy σ, an agent indexed by ω with skill history θ^T gets the consumption and output allocation meant for the skill history $\sigma(\theta^T)$ instead of the allocation meant for the skill history θ^T. Note that σ_t is a function of θ^t, so that a mimicking strategy is a complete contingent plan of how the agent plans to act in every positive probability history.

Because θ_t is always private information, an agent can potentially use *any* mimicking strategy. Let Σ be the set of all mimicking strategies. Given an allocation (c, y), an agent with index ω gets *ex ante* utility

$$V(\sigma; c, y, \omega)$$

$$= \sum_{\theta^T \in D} \pi_\Theta(\theta^T)$$

$$\times \sum_{t=1}^{T} \beta^{t-1} \left[u(c_t(\omega, \sigma(\theta^T))) - v\left(\frac{y_t(\omega, \sigma(\theta^T))}{\theta_t} \right) \right]$$

$$\tag{3.6}$$

from using mimicking strategy σ. (He gets the consumption and output associated with $\sigma(\theta^T)$, but must provide effort according to his true skill θ_t.) Let σ_{TT} be the nonmimicking[3] strategy, so that $\sigma_{TT}(\theta^T) = \theta^T$, and suppose $V(\sigma_{TT}; c, y, \omega) < V(\sigma; c, y, \omega)$. Then, agents with characteristic ω will use mimicking strategy σ, and will not consume/produce according to the allocation (c, y). We can conclude that for an

---

[3] I use the subscript "TT" to denote "truth-telling."

allocation (c, y) to be achievable, it must satisfy

$$V(\sigma_{TT}; c, y, \omega) \geqslant V(\sigma; c, y, \omega)$$
$$\text{for all } \omega \text{ in } \Omega \text{ and all } \sigma \text{ in } \Sigma.$$
$$(3.7)$$

The above argument implies that the restriction (3.7) is *necessary* if an allocation is to be achievable in the presence of private information. The restriction is also *sufficient* in the following sense. Suppose (c, y) satisfies (3.7) and is also feasible. Then, we can design a game for the agents in the economy to play such that (c, y) is a (Bayesian–Nash) equilibrium outcome of that game. There are many such games that can be used, but the simplest one is what is known as a *direct mechanism*. The direct mechanism works as follows. At each date, agents report their current skills to a centralized authority. They receive $(c, y)(\omega, a^T)$, where a^T is the sequence of reported skills. In this game, the set of possible strategies corresponds to Σ, and the restriction (3.7) implies that truth-telling (the strategy σ_{TT} in Σ) is a (Bayesian–Nash) equilibrium in this game.

Thus, the set of allocations that are achievable in this setting given that skills are private information are exactly the ones that satisfy the *incentive constraints* (3.7) and the usual *feasibility constraints*. In what follows, I refer to the allocations that satisfy (3.7) as being *incentive-compatible* (this is the standard terminology for allocations that remain achievable, given the presence of an incentive problem).[4] Allocations that are

---

[4] Throughout this book, I rule out stochastic allocations in which agents receive random consumptions and outputs as a function of their realized skills. It is readily shown that randomized consumption allocations are suboptimal. (Intuitively, we can

simultaneously feasible and incentive-compatible are called *incentive-feasible.*

3.3 Remarks on Incentive-Compatibility

This section addresses some possible concerns with the above definition of incentive-compatibility in this dynamic setting. (Readers who are not concerned about the definition can safely skip it.)

3.3.1 But People Do Lie in the Real World!

In the previous subsection, I described how, if an allocation satisfies (3.7), there is a game in which that allocation is an equilibrium outcome. The constructed game was a direct mechanism, in which agents simply reported their information to a centralized authority, which allocates resources based on these reports. The equilibrium strategy in this game was to tell the truth.

It is important to realize though that there is no intrinsic connection between truth-telling and incentive constraints. Many allocations can emerge as equilibrium outcomes of some direct mechanism, even though agents are lying in equilibrium about their types. To take an extreme, suppose we have an allocation with the property that all types get the same consumption and output sequences. Such an allocation is an equilibrium outcome of the direct mechanism, in which agents tell the truth. However, this allocation is also an equilibrium outcome, given an equilibrium strategy that involves lying with positive probability.

---

simply replace the stochastic allocation with its certainty equivalent to create a welfare-equivalent incentive-compatible allocation and free up resources.) It may be optimal though to use stochastic allocations of output.

More generally, direct mechanisms with truth-telling equilibrium strategies are but one way to derive the sufficiency of incentive constraints. There are many others.

3.3.2 The Range of Mimicking Strategies

In the above formulation of incentive-compatibility, we restrict agents to mimic positive probability types (elements of D). For example, suppose $T = 2$, and $\pi(1,0) = \pi(0,1) = 1/2$. In this setting, an agent has two choices of mimicking strategies available in period 1. Whatever he chooses in period 1, though, pins down what he can do in period 2. Thus, if he acts like an unskilled agent in period 1, he cannot also act unskilled in period 2.

In some ways, this restriction builds a large amount of commitment into the environment. In some allocations, an agent who claims to be unskilled in period 1 will receive some consumption, while giving up consumption in period 2. Such a person is in some sense a borrower. He is required to repay the loan, because he is unable to mimic a low-skilled type in period 2. (The term "mimic" is in fact fundamentally wrong here, because there is no one of this type to mimic.)

There are two possible reasons why one might be concerned about this level of commitment. One is that, implicitly, we are assuming that it is possible to impose an infinite penalty for nonrepayments of debts. In reality, there may well be limits to the kinds of penalties that can be imposed. But if they exist, these enforcement limits should be incorporated fully into our analysis, not just for zero-probability events. Doing so remains technically challenging.

The other concern is that there are no truly zero-probability events. If $\pi(0,0) = \varepsilon > 0$, no matter how small ε is, it becomes believable for a person to act low-skilled in both periods. Incentive constraints are fundamentally different in this case, and it becomes possible for a borrower in period 1 to claim to be unable to repay in period 2. From a technical point of view, this concern is easy to handle: just change π so that $\pi(1,1)$ and $\pi(0,0)$ are nonzero.

3.3.3 Centralization?

It is not controversial that any achievable allocation in this setting must satisfy the incentive constraints (3.7). Take any game that these agents could possibly play. (Here, by "game," I mean any possible rules of interaction, including competitive trade modulated by taxes or some more or less centralized system.) In any such game, any of them can mimic any other type. It follows trivially that any equilibrium outcome of any game that gets played between these agents will have to satisfy (3.7).

The converse—that any allocation that satisfies (3.7) is achievable—is more controversial. Recall that, to establish this converse, we use a mechanism in which all information gets reported to a centralized authority, and then that authority allocates resources based on that information. This degree of centralization seems unappealing to many economists. They express two distinct concerns.

The first is that agents can circumvent the dictates of the centralized authority. In the direct mechanism contemplated earlier, the centralized authority allocated resources and then no further trade took place.

But how (ask these critics) is the centralized authority supposed to prevent such retrading?[5] The second kind of concern is that there are significant costs associated with centralization, and the above analysis ignores those costs. To cite but one example, informational transmission and processing is assumed to be costless.[6]

These two concerns are often confused, and so it is important to realize they are quite distinct. The first says that centralization may well be desirable, but argues that it is impossible. The second argues that centralization is not desirable, because it may have significant costs. I am especially sympathetic to the latter concern, and would like to see useful formalizations of its impact.

3.4 Pareto Optimal Allocations

I focus on the properties of (*ex ante*) Pareto optimal allocations. I define an incentive-feasible allocation (c, y) to be *Pareto optimal* if there exists no other incentive-feasible allocation (c', y') such that

$$\sum_{\theta^T \in \Theta^T} \sum_{t=1}^{T} \beta^{t-1} \pi_\Theta(\theta^T) [u(c'_t(\omega, \theta^T)) \\ - v(y'_t(\omega, \theta^T)/\theta_t)]$$

$$\geq \sum_{\theta^T \in \Theta^T} \sum_{t=1}^{T} \beta^{t-1} \pi_\Theta(\theta^T) [u(c_t(\omega, \theta^T)) \\ - v(y_t(\omega, \theta^T)/\theta_t)] \tag{3.8}$$

---

[5] See Ales and Maziero (2009) for a discussion of how such retrading affects the structure of optimal allocations.

[6] See Segal (2006) for a discussion of how to take information transmission costs into account in social contracting problems.

for all ω in Ω, with a strict inequality for some ω. Hence, an allocation is Pareto optimal if it is impossible to make some ω better off without making some other ω' worse off.

It is straightforward to provide a useful mathematical characterization of Pareto optimal allocations. Fix ω^* to be some element of Ω. An allocation (c^*, y^*) is Pareto optimal if and only if there exists a vector of *ex ante* utility levels U_ω, $\omega \in \Omega - \{\omega^*\}$, such that

$$(c^*, y^*) \in \arg\max_{(c,y)} \sum_{\theta^T \in \Theta^T} \sum_{t=1}^{T} \beta^{t-1} \pi_\Theta(\theta^T)$$

$$\times \left[u(c_t(\omega^*, \theta^T)) - v(y_t(\omega^*, \theta^T)/\theta_t) \right]$$

$$(3.9)$$

$$\text{s.t.} \sum_{\theta^T \in \Theta^T} \sum_{t=1}^{T} \beta^{t-1} \pi_\Theta(\theta^T)$$

$$\times \left[u(c_t(\omega, \theta^T)) - v(y_t(\omega, \theta^T)/\theta_t) \right]$$

$$\geqslant U_\omega, \quad \omega \in \Omega - \{\omega^*\},$$

$$\sum_{\omega \in \Omega} \sum_{\theta^T \in \Theta^T} \sum_{t=1}^{T} R^{-t} \pi_\Omega(\omega) \pi_\Theta(\theta^T)$$

$$\times \{ c_t(\omega, \theta^T) - y_t(\omega, \theta^T) \} \leqslant 0,$$

$$V(\sigma_{\text{TT}}; c, y, \omega) \geqslant V(\sigma; c, y, \omega)$$

$$\text{for all } \sigma \text{ in } \Sigma \text{ and } \omega \text{ in } \Omega,$$

$$c_t(\omega, \theta^T) \geqslant 0, \quad y_t(\omega, \theta^T) \geqslant 0, \quad y_t(\omega, \theta^T) \leqslant \bar{y}$$

$$\text{for all } t, \omega, \theta^T,$$

$$(c_t, y_t) \text{ is } (\omega, \theta^t)\text{-measurable.}$$

In this programming problem, an artificial planner seeks to maximize the *ex ante* utility of type ω^* agents, subject to delivering a certain amount of reservation *ex ante* utility to all other agents. By varying the reservation utilities $(U_\omega)_{\omega \in \Omega - \{\omega^*\}}$, we can sketch out a frontier of Pareto optimal allocations.[7]

3.5 The Reciprocal Euler Equation

In this subsection, I provide an important intertemporal characterization of Pareto optimal allocations.

3.5.1 Pareto Optima Without Private Information: Two Euler Equations

Consider a version of the planner's problem without any incentive-compatibility restrictions, and suppose a positive (c, y) solves this planner's problem. Such an allocation (c, y) is Pareto optimal in an environment without private information. The consumption allocation satisfies the first-order necessary conditions that, for all θ^T in D,

$$\beta^{t-1} u'(c_t(\omega^*, \theta^T)) = \lambda R^{-t} \pi_\Omega(\omega^*),$$
$$\beta^{t-1} u'(c_t(\omega, \theta^T)) \phi(\omega) = \lambda R^{-t} \pi_\Omega(\omega), \qquad (3.10)$$
$$\omega \in \Omega - \{\omega^*\},$$

where λ is the multiplier on the resource constraints and $\phi(\omega)$ is the multiplier on the ω reservation utility constraint. These first-order conditions tell us

---

[7] This definition of Pareto optimality is an *ex ante* one, because it calculates agents' utilities before the realization of any skill shocks. The results in this chapter also apply to an interim notion of Pareto optimality, in which agents' utilities are calculated conditional on the realization of period 1 skills.

$c_t(\omega, \theta^T)$ may depend on t and ω, but is independent of θ^T. Agents are fully insured against their productivity shocks in a Pareto optimal allocation without private information.

Full risk-sharing implies two types of intertemporal Euler equations. The first one takes the form

$$u'(c_t(\omega, \bar{\theta}^t, \theta_{t+1}^T))$$

$$= \beta R \frac{\sum_{\theta^T \geqslant \bar{\theta}^t} \pi(\theta^T) u'(c_{t+1}(\omega, \theta^T))}{\sum_{\theta^T \geqslant \bar{\theta}^t} \pi(\theta^T)} \quad (3.11)$$

$$= \beta R E\{u'(c_{t+1}(\omega, \theta^T)) \mid \theta^t = \bar{\theta}^t\} \quad (3.12)$$

for any ω in Ω and for any $\bar{\theta}^t$ that can occur with positive probability. (The notation θ_{t+1}^T refers to the partial history $(\theta_{t+1}, \ldots, \theta_T)$. The notation $\theta^T \geqslant \bar{\theta}^t$ refers to any positive probability θ^T with initial history $\bar{\theta}^t$.) In words, the marginal utility of consumption in history $\bar{\theta}^t$ equals βR multiplied by the expected marginal utility of consumption in period $(t + 1)$. This Euler equation says that, in a Pareto optimal allocation, agents are left marginally indifferent between further borrowing and lending in the asset market. Put another way, if agents are endowed with a Pareto optimal allocation (c, y), they will not trade away from this allocation by borrowing and lending.

The second intertemporal Euler equation is more unusual. It takes the form that, for all $\bar{\theta}^T$ in D,

$$\frac{1}{u'(c_t(\omega, \bar{\theta}^T))}$$

$$= \beta^{-1} R^{-1} \frac{\sum_{\theta^T \geqslant \bar{\theta}^t} \pi(\theta^T) u'(c_{t+1}(\omega, \theta^T))^{-1}}{\sum_{\theta^T \geqslant \bar{\theta}^t} \pi(\theta^T)}$$

$$\quad (3.13)$$

$$= \beta^{-1} R^{-1} E\left\{ \frac{1}{u'(c_{t+1}(\omega, \theta^T))} \,\middle|\, \theta^t = \bar{\theta}^t \right\}. \quad (3.14)$$

In words, this equation says that the reciprocal of marginal utility in period t equals $\beta^{-1}R^{-1}$ multiplied by the expectation of the reciprocal of marginal utility in period $(t+1)$. This equation is often called the *reciprocal Euler equation* because it applies to the reciprocal of marginal utility.

The intuition behind this restriction is less familiar. It comes from thinking about the planner as using resources to produce utility. The planner's goal is to smooth the marginal cost of utility production over time. Mathematically, if $C(U)$ is the period t resource cost of producing U utiles in period t, this desire for smoothing implies that

$$C'(U_t(\omega, \bar{\theta}^T))$$
$$= \beta^{-1}R^{-1}E\{C'(U_{t+1}(\omega, \theta^T)) \mid \theta^t = \bar{\theta}^t\}. \quad (3.15)$$

Note though that $C'(U) = 1/u'(C(U))$. Hence, the marginal cost-smoothing condition (3.15) is exactly the same as (3.14).

3.5.2 Reciprocal Euler Equation: Derivation with Private Information

At this point, I turn back to the planner's problem (3.9) with private information. I derive a set of necessary conditions of Pareto optimality, designed to capture the intertemporal trade-off in consumption. The derivation takes the usual form of finding conditions that ensure that there is no way to increase the objective by perturbing the optimum in a limited set of directions that lie inside the constraint set.

In particular, suppose (c^*, y^*) is Pareto optimal and there exists t and ω' such that

$$c_t^*(\omega', \theta^T), c_{t+1}^*(\omega', \theta^T) > 0 \quad \text{for all } \theta^T \text{ in } D.$$

Then, pick any $\varepsilon : \Theta^t \to R$ and any constant Δ. We can use these to construct a perturbed allocation (c', y^*), where $c'_s(\omega, .) = c^*_s(\omega, .)$ if $s \notin \{t, t+1\}$ or $\omega' \neq \omega$, and (c'_t, c'_{t+1}) satisfies

$$u(c'_t(\omega', \theta^T)) = u(c^*_t(\omega', \theta^T)) + \Delta + \varepsilon(\theta^t)$$

$$\text{for all } \theta^T \in D,$$

$$(3.16)$$

$$u(c'_{t+1}(\omega', \theta^T)) = u(c^*_{t+1}(\omega', \theta^T)) - \beta^{-1}\varepsilon(\theta^t)$$

$$\text{for all } \theta^T \in D,$$

$$(3.17)$$

$$\sum_{\theta^T}(c'_t(\omega', \theta^T) - c^*_t(\omega', \theta^T))\pi_\Theta(\theta^T)$$

$$+ R^{-1}\sum_{\theta^T}(c'_{t+1}(\omega', \theta^T) - c^*_{t+1}(\omega', \theta^T))\pi_\Theta(\theta^T)$$

$$= 0. \qquad (3.18)$$

The first restriction says that for type ω' agents, we change utility in each history θ^t. This utility change has two pieces: $\varepsilon(\theta^t)$ and Δ. The second restriction says that we undo the change $\varepsilon(\theta^t)$ by subtracting $\beta^{-1}\varepsilon(\theta^t)$ in all successor nodes. Note that the perturbation adds the same amount of utility Δ along every sample path θ^T. The third restriction ensures that c' uses up the same resources as c^* does.

Our goal is to derive necessary conditions of optimality. Hence, if this perturbation is to be of use to us, it must lie within the constraint set. It is clear that (c', y^*) is feasible, because it uses up the same resources as (c^*, y^*). Also, we have added the same utility to (c^*, y^*) for all θ^T sequences that occur with positive probability. Hence, for any mimicking strategy σ,

$$V(\sigma; c', y^*, \omega') - V(\sigma; c^*, y^*, \omega') = \Delta.$$

It follows that the *ranking* of mimicking strategies is the same under (c', y^*) as under (c^*, y^*), and so (c', y^*) must be incentive-compatible if (c^*, y^*) is.

In this fashion, given any incentive-feasible allocation (c^*, y^*), we can construct a set of incentive-feasible allocations (c', y^*). (Note that this set is a proper subset of all incentive-feasible allocations. Indeed, it is a proper subset of all incentive-feasible allocations with output given by y^*.) If (c^*, y^*) is to be Pareto optimal, it must be true that $(0, c_t^*, c_{t+1}^*)$ solves

$$\max_{\Delta, c_t', c_{t+1}'} \Delta \tag{3.19}$$

$$\text{s.t. } u(c_t'(\omega', \theta^T)) + \beta u(c_{t+1}'(\omega', \theta^T))$$
$$= u(c_t^*(\omega', \theta^T)) + \beta u(c_{t+1}^*(\omega', \theta^T)) + \Delta$$
$$\text{for all } \theta^T \in D,$$

$$\sum_{\theta^T \in D} (c_t'(\omega', \theta^T) - c_t^*(\omega', \theta^T)) \pi_\Theta(\theta^T)$$
$$+ R^{-1} \sum_{\theta^T \in D} (c_{t+1}'(\omega', \theta^T) - c_{t+1}^*(\omega', \theta^T)) \pi_\Theta(\theta^T)$$
$$= 0,$$

$c_t'(\omega', .)$ is θ^t-measurable,

$c_{t+1}'(\omega', .)$ is θ^{t+1}-measurable,

$c_t'(\omega', \theta^T), c_{t+1}'(\omega', \theta^T) \geqslant 0 \quad \text{for all } \theta^T \text{ in } D.$

By varying the constant Δ, we are varying the amount of extra *ex ante* utility that we can deliver to type ω' agents over (c^*, y^*), while keeping the utility delivered to other agents the same. If (c^*, y^*) is Pareto optimal, then we should not be able to deliver any extra utility. By varying c', we are varying the timing of when agents receive their utility from consumption. A

Pareto optimal allocation must deliver this utility in an optimal fashion over time.

We can attack this constrained optimization problem (3.19) using Lagrangian methods. Let $\eta_t(\theta^T)$ be the multiplier on the first constraint, and λ be the multiplier on the second constraint. The first-order necessary conditions with respect to (c_t', c_{t+1}', Δ) are

$$u'(c_t^*(\omega', \bar{\theta}^T)) \sum_{\theta^T \geqslant \bar{\theta}^t} \eta_t(\theta^T)$$

$$= \lambda \sum_{\theta^T \geqslant \bar{\theta}^t} \pi_\Theta(\theta^T) \quad \text{for all } \bar{\theta}^T \text{ in } D, \quad (3.20)$$

$$\beta u'(c_{t+1}^*(\omega', \bar{\theta}^T)) \sum_{\theta^T \geqslant \bar{\theta}^{t+1}} \eta_{t+1}(\theta^T)$$

$$= \lambda R^{-1} \sum_{\theta^T \geqslant \bar{\theta}^{t+1}} \pi_\Theta(\theta^T) \quad \text{for all } \bar{\theta}^T \text{ in } D,$$

$$(3.21)$$

$$\sum_{\theta^T} \eta_t(\theta^T) = 1. \quad (3.22)$$

The different sums of $\eta_t(\theta^T)$ in the various first-order conditions capture various measurability restrictions. In particular, because c_t' is θ^t-measurable, we sum across all η_ts that have the same $\bar{\theta}^t$. We can combine (3.20) and (3.21) to get

$$\frac{1}{u'(c_t^*(\omega', \bar{\theta}^T))}$$

$$= \beta^{-1} R^{-1} \left\{ \sum_{\theta^T \geqslant \bar{\theta}^t} \frac{\pi_\Theta(\theta^T)}{u'(c_{t+1}^*(\omega', \theta^T))} \right\} \bigg/ \sum_{\theta^T \geqslant \bar{\theta}^t} \pi_\Theta(\theta^T).$$

$$(3.23)$$

This can be rewritten as

$$\frac{1}{u'(c_t^*(\omega', \bar{\theta}^T))}$$
$$= \beta^{-1} R^{-1} E \left\{ \frac{1}{u'(c_{t+1}^*(\omega', \theta^T))} \;\middle|\; \theta^t = \bar{\theta}^t \right\}$$

for all $\bar{\theta}^T$ in D,

(3.24)

which is the same as the reciprocal Euler equation (3.14) derived earlier.

This result is sufficiently important so as to merit being labeled a theorem.

Theorem 3.1. *Suppose* (c^*, y^*) *is a Pareto optimal allocation such that* $c_t^*(\omega, \theta^T) > 0$ *and* $c_{t+1}^*(\omega, \theta^T) > 0$ *for all* θ^T *in* D. *Then, for all* $\bar{\theta}^T$ *in* D,

$$\frac{1}{u'(c_t^*(\omega, \bar{\theta}^T))}$$
$$= \beta^{-1} R^{-1} E \left\{ \frac{1}{u'(c_{t+1}^*(\omega, \theta^T))} \;\middle|\; \theta^t = \bar{\theta}^t \right\}.$$

(3.25)

3.5.3 Robustness of the Reciprocal Euler Equation

We earlier demonstrated that any Pareto optimal allocation must satisfy the reciprocal Euler equation when θ is public information. The content of theorem 3.1 is that Pareto optimal allocations must satisfy this restriction even if θ is private information. A remarkable feature of theorem 3.1 is that it is true regardless of π_Θ. In contrast, the specification of π_Θ has a great impact on the overall properties of optimal allocations. (For example, we cannot conclude that preferences over consumption and output display single-crossing without knowing π_Θ.)

The proof of theorem 3.1 works because consumption and the utility from consumption are both publicly observable. The proof can be readily extended to much richer environments if they have this same property. For example, in this economy, skills evolve exogenously. Theorem 3.1 will still apply if we change the environment to allow for skill augmentation via hidden effort.

On the other hand, the proof breaks down if agents face privately observed shocks to their marginal utilities of consumption, if they can consume secretly, or if agents' discount factors are private information (as in Townsend (1982), Green (1987), or Atkeson and Lucas (1992)). More subtly, if preferences are nonseparable between consumption and labor, then the marginal utility of consumption is private information, and we cannot prove theorem 3.1.

We have restricted π_Θ to have finite support. However, Golosov et al. (2003) extend the proof of theorem 3.1 to cases in which Θ is infinite (for example, an interval). I discuss some aspects of this extension in the technical notes at the end of this chapter.[8]

3.5.4 Failure of the Standard Euler Equation

Theorem 3.1 demonstrates that the reciprocal Euler equation generalizes in the presence of private information. This subsection shows that the standard Euler equation does not.

---

[8] Farhi and Werning (2008) extend theorem 3.1 to settings with nonexpected utility preferences. However, much of their analysis relies on the assumption that (the private information components of) individual skills are i.i.d. over time. Grochulski and Kocherlakota (2008) extend theorem 3.1 to a class of environments in which preferences are nonseparable over time, but are restricted to be weakly separable between consumption and labor.

The reciprocal Euler equation tells us that

$$u'(c_t^*(\omega, \bar{\theta}^T))$$

$$= \beta R \left[E \left\{ \frac{1}{u'(c_{t+1}^*(\omega, \theta^T))} \, \middle| \, \theta^t = \bar{\theta}^t \right\} \right]^{-1}.$$
(3.26)

In a Pareto optimal allocation *without* private information, c_{t+1}^* depends on ω but is independent of θ^T. We can get rid of the expectation on the right-hand side, and conclude that the standard Euler equation applies, because

$$u'(c_t^*(\omega, \bar{\theta}^T))$$

$$= \beta R u'(c_{t+1}^*(\omega, \theta^T)) \quad \text{for all } \theta^T \geqslant \bar{\theta}^t \quad (3.27)$$

$$= \beta R E\{u'(c_{t+1}^*(\omega, \theta^T)) \mid \theta^t = \bar{\theta}^t\}.$$

However, in a Pareto optimal allocation with private information, c_t^* typically depends on θ^T as well as on ω. Without this kind of dependence, people who are highly skilled in period t will never choose to produce more than low-skilled people in that period. So, in a Pareto optimal allocation, we can typically expect that $\text{Var}(c_{t+1}^* \mid \theta^t = \bar{\theta}^t) > 0$. Given this variability, we can apply Jensen's inequality to the reciprocal function on the right-hand side of (3.26) and conclude that

$$u'(c_t^*(\omega, \bar{\theta}^T)) < \beta R E\{u'(c_{t+1}^*(\omega, \theta^T)) \mid \theta^t = \bar{\theta}^t\}.$$
(3.28)

The marginal utility of consumption in period t is strictly *lower* than the expected discounted marginal utility of consumption in period $(t + 1)$.

In a Pareto optimal allocation with private information, there is a wedge in the intertemporal Euler equation. This wedge means it is impossible to obtain a Pareto optimal allocation while allowing agents to undertake unlimited trading of bonds. Note that the wedge is the opposite of what emerges from models with borrowing constraints. In such models, agents would like to move consumption to period t from period $(t + 1)$ but cannot do so. In a Pareto optimal allocation, agents would like to move consumption from period t to period $(t + 1)$. They must be prevented from doing so in some fashion.

There is a basic intuition for why consumption-smoothing (that is, (3.12)) is not satisfied by Pareto optimal allocations. For simplicity, assume that $\Theta = \{\theta_H, \theta_L\}, \theta_H > \theta_L$ and Ω has one element. Suppose that (c, y) is a Pareto optimal allocation in which c satisfies

$$u'(c_t(\theta^t)) = \beta R \pi_H u'(c_{t+1}(\theta^t, \theta_H))$$
$$+ \beta R \pi_L u'(c_{t+1}(\theta^t, \theta_L)), \tag{3.29}$$

$$u'(c_{t+1}(\theta^t, \theta_H)) < u'(c_{t+1}(\theta^t, \theta_L)). \tag{3.30}$$

(Here, π_i represents the probability of $\theta_{t+1} = \theta_i$, conditional on θ^t.) This contract provides perfect smoothing but limited insurance in period $(t + 1)$. Intuitively, the planner should be able to lower costs by offering a contract that pays the second-order cost of reducing smoothing to get the first-order benefit of improving insurance.

To be more specific, suppose the planner changes the allocation by lowering $c_{t+1}(\theta^t, \theta_L)$ by ε_L, lowering $c_{t+1}(\theta^t, \theta_H)$ by ε_H, and raising $c_t(\theta^t)$ by ε. The planner chooses $(\varepsilon_H, \varepsilon_L, \varepsilon)$ so that there exists some δ with the property that

$$\delta = -\beta u(c_{t+1}(\theta^t, \theta_H) - \varepsilon_H) + \beta u(c_{t+1}(\theta^t, \theta_H)) \tag{3.31}$$

$$= -\beta u(c_{t+1}(\theta^t, \theta_L) - \varepsilon_L) + \beta u(c_{t+1}(\theta^t, \theta_L)) \tag{3.32}$$

$$= -u(c_t(\theta^t)) + u(c_t(\theta^t) + \varepsilon). \tag{3.33}$$

(In words, the utility loss in period $(t + 1)$ is the same across the two states, and equals the utility gain in period t.) Because u is concave, such a contract must necessarily have the property that $\varepsilon_H > \varepsilon_L$. Hence, while it necessarily worsens smoothing, the alternative contract provides superior risk-sharing in period t.

We can approximate the changes as

$$\varepsilon \approx \frac{\delta}{u'(c_t(\theta^t))}, \tag{3.34}$$

$$\varepsilon_L \approx \beta^{-1} \frac{\delta}{u'(c_{t+1}(\theta^t, \theta_L))}, \tag{3.35}$$

$$\varepsilon_H \approx \beta^{-1} \frac{\delta}{u'(c_{t+1}(\theta^t, \theta_H))}. \tag{3.36}$$

If we apply Jensen's inequality to the smoothing condition (3.29) and multiply through by δ, we know that

$$\frac{\delta}{u'(c_t(\theta^t))} < \beta^{-1} R^{-1} \pi_H \frac{\delta}{u'(c_{t+1}(\theta^t, \theta_H))}$$
$$+ \beta^{-1} R^{-1} \pi_L \frac{\delta}{u'(c_{t+1}(\theta^t, \theta_L))}, \tag{3.37}$$

which implies that

$$-\varepsilon + R^{-1} \pi_H \varepsilon_H + R^{-1} \pi_L \varepsilon_L > 0. \tag{3.38}$$

The new allocation lowers the society's costs of generating output y. In this fashion, the planner is able to provide better risk-sharing by front-loading consumption.

3.6 Dynamics of Pareto Optimal Consumption

When θ is publicly observable, a Pareto optimal consumption allocation c_t^* is independent of θ^T for all t and ω. There is no reason for agents to face consumption risk, and so past (and current) realizations of θ have no impact on consumption. At the same time, there are differences in consumption because the planner might treat agents with different ωs differently. If $\beta R = 1$, these differences stay fixed over time. In this case, consumption inequality is constant over time in any Pareto optimal allocation (when θ is publicly observable).

In the remainder of this section, we explore to what extent these two properties (history independence and constant inequality) are valid when θ is private information.

3.6.1 History Independence

With private information, it is no longer Pareto optimal to give agents full consumption insurance. Differently skilled agents should produce different levels of output, and they can only be given the incentive to do so if they receive different consumptions. It follows that shocks to skills are inherited (at least in part) by consumption.

More interestingly, the reciprocal Euler equation implies that a shock to skills in period t impacts consumption at future dates. Suppose $\beta R = 1$. The private information problem implies that in period t, agents may not know their marginal utilities of consumption in period $(t+1)$. Define their innovation in information about $1/u'(c_{t+1})$ to be Δ_{t+1}:

$$\Delta_{t+1} \equiv 1/u'(c_{t+1}) - E_t\{1/u'(c_{t+1})\}. \qquad (3.39)$$

This innovation in information also affects the *forecasts* of future reciprocals of marginal utilities. We can measure this change in forecasts as

$$E_{t+1}\frac{1}{u'(c_{t+s+1})} - E_t\frac{1}{u'(c_{t+s})}, \quad s > 0. \qquad (3.40)$$

The reciprocal Euler equation implies that in a Pareto optimal allocation, $1/u'(c_t)$ is a *martingale*:[9]

$$\frac{1}{u'(c_t)} = E_t\frac{1}{u'(c_{t+1})}. \qquad (3.41)$$

We can use this formula, and the law of iterated expectations, to conclude that the change in agents' forecasts (3.40) is exactly equal to their new information Δ_{t+1} about $1/u'(c_{t+1})$. In words, any shock that leads to a change of Δ_{t+1} in $1/u'(c)$ leads to a change of Δ_{t+1} in agents' forecasts of $1/u'(c)$ at any future date. In this sense, skill shocks—regardless of their own data-generation process—have a *permanent* impact on the reciprocal of marginal utility. If utility is logarithmic, these permanent effects show up in the level of consumption itself.

The intuition behind this result is similar to that underlying the permanent income hypothesis. It is efficient to require higher output from a person who gets a higher skill realization in period t. However, given that θ is private information, a Pareto optimal allocation can only generate this higher output by rewarding this agent with an increase in his lifetime utility of consumption. The reciprocal Euler equation governs how this increase is spread over time. When $\beta R = 1$,

---

[9] A martingale is a stochastic process x that satisfies the property that $x_t = E_t x_{t+1}$. A random walk is a special kind of martingale such that the increments $(x_{t+1} - x_t)$ are i.i.d. over time.

it is efficient to spread the utility increase evenly over time, which means that even temporary shocks can translate into permanent changes in $1/u'$.

3.6.2 Consumption Inequality

The cross-sectional distribution of consumption never changes in a Pareto optimal allocation if θ_t is publicly observable. However, this result does not apply once θ is private information.

To see why, suppose $\beta R = 1$. Then, the reciprocal Euler equation says that

$$\frac{1}{u'(c_t)} = E_t \frac{1}{u'(c_{t+1})}. \qquad (3.42)$$

This property implies that

$$\frac{1}{u'(c_{t+1})} = \frac{1}{u'(c_t)} + \varepsilon_{t+1}, \qquad (3.43)$$

where ε_{t+1} is mean zero and is uncorrelated with $1/u'(c_t)$. It follows that

$$\text{Var}\left(\frac{1}{u'(c_{t+1})}\right) = \text{Var}\left(\frac{1}{u'(c_t)}\right) + \text{Var}(\varepsilon_{t+1}), \quad (3.44)$$

where Var represents the unconditional variance of the relevant random variable. Because the population of agents is so large, this statement about *unconditional* variances translates directly into a statement about *cross-sectional* variances within the population.

As we have seen, the private information problem implies that in a Pareto optimal allocation, $1/u'(c_{t+1})$ typically depends on new information revealed at date $(t + 1)$. This dependence means that $\text{Var}(\varepsilon_{t+1})$ is positive. It follows that in a Pareto optimal allocation

$$\text{Var}\left(\frac{1}{u'(c_{t+1})}\right) > \text{Var}\left(\frac{1}{u'(c_t)}\right). \qquad (3.45)$$

In a Pareto optimal allocation, the cross-sectional distribution of the reciprocal of marginal utility grows over time. If u is logarithmic, this statement translates into growing inequality in consumption itself.

3.7 Long-Run Properties of Pareto Optima

In the above section, we established two important properties of Pareto optimal allocations of consumption. These properties concern what happens for any finite period t. In this subsection, we turn to the long-run properties of Pareto optima.[10]

3.7.1 Long-Run Convergence

Suppose again that $\beta R = 1$, so that if (c, y) is Pareto optimal, then $1/u'(c_t)$ is a nonnegative martingale. (In addition, because Θ is finite, $1/u'(c_t)$ must have a finite mean.) As it turns out, much is known about the long-run properties of nonnegative martingales. Take a sample path θ^∞ of skill realizations. There are three logical possibilities for the behavior of the reciprocal of marginal utility along this sample path:

$$\lim_{t \to \infty} \frac{1}{u'(c_t(\omega, \theta^\infty))} < \infty, \tag{3.46}$$

$$\lim_{t \to \infty} \frac{1}{u'(c_t(\omega, \theta^\infty))} = \infty, \tag{3.47}$$

---

[10] To derive these results, we need to extend the class of environments to allow the horizon length T to equal infinity. We can do so by making only minimal changes in the basic model. The main change is that we now need to assume that π_Θ is a probability density function over the countable set Θ^∞. With this change in hand, the proof of theorem 3.1 carries over to infinite horizon settings.

$$\lim_{t \to \infty} \frac{1}{u'(c_t(\omega, \theta^\infty))} \quad \text{does not exist.} \quad (3.48)$$

The first possibility is that the reciprocal of marginal utility converges along the sample path to a finite (non-negative) limit. The second possibility is that the reciprocal of marginal utility grows along the sample path without bound. The final possibility is that the reciprocal of marginal utility cycles forever (possibly aperiodically) between two values.

The *martingale convergence theorem* states that for a nonnegative martingale with finite first moment, almost all sample paths are of the first kind. This theorem governs the long-run behavior of Pareto optima as follows.

Theorem 3.2. *Let* $\beta R = 1$, *and suppose* (c^*, y^*) *is a Pareto optimal allocation. Then, there exists a random variable* $X^* : \Omega \times \Theta^\infty \to R_+$ *such that*

$$\lim_{t \to \infty} \frac{1}{u'(c_t^*(\omega, \theta^\infty))} = X^*(\omega, \theta^\infty) \quad (3.49)$$

for all ω *in* Ω *and almost all* θ^∞ *in* Θ^∞. *If*

$$\lim_{c \to \infty} u'(c) = 0,$$

then there exists a finitely valued random variable c^∞ *such that*

$$\lim_{t \to \infty} c_t^*(\omega, \theta^\infty) = c^\infty(\omega, \theta^\infty) \quad (3.50)$$

for all ω *in* Ω *and almost all* θ^∞ *in* Θ^∞.

Note that the limiting random variable X^* itself is random over sample paths. Hence, theorem 3.2 only tells us that $1/u'(c)$ converges *along* almost every sample path. It says nothing about how these limits vary *across* sample paths. This distinction is important in what follows.

I provide some (relatively crude) intuition for the martingale convergence theorem in the technical notes that follow the chapter. For a complete proof, interested readers should consult an advanced book in probability theory like Billingsley (1986).

3.7.2 Immobility of Consumption

In a Pareto optimal allocation when θ is publicly observable, consumption is highly immobile if $\beta R = 1$. Agents' consumptions are constant over time at possibly distinct values pinned down by ω. Hence, it is impossible for agents' consumption rankings to change over time.

When θ is private information, it is Pareto optimal for consumption rankings to change over time. For example, suppose $c_t^*(\omega, \theta^t) > c_t^*(\omega', \theta^{t'})$, but only slightly. The need to provide for incentives may well imply that

$$c_{t+1}^*(\omega, \theta^t, \theta^L) < c_{t+1}^*(\omega', \theta^{t'}, \theta^H) \quad \text{if } \theta^H > \theta^L.$$

However, theorem 3.2 tells us that consumption *is* immobile in the long run. In particular, consider the limit

$$L_t(\omega, \theta^\infty) = \lim_{\tau \to \infty} |c_t^*(\omega, \theta^\infty) - c_{t+\tau}^*(\omega, \theta^\infty)|$$

of the difference between consumption at date t and consumption in the sufficiently distant future. Then, consider the limit of this difference as date t gets sufficiently large (that is, $\lim_{t \to \infty} L_t(\omega, \theta^\infty)$). By the triangle inequality, this limit can be bounded from above by

$$\lim_{t \to \infty} L_t(\omega, \theta^\infty)$$

$$\leqslant \lim_{t \to \infty} \lim_{\tau \to \infty} |c_t^*(\omega, \theta^\infty) - c^\infty(\omega, \theta^\infty)|$$

$$+ \lim_{t \to \infty} \lim_{\tau \to \infty} |c_{t+\tau}^*(\omega, \theta^\infty) - c^\infty(\omega, \theta^\infty)|$$

$$\tag{3.51}$$

$$= 0 + 0.$$

It follows that the difference between current consumption and very long-run consumption gets smaller as time passes. In other words, agents' consumptions don't change very much in the long run.

3.7.3 Long-Run Distribution of Consumption

As I indicated earlier, theorem 3.2 provides little information about the variance of long-run consumption *across* sample paths. In this subsection, I provide three examples that illustrate the range of possible long-run outcomes. Throughout I assume that $\beta R = 1$, and I let $u(c) = \ln(c)$.

3.7.3.1 *Example 1: A Two-Caste System*

In this example, I suppose that the skill process is such that θ_t is equally likely to be θ_H or θ_L, regardless of the history of past skills. I assume that $v'(0) > 0$, and $v'(\bar{y}) < \infty$. Under these restrictions, the long-run behavior of consumption in a Pareto optimal allocation depends on the reservation utility U_ω. First, and less interestingly, if U_ω is sufficiently high or sufficiently low, there is no incentive problem, and so the agent's consumption is constant over time in a Pareto optimal allocation. More specifically, suppose an agent's reservation utility U_ω is larger than $\overline{U}_\omega$, where

$$\overline{U}_\omega = \frac{\ln(\bar{c}) - v(0)}{1 - \beta}, \tag{3.52}$$

$$\bar{c} \equiv \frac{\theta_H}{v'(0)}, \tag{3.53}$$

Then, $c_t^*(\omega, \theta^t)$ is constant at some consumption level higher than $\bar{c}$, and $y_t^*(\omega, \theta^t)$ is constant at 0. Intuitively, preferences exhibit wealth effects, and having a high reservation utility is akin to having lots of wealth. When $U_\omega \geqslant \overline{U}_\omega$, the agent has so much "wealth" that it is efficient for him never to work regardless of his skill realization.

Similarly, suppose the reservation utility U_ω is lower than $\underline{U}_\omega$, where

$$\underline{U}_\omega = \frac{\ln(\underline{c}) - v(\bar{y}/\theta_H)/2 - v(\bar{y}/\theta_L)/2}{1 - \beta}$$

$$\underline{c} \equiv \frac{\theta_L}{v'(\bar{y})}.$$

Then, $c_t^*(\omega, \theta^t)$ is constant at some consumption level less than $\underline{c}$, and $y_t^*(\omega, \theta^t)$ is constant at $\bar{y}$. The intuition is the same as before: when the agent's reservation utility level is so low, he is so "poor" that it is efficient for him to produce the maximal level of output regardless of his skill realization.

The more interesting case is if the reservation utility U_ω lies in the open interval $(\underline{U}_\omega, \overline{U}_\omega)$. In that case, in a Pareto optimal allocation, consumption $c_t^*(\omega, \theta^t)$ lies in the open interval $(\underline{c}, \bar{c})$ for all (t, θ^t). At the same time, the reciprocal Euler equation (applied to a log utility function) implies that consumption itself follows a martingale. Hence, $c_t^*(\omega, \theta^t)$ must converge along almost every sample path θ^∞. I will not do so here[11], but one can show that it is impossible for the limiting consumption to be an element of the open interval $(\underline{c}, \bar{c})$. Instead, consumption must converge to one of the endpoints of this interval, so that

$$\lim_{t \to \infty}(c_t^*(\omega, \theta^t), y_t^*(\omega, \theta^t)) \in \{(\bar{c}, 0), (\underline{c}, \bar{y})\}$$

for almost all θ^∞.

Thus, given U_ω lies in $(\underline{U}_\omega, \overline{U}_\omega)$, the long-run distribution of consumption has a support of at most two points. Is it possible that all of the consumption paths converge to the same limit? The answer is no. Consumption is a martingale, which implies that, for any $t > s$,

$$c_s^*(\omega, \theta^s) = E(c_t^*(\omega, \theta^t) \mid \theta^s).$$

If we take limits of the right-hand side, we get

$$c_s^*(\omega, \theta^s) = \lim_{t \to \infty} E(c_t^*(\omega, \theta^t) \mid \theta^s)$$
$$= E\left(\lim_{t \to \infty} c_t^*(\omega, \theta^t) \; \middle| \; \theta^s \right),$$

where the second equality relies on consumption being uniformly bounded from above and below. Since $c_s^*(\omega, \theta^s)$ lies in the open interval $(\underline{c}, \bar{c})$, it must be true that the event

$$\left\{ \theta^\infty \; \middle| \; \lim_{t \to \infty} c_t^*(\omega, \theta^t) = \bar{c} \right\}$$

---

[11] The proof relies on results in chapter 6. In that chapter, I show that when skills are i.i.d., we can set up the planner's problem as a dynamic program in which continuation utility is the lone state variable. The dynamic programming formulation can be used to rationalize my description of long-run behavior of consumption in this particular example.

has positive probability and the event

$$\left\{ \theta^\infty \mid \lim_{t \to \infty} c_t^*(\omega, \theta^t) = \underline{c} \right\}$$

has positive probability.

We conclude that, we end up with two distinct castes in the long run in a Pareto optimal allocation. The first caste produces no output, and consumes (at least) $\bar{c}$. The second caste produces $\bar{y}$ units of output and consumes (no more than) $\underline{c}$. However, convergence to these castes takes an infinite amount of time if $U_\omega \in (\underline{U}_\omega, \overline{U}_\omega)$.

3.7.3.2 Example 2: Immiseration

The above analysis relies crucially on the binding lower bound on output. Suppose we assume that we change the above example by setting $v'(0)$ equal to 0, so that the marginal disutility of labor is zero for agents who are not working. This change in preferences has a big effect on the the long-run behavior of consumption in Pareto optimal allocations.

It is still true that if agent ω's reservation utility U_ω is sufficiently low (that is, $U_\omega \leq \underline{U}_\omega$), then ω's consumption is constant at some amount less than $\underline{c}$. The change in long-run allocations occurs if $U_\omega > \underline{U}_\omega$. In the preceding example, when U_ω is larger than $\underline{U}_\omega$, consumption converges to $\bar{c}$ along a positive fraction of paths. But in this example, in which $v'(0)$ equals 0, $\bar{c}$ is infinite. By the martingale convergence theorem, consumption converges to a *finite* limit along almost every sample path, and so it can only converge to $\bar{c}$ along a set of paths with probability zero. Instead, if $U_\omega > \underline{U}_\omega$, consumption must converge to the lower bound $\underline{c}$ along almost every sample path.

This property is known as *immiseration*, because almost all agents' consumptions converge to the same low level. Immiseration takes its most striking form when $v'(\bar{y}) = \infty$. In that case, $\underline{c}$ equals zero. It follows that in any Pareto optimal allocation, almost all agents' consumptions converge to *zero*!

This result often strikes people as counterintuitive. Among other subtleties, it is still true that the unconditional expectation of consumption is time-invariant for any agent ω. How then is it that almost all agents' consumptions converge to zero? The trick is that there is no upper bound on consumption. As time passes, an increasingly small fraction of agents consumes an increasingly large amount of consumption. This fraction eventually converges to zero, while the amount eventually converges to infinity, in such a way so as to keep the average level always the same.[12]

3.7.3.3 Example 3: Permanent Disability Shocks

In the above examples, the history of skill realizations has little impact on the long-run limit of consumption. In example 2, given ω, almost all sample paths of consumption converge to the same limit. Even in example 1, given ω, different histories of skill realizations generate at most two possible limiting levels of consumption.

Suppose $v(y) = y^2/2$, $\theta_H = 1$, and $\theta_L = 0$. Assume that $\pi(\theta_{t+1} = 1 \mid \theta^t) = 1/2$ if $\theta_s = 1$ for all $s \leqslant t$, and $\pi(\theta_{t+1} = 1 \mid \theta^t) = 0$ if $\theta_s = 0$ for some $s \leqslant t$. This stochastic process for skills is such that agents

---

[12] For example, suppose θ is uniform over $[0, 1]$ and consider the sequence of random variables $\{x_n\}_{n=1}^{\infty}$, where $x_n : [0, 1] \to R_+$, and $x_n(\theta) = 0$ if $\theta \geqslant 1/n$ and $x_n(\theta) = n$ if $\theta < 1/n$. Here, the expectation of x_n is 1 for all n, but x_n converges to 0 almost everywhere.

are either able to produce or not. Being disabled is an absorbing state.

Given the stochastic process, there is no remaining incentive problem once an agent becomes disabled. Hence, if $\beta R = 1$, then consumption remains constant for such agents in any Pareto optimal allocation. The resulting constant level of consumption does depend on exactly *when* the agent becomes disabled. Agents who stay abled for longer periods of time must be rewarded for not falsely declaring themselves disabled. Hence, an agent who becomes disabled in period $s < t$ receives less perpetual consumption than an agent who becomes disabled in period t.

It follows that in this setting, the long-run distribution of consumption in a Pareto optimal allocation, for any ω, has a countable support. The eventual limit of any agent's consumption depends on the exact history of shocks that agent faces.

3.8 Summary

People differ in skills at the beginning of their lives, and those differences fluctuate stochastically. If skills can be observed, then it is Pareto optimal for consumption to be independent of skill realizations. However, in a world in which skills are private information, high-skill agents must get more consumption if they are to produce more output. In this fashion, private information about skills induce a Pareto optimal dependence of consumption on skills.

In this section, we have seen that in intertemporal contexts, this dependence of consumption on skills has a large impact on the evolution of consumption. Regardless of whether skills are private information or not, and regardless of the law of motion of skills themselves, the reciprocal of marginal utility follows the law of motion

$$1/u'(c_{t+1}) = \beta R/u'(c_t) + \varepsilon_{t+1}, \qquad (3.54)$$

where ε_{t+1} is a martingale difference. If skills are private information, and it is Pareto optimal to elicit more output from highly skilled agents in period $(t + 1)$, then the conditional variance of ε_{t+1} is nonzero. This nonzero variance has two critical consequences for the Pareto optimal evolution of consumption. First, $u'(c_t) < \beta R E_t u'(c_{t+1})$, so that agents cannot be allowed to borrow and lend freely at interest rate R. Second, the ε innovations to $1/u'(c_{t+1})$ persist over time to a degree governed by the size of βR.

If $\beta R = 1$, $1/u'(c_t)$ follows a martingale and we can exploit the martingale convergence theorem to reach useful conclusions about the long-run properties of $1/u'(c)$. The general result is that along almost all histories, $1/u'(c_t)$ converges and if $u'(\infty) = 0$, so does c_t itself. The nature of the limit depends on the exact features of the environment.

The literature (see, among others, Farhi and Werning 2007) has put a great deal of emphasis on the immiseration result. Indeed, it is often regarded as being the hallmark result of dynamic social contracting in the presence of private information. In my view, this particular limiting result should be seen only as an example of a more general finding that it is Pareto optimal for consumption to be unresponsive to skill shocks in the long run. The lesson of the martingale convergence theorem is that any distortions associated with incentives must be front-loaded.[13]

---

[13] See Albanesi and Armenter (2007) for a more general discussion of front-loading in problems of the second-best.

3.9 Technical Notes

In this section, I describe how to generalize theorem 3.1 to allow Θ to be any Borel set, and I provide a heuristic justification for the martingale convergence theorem.

3.9.1 Generalizing Theorem 3.1 to Intervals

In the body of the section, I assumed that the set Θ of skills was finite. It is more traditional in public finance to assume, following Mirrlees (1971), that the set of skills is an interval. Golosov et al. provide a proof of theorem 3.1 that is valid given that Θ is any Borel[14] subset of R_+. This kind of generality is important, because it allows us to form connections between the work in macroeconomics on dynamic contracting and work in public finance on optimal taxation. For this reason, I now go through this extension in some detail. The discussion requires some knowledge of basic measure theory.

This more general proof builds on the same basic perturbation. We do have to generalize the notion of probabilities in the setup. To simplify matters, assume Ω has only one point. Let μ be a probability measure over the Borel subsets of Θ^T, with support equal to $D \subseteq \Theta^T$. Here, $\mu(A)$ represents the probability that a given agent receives a skill sequence in A. Now, suppose (c^*, y^*) is optimal and there exists $\delta > 0$ such that $c_t^*(\omega, \theta^T), c_{t+1}^*(\omega, \theta^T) \geq \delta$ for almost all θ^T in D. Then, using the same argument as in the body of the

---

[14]The Borel σ-algebra B is the smallest collection of subsets of R_+ that satisfies four properties. First, B contains the empty set. Second, any countable union of elements of B is contained in B. Third, the complement of any element of B is contained in B. Finally, any interval in R_+ is contained in B.

paper, we know that $(0, c_t^*, c_{t+1}^*)$ solves the following programming problem:

$$\max_{\Delta, c_t', c_{t+1}'} \Delta \tag{3.55}$$

s.t. $u(c_t'(\theta^T)) + \beta u(c_{t+1}'(\theta^T))$

$\qquad = u(c_t^*(\theta^T)) + \beta u(c_{t+1}^*(\theta^T)) + \Delta \quad$ for all $\theta^T \in D$

$\qquad \int_D (c_t' - c_t^*) \, d\mu + R^{-1} \int_D (c_{t+1}' - c_{t+1}^*) \, d\mu = 0,$

$\qquad c_t'$ is θ^t-measurable,

$\qquad c_{t+1}'$ is θ^{t+1}-measurable,

$\qquad c_t'(\theta^T), c_{t+1}'(\theta^T) \geqslant 0 \quad$ for all θ^T in D.

Note that this programming problem closely resembles (3.19), except that I have generalized the feasibility restriction to be an integral with respect to μ.

We now need to derive the first-order necessary conditions to this problem. To do so, though, we need to deal with three mathematical issues.

3.9.1.1 Issue 1: Almost Everywhere versus Everywhere

The constraint set in (3.55) treats (c_t', c_{t+1}') as distinct from (c_t^*, c_{t+1}^*) if they differ for any sequence θ^T in D. This formulation makes sense economically because the agent has the ability to pretend to be any θ^T in D. But, from the point of view of the probability measure μ, c_t' and c_t^* are indistinguishable if they differ only on a subset A of D such that $\mu(A) = 0$ (that is, they are equal almost everywhere). There is an intrinsic incompatibility between our formulation of the constraint set (3.55) and μ.

We can readily fix this difficulty by considering the problem:

$$\max_{\Delta, c_t', c_{t+1}'} \Delta \tag{3.56}$$

$$\text{s.t. } u(c_t'(\theta^T)) + \beta u(c_{t+1}'(\theta^T))$$
$$= u(c_t^*(\theta^T)) + \beta u(c_{t+1}^*(\theta^T)) + \Delta$$
$$\text{for almost all } \theta^T \in D,$$

$$\int_D (c_t' - c_t^*) \, d\mu + R^{-1} \int_D (c_{t+1}' - c_{t+1}^*) \, d\mu = 0,$$

c_t' is θ^t-measurable,

c_{t+1}' is θ^{t+1}-measurable,

$c_t'(\theta^T), c_{t+1}'(\theta^T) \geqslant 0$ for almost all θ^T in D,

instead. This problem expands the constraint set of (3.55), and so could potentially have a different (superior) solution. However, suppose $(\Delta^*, c_t', c_{t+1}')$, with $\Delta^* > 0$, solves (3.56). Then, there exists $A \subset D$, $\mu(A) = 0$, such that

$$u(c_t'(\theta^T)) + \beta u(c_{t+1}'(\theta^T))$$
$$= u(c_t^*(\theta^T)) + \beta u(c_{t+1}^*(\theta^T)) + \Delta^*,$$
$$c_t'(\theta^T), c_{t+1}'(\theta^T) \geqslant 0 \tag{3.57}$$

for all θ^T in $D - A$. Define a new pair of consumptions (c_t'', c_{t+1}'') so that (c_t'', c_{t+1}'') equals (c_t', c_{t+1}') except

$$c_t''(\theta^T) = c_t^*(\theta^T) + \varepsilon(\theta^T) \quad \text{if } \theta^T \text{ is in } A, \tag{3.58}$$

$$c_{t+1}''(\theta^T) = c_{t+1}^*(\theta^T) \quad \text{if } \theta^T \text{ is in } A, \tag{3.59}$$

where

$$\varepsilon(\theta^T) = u^{-1}(u(c_t^*(\theta^T)) + \Delta^*) - c_t^*(\theta^T). \tag{3.60}$$

The triple $(\Delta^*, c''_t, c''_{t+1})$ lies in the constraint set of the original problem, and so we have a contradiction to the supposition that (c^*, y^*) is optimal.

This argument implies that $(0, c^*_t, c^*_{t+1})$ must satisfy the first-order necessary conditions to (3.56) if it is to be optimal.

3.9.1.2 Issue 2: A Useful Metric

To derive first-order necessary conditions, we need to be able to take derivatives of functions of c^*. At its most basic level, a derivative is a measure of the change in a function relative to the change in its arguments. In order to differentiate, we need to have a measure of distance between (c'_t, c'_{t+1}) and (c^*_t, c^*_{t+1}).

Not all measures of distance will work. To generate a first-order necessary condition like (3.14), it must be true that if (c'_t, c'_{t+1}) is "close to" (c^*_t, c^*_{t+1}), then (c'_t, c'_{t+1}) is positive almost everywhere. (Otherwise, we have to worry about the possibility of binding non-negativity constraints in formulating our first-order conditions.) This requirement is trivially satisfied by the Euclidean norm when Θ is finite and the pair (c^*_t, c^*_{t+1}) is positive. However, for an arbitrary Borel set Θ, many standard measures of distance will not have this property.

For example, suppose $\Theta = [0, 1]$, and consider any L^p metric, $p < \infty$. This metric measures the distance between two random variables c^*_t and c'_t as the pth moment of the absolute difference between those random variables. Suppose c^*_t is positive almost everywhere (in fact, uniformly bounded away from zero almost everywhere). Pick any δ, no matter how small. We can find some c'_t such that the L^p-distance between c'_t and c^*_t is less than δ, and c'_t has a positive probability of being less than 0. The construction of c_t' works by squeezing the negative portion of c_t' onto a smaller set of θ^T as δ shrinks.

One measure of distance that does work is the *essential-supremum (ess-sup)* metric. The ess-sup of a random variable x is the smallest number M such that $|x| \leqslant M$ almost everywhere. The ess-sup metric measures the distance between c_t^* and c_t' as the ess-sup of $|c_t^* - c_t'|$. The squeezing trick described in the above paragraph doesn't work with the ess-sup metric, because it definitionally covers almost all θ^T. Hence, if c_t^* is uniformly bounded away from zero, then there exists some δ such that if c_t' is within δ of c_t^* in terms of the ess-sup metric, then c_t' is also uniformly bounded away from zero.

With the ess-sup measure of distance, we can, without loss, change the problem (3.56) one more time. In this final change, we drop the nonnegativity constraints, and impose the requirement that c_t' and c_{t+1}' lie in L^∞ (that is, they have essential suprema that are finite):

$$\max_{\Delta, c_t', c_{t+1}'} \Delta \tag{3.61}$$

$$\text{s.t. } u(c_t'(\theta^T)) + \beta u(c_{t+1}'(\theta^T))$$
$$= u(c_t^*(\theta^T)) + \beta u(c_{t+1}^*(\theta^T)) + \Delta$$
$$\text{for almost all } \theta^T \in D,$$

$$\int_D (c_t' - c_t^*) \, d\mu + R^{-1} \int_D (c_{t+1}' - c_{t+1}^*) \, d\mu = 0,$$

c_t' is θ^t-measurable,

c_{t+1}' is θ^{t+1}-measurable,

$c_t', c_{t+1}' \in L^\infty$.

3.9.1.3   Issue 3: Lagrangians in L^∞

The putative optimum $(0, c_t^*, c_{t+1}^*)$ is, in the language of Luenberger (1969), a regular point of the above constraint set. (Intuitively, we can move in at least one direction away from $(0, c_t^*, c_{t+1}^*)$ and stay within the constraint set.) This means that we can attack this problem using Lagrangian analysis, and that $(0, c_t^*, c_{t+1}^*)$ must be a stationary point of the functional:

$$L(\Delta, c_t', c_{t+1}') = \Delta + \langle z^*, u(c_t') + \beta u(c_{t+1}') - \Delta \rangle$$

$$- \lambda \int_D c_t' + R^{-1} c_{t+1}' \, d\mu. \qquad (3.62)$$

Here, λ is a standard Lagrange multiplier. The notation $\langle z^*, x \rangle$ represents a linear operator that inputs elements x of L^∞ and outputs elements of R. It would be desirable to transform this linear operator into a more interpretable form. The Riesz representation theorem guarantees that linear operators that map L^p into R can be written as the integral of the product of the input x with a fixed element z^* of L^q, where $1/p + 1/q = 1$. Unfortunately, this theorem does not apply when $p = \infty$.

Nonetheless, Golosov et al. (2003) show how one can use the above Lagrangian (3.62) to derive the reciprocal Euler equation. Let L_t^∞ be the set of elements of L^∞ that are θ^t-measurable and L_{t+1}^∞ be the set of elements of L^∞ that are θ^{t+1}-measurable. To be a stationary point of L, $(0, c_t^*, c_{t+1}^*)$ must satisfy

$$\langle z^*, u'(c_t^*) \delta_t \rangle$$

$$- \lambda \int_D \delta_t \, d\mu = 0 \quad \text{for all } \delta_t \text{ in } L_t^\infty, \qquad (3.63)$$

$$\langle z^*, \beta u'(c_{t+1}^*)\delta_{t+1}\rangle$$

$$-\lambda R^{-1} \int_D \delta_{t+1} \, d\mu = 0 \quad \text{for all } \delta_{t+1} \text{ in } L_{t+1}^\infty. \quad (3.64)$$

Given any δ_t' in L_t^∞, define an element δ_t of L_t^∞ by $\delta_t = \delta_t'/u'(c_t^*)$. Similarly, given any δ_t' in L_t^∞, define an element δ_{t+1} of L_{t+1}^∞ by $\delta_{t+1} = \beta^{-1}\delta_t'/u'(c_{t+1}^*)$. Substituting into (3.63) and (3.64), we obtain

$$\langle z^*, \delta_t'\rangle - \lambda \int_D \frac{\delta_t'}{u'(c_t^*)} \, d\mu = 0$$

$$\text{for all } \delta_t' \text{ in } L_t^\infty,$$

$$\langle z^*, \delta_t'\rangle - \beta^{-1}R^{-1}\lambda \int_D \frac{\delta_t'}{u'(c_{t+1}^*)} \, d\mu = 0$$

$$\text{for all } \delta_t' \text{ in } L_t^\infty.$$

We can substitute out the z^* operators to get

$$\lambda \int_D \frac{\delta_t'}{u'(c_t^*)} \, d\mu$$

$$= \lambda R^{-1}\beta^{-1} \int_D \frac{\delta_t'}{u'(c_{t+1}^*)} \, d\mu \quad \text{for all } \delta_t \text{ in } L_t^\infty.$$
$$(3.65)$$

We can pick δ_t' to be any element of L_t^∞. In particular, we can choose δ_t' to be the indicator variable of any Borel set in Θ^t. We can conclude, from the definition of conditional expectation (in, for example, Billingsley 1986) that

$$\frac{1}{u'(c_t^*)} = \beta^{-1}R^{-1}E\left\{ \frac{1}{u'(c_{t+1}^*)} \,\middle|\, \theta^t \right\}. \quad (3.66)$$

3.9.2 Heuristic Argument for the Martingale Convergence Theorem

In this subsection, I follow Chamley (2003) and sketch a proof of the martingale convergence theorem. Be forewarned: the proof of the general theorem is considerably deeper than the following discussion indicates.

Let X_t be a nonnegative martingale. To simplify the argument, I assume that the probability density function of $X_{t+T} - X_t$, conditional on X_t, is symmetric around 0 for any t, T. Recall that, along a given sample path, X_t must either converge to infinity, converge to a finite nonnegative number, or fail to converge. The fact that $E(X_t)$ is constant and finite immediately implies that the probability that X_t converges to infinity is zero. It remains to be shown that X_t must converge along almost all sample paths.

The martingale property implies that first-differenced X_t has an autocorrelation of zero. Hence,

$$\text{Var}(X_{t+T} \mid X_t) = \text{Var}(X_{t+T} - X_t \mid X_t) \quad (3.67)$$

$$= \sum_{k=1}^{T} \text{Var}(X_{t+k} - X_{t+k-1} \mid X_t). \quad (3.68)$$

The density of $X_{t+T} - X_t$, conditional on X_t, is symmetric around 0 (by assumption). Since X_{t+T} is nonnegative, we know that $X_{t+T} - X_t$ is bounded from below by $-X_t$; symmetry implies that $X_{t+T} - X_t$ is bounded from above by X_t. Hence,

$$X_t^2 \geqslant \lim_{T \to \infty} \sum_{k=1}^{T} \text{Var}(X_{t+k} - X_{t+k-1} \mid X_t). \quad (3.69)$$

Since the right-hand side sum converges, we know that its tail partial sums converge to zero:

$$0 = \lim_{T \to \infty} \lim_{S \to \infty} \sum_{s=1}^{S} \text{Var}(X_{t+T+s} - X_{t+T+s-1} \mid X_t) \quad (3.70)$$

$$= \lim_{T \to \infty} \lim_{S \to \infty} E\{(X_{t+T+S} - X_{t+T})^2 \mid X_t\}. \quad (3.71)$$

Thus, $|X_{t+T+S} - X_{t+T}|^2$ is converging to zero almost everywhere as T, S converge to infinity. We can conclude that X_{t+T} converges to some (possibly random) X_∞ as T goes to infinity.

References

Albanesi, S., and R. Armenter. 2007. Intertemporal distortions in the second-best. Working Paper, Columbia University.

Ales, L., and P. Maziero. 2009. Non-exclusive dynamic contracts, competition, and the limits of insurance. Working Paper, University of Minnesota.

Atkeson, A., and R. E. Lucas, Jr. 1992. On efficient distribution with private information. *Review of Economic Studies* 59:427–53.

Billingsley, P. 1986. *Probability and Measure*, 2nd edn. New York: John Wiley & Sons.

Chamley, C. 2003. *Rational Herds: Economic Models of Social Learning.* Cambridge University Press.

Diamond, P., and J. A. Mirrlees. 1978. A model of social insurance with variable retirement. *Journal of Public Economics* 10:295–336.

Farhi, E., and I. Werning. 2007. Inequality and social discounting. *Journal of Political Economy* 115:365–402.

———. 2008. Optimal savings distortions with recursive preferences. *Journal of Monetary Economics* 55:21–42.

Golosov, M., N. Kocherlakota, and A. Tsyvinski. 2003. Optimal indirect and capital taxation. *Review of Economic Studies* 70:569–87.

Green, E. 1987. Lending and the smoothing of uninsurable income. In *Contractual Arrangements for Intertemporal Trade* (ed. E. C. Prescott and N. Wallace). University of Minnesota Press.

Grochulski, B., and N. Kocherlakota. 2008. Nonseparable preferences and optimal social security systems. Working Paper, University of Minnesota.

Luenberger, D. 1969. *Optimization by Vector Space Methods.* New York: John Wiley & Sons.

Mirrlees, J. A. 1971. An exploration in the theory of optimum income taxation. *Review of Economic Studies* 38: 175–208.

Rogerson, W. 1985. Repeated moral hazard. *Econometrica* 53:69–76.

Segal, I. 2006. Communication in economic mechanisms. In *Advances in Economics and Econometrics: Theory and Application, Ninth World Congress* (ed. R. Blundell, W. K. Newey, and T. Persson). Cambridge University Press.

Sun, Y. 2006. The exact law of large numbers via Fubini extension and characterization of insurable risks. *Journal of Economic Theory* 126:31–69.

Townsend, R. 1982. Optimal multiperiod contracts and the gain from enduring relationships under private information. *Journal of Political Economy* 90:1166–86.

4

Dynamic Optimal Taxation:
Lessons for Macroeconomists

In this chapter, we return to the fiscal policy issues that lay at the heart of chapter 2. I augment the model from that chapter so as to include agent heterogeneity and aggregate shocks to the aggregate production function. As in chapter 3, the agent heterogeneity takes the form of differences in skills (labor productivities), and these differences can fluctuate stochastically over time. Within this class of environments, I set up a canonical optimal *nonlinear* taxation problem for the government. I assume that the government has access to a complete record of the history of an agent's labor incomes and can also observe an agent's current capital income. The government is able to contemplate *any* tax schedule as a function of these agent-specific variables, and can also condition the tax schedule on the aggregate shocks.

The government's ability to tax is limited, though: it cannot condition tax payments directly on agents' skills. From a strictly mathematical point of view, this restriction is simply one more ad hoc limitation on the functional form of taxes (like linearity in chapter 2). However, from an economic point of view, this restriction is a much more natural one because it emerges *endogenously* when skills are private information (as in chapter 3).

The key to the analysis in this chapter is that, in many circumstances, the quantities in the solution to this canonical optimal tax problem also solve the social planner's problem in chapter 3. This result allows us to use the characterizations of optimal quantities in chapter 3 to reach important conclusions about the nature of optimal capital income taxes, labor income taxes, government debt, and monetary policy.

4.1 A Nonlinear Tax Problem

In this section, I describe a canonical nonlinear taxation problem for a class of dynamic economies with heterogeneous agents. Suppose there is a unit measure of agents in a T period economy, $T < \infty$. The agents have identical preferences,

$$\sum_{t=1}^{T} \beta^{t-1}[u(c_t) - v(l_t)],$$

where c_t is consumption in period t, l_t is effort in period t, and θ_t represents the agent's level of skill in period t. We assume u is increasing and v is increasing.

The shock structure works as follows. Let Z and Θ be finite sets. Nature first draws a T period sequence z^T of aggregate shocks from the set Z^T according to π_Z. Then, she draws θ^T from the set Θ^T for each agent, according to the probability density function $\pi_\Theta(\cdot \mid z^T)$. For convenience, assume that both probability density functions π_Z and π_Θ put positive probability on all elements of Z^T and Θ^T respectively. We assume that a law of large numbers holds: for each z^T, the fraction of agents who have history θ^T is given by $\pi_\Theta(\theta^T \mid z^T)$.

I assume that, for all θ^t, the conditional density,

$$\pi_\theta(\theta^t \mid z^T) \equiv \sum_{(\theta_{t+1},\dots,\theta_T)} \pi_\theta(\theta^t, \theta_{t+1},\dots,\theta_T \mid z^T),$$

(4.1)

is independent of $z^T_{t+1} \equiv (z_{t+1},\dots,z_T)$. This restriction says that, conditional on z^t, θ^t and z^T_{t+1} are independent.[1] It has two consequences. First, given z^t, we know the cross-sectional distribution of the agents' personal histories (θ^t). Second, an agent's personal history in period t reveals nothing to him about future aggregate shocks beyond what is in z^t.

At each date, agents can produce effective labor using effort, according to the technology

$$y_t = \theta_t l_t.$$

As we shall see, effective labor is then used together with capital to produce output. Note that as in chapter 3, I am imposing few restrictions on the data-generation processes for shocks (both individual and aggregate).

There is a government with a technology that can turn private goods one-for-one into public goods. We assume that the government's production of public goods is governed by the (exogenous) stochastic process G, where $G = (G_t)_{t=1}^T$, $G_t : Z^T \to R_+$, and G_t is z^t-measurable.

All agents in the economy are initially endowed with $\bar{K}_1$ units of capital. Then, an allocation is a mapping

---

[1] In the technical notes to this chapter, I discuss some of the issues that emerge when this restriction is relaxed.

(c, y, k) such that

$$
\begin{aligned}
c &: \quad \Theta^T \times Z^T \to R_+^T, \\
y &: \quad \Theta^T \times Z^T \to [0, \bar{y}]^T, \\
k &: \quad \Theta^T \times Z^T \to R_+^{T-1},
\end{aligned}
$$

where $(c_t, y_t, k_{t+1})_{t=1}^T$ is measurable with respect to (θ^t, z^t). Let $F(K, Y, z)$ be an aggregate production function such that F is homogeneous of degree 1 in its first two arguments, and suppose capital depreciates at rate δ from one period to the next. Then, a feasible allocation must satisfy

$$
\begin{aligned}
C_t(z^T) &+ K_{t+1}(z^T) + G_t(z^T) \\
&\leqslant (1 - \delta)K_t(z^T) + F(K_t(z^T), Y_t(z^T), z_t) \\
&\qquad\qquad\qquad\qquad\qquad\qquad \text{for all } t, z^T,
\end{aligned}
$$

$$
K_1 \leqslant \overline{K}_1,
$$

where

$$
\begin{aligned}
C_t(z^T) &\equiv \sum_{\theta^T \in \Theta^T} \pi_\Theta(\theta^T \mid z^T) c_t(\theta^T, z^T), \\
Y_t(z^T) &\equiv \sum_{\theta^T \in \Theta^T} \pi_\Theta(\theta^T \mid z^T) y_t(\theta^T, z^T), \\
K_t(z^T) &\equiv \sum_{\theta^T \in \Theta^T} \pi_\Theta(\theta^T \mid z^T) k_t(\theta^T, z^T)
\end{aligned}
$$

represent per-capita consumption, effective labor, and capital respectively.

There is a large number of identical competitive firms. The firms rent capital and hire effective labor from the agents, taking wages $w_t(z^T)$ and rental rates $r_t(z^T)$ as given in period t. At each date t, agents can trade capital with one another, lease capital to the firms, and provide effective labor to the firms.

Before period 1, the government commits to a tax schedule $\tau = (\tau_t)_{t=1}^T$, where $\tau_t : R^t \times R \times Z^t \to R$ maps the agent's history of labor incomes, his period t capital income, and the history of aggregate shocks z^t into taxes. Note that, as mentioned above, taxes do not depend directly on agents' skills. Given τ, and stochastic processes w and r for wages and rents respectively, the agent solves the problem

$$\max_{c,y,k} \sum_{z^T \in Z^T} \sum_{\theta^T \in \Theta^T} \sum_{t=1}^{T} \pi_\Theta(\theta^T \mid z^T) \pi_Z(z^T)$$
$$\times [u(c_t(\theta^T, z^T)) - v(y_t(\theta^T, z^T)/\theta_t)] \beta^{t-1}$$
$$\text{s.t. } c_t(\theta^T, z^T) + k_{t+1}(\theta^T, z^T)$$
$$+ \tau_t((w_s(z^T)y_s(\theta^T, z^T))_{s=1}^t, r_t(z^T)k_t(\theta^T, z^T), z^t)$$
$$\leqslant (1 - \delta + r_t(z^T))k_t(\theta^T, z^T)$$
$$+ w_t(z^T)y_t(\theta^T, z^T) \quad \text{for all } (t, \theta^T, z^T)$$

$(c_t, y_t, k_{t+1}, \bar{y} - y_t)$ is nonnegative and
$$(\theta^t, z^t)\text{-measurable,}$$

$k_1 \leqslant \overline{K}_1$.

(I ignore firm profits; with the constant returns to scale technology, profits are zero in equilibrium.)

Then, given a government's choice τ, an equilibrium in this economy is an allocation (c, y, k) and prices (r, w) such that (c, y, k) solves the agent's problem given (τ, r, w) and markets clear in every date and history:

$$C_t(z^T) + K_{t+1}(z^T) + G_t(z^T)$$
$$= (1 - \delta)K_t(z^T) + F(K_t(z^T), Y_t(z^T), z_t)$$
$$\text{for all } t, z^T,$$

$K_1 = \overline{K}_1$.

As was true in the Ramsey model, given that G is exogenously specified, there is no equilibrium for most specifications of τ. (Thus, if we set $\tau = 0$ and G is positive in all dates and states, then there is no equilibrium.) I denote the set of equilibrium allocations (c, y, k) for a given τ and G by $\text{EQM}_{\text{NL}}(\tau, G)$ (where the subscript "NL" represents nonlinear). Note that in any equilibrium, since F is homogeneous of degree 1, we know that, for all t, z^T,

$$C_t(z^T) + K_{t+1}(z^T)$$

$$+ \sum_{\theta^T \in \Theta^T} [\pi_\Theta(\theta^T \mid z^T)\tau_t((w_s(z^T)y_s(\theta^T, z^T))_{s=1}^t,$$

$$r_t(z^T)k_t(\theta^T, z^T), z^t)]$$

$$= (1 - \delta)K_t(z^T) + F(K_t(z^T), Y_t(z^T), z_t).$$

Market-clearing then implies that, for all t, z^T,

$$G_t(z^T)$$

$$= \sum_{\theta^T \in \Theta^T} [\pi_\Theta(\theta^T \mid z^T)\tau_t((w_s(z^T)y_s(\theta^T, z^T))_{s=1}^t,$$

$$r_t(z^T)k_t(\theta^T, z^T), z^t)].$$

We can conclude that in any equilibrium, the government maintains budget balance in each period.

Before period 1, the government chooses tax system τ so as to maximize *ex ante* utility. Hence, the government's problem in this economy is akin to that in the Ramsey model:

$$\max_{(c, y, k, \tau)} \sum_{\theta^T \in \Theta^T} \sum_{z^T \in Z^T} \sum_{t=1}^T \beta^{t-1} \left[\pi_\Theta(\theta^T \mid z^T)\pi_Z(z^T) \right.$$

$$\left. \times \left\{ u(c_t(\theta^T, z^T)) - v\left(\frac{y_t(\theta^T, z^T)}{\theta_t}\right) \right\} \right]$$

s.t. $(c, y, k) \in \text{EQM}_{\text{NL}}(\tau, G)$.   (4.2)

The objective in this problem assumes that the government treats all agents symmetrically. However, the results in this chapter are also valid if the government uses an objective that distinguishes among individuals based on attributes like the ωs described in chapter 3 or based on first period realizations of skills.

4.2 Any Tax Equilibrium Is Incentive-Compatible

In developing the model in this chapter, I have made no reference to an agent's personal history of shocks actually being private information. Nonetheless, I now prove that any equilibrium allocation is in fact incentive-compatible in the sense described in chapter 3. This crucial result is implied by our assumption in the preceding section that taxes cannot be conditioned directly on skills. The result allows us to connect our study of optimal incentive-feasible allocations in chapter 3 with the study of optimal tax systems.

To prove this result, we first need to develop a definition of incentive-compatibility in this economy with macroeconomic shocks. Define a mimicking strategy to be a mapping,

$$\sigma : \Theta^T \times Z^T \to \Theta^T,$$

where σ_t is (θ^t, z^t)-measurable for all t. This definition is completely analogous to that in chapter 3 except that we allow the agent to condition his choices on the history of aggregate shocks and in this case all histories have positive probability. Let Σ be the set of all mimicking strategies and define

$$V(\sigma; c, y)$$

$$\equiv \sum_{z^T \in Z^T} \pi_Z(z^T) \sum_{t=1}^{T} \beta^{t-1} \sum_{\theta^T \in \Theta^T} \pi_\Theta(\theta^T \mid z^T)$$
$$\times [u(c_t(\sigma(\theta^T, z^T), z^T))$$
$$- v(y_t(\sigma(\theta^T, z^T), z^T)/\theta_t)]$$

to be the utility that an agent receives from using mimicking strategy σ given allocation (c, y). Let σ_{TT} be the truth-telling strategy such that $\sigma(\theta^T, z^T) = \theta^T$ for all (θ^T, z^T). Then, an allocation (c, y, k) is incentive-compatible if and only if

$$V(\sigma_{TT}; c, y) \geqslant V(\sigma; c, y)$$

for all σ in Σ. Note that if (c, y, k) is incentive-compatible, so is (c, y, k') for any k'.

With this definition of incentive-compatibility in hand, we can prove that equilibrium outcomes are in fact incentive-compatible. The proof is essentially an application of the Revelation Principle.

Proposition 4.1. *Suppose an allocation* (c, y, k) *is an equilibrium given some tax function* τ, *so that* $(c, y, k) \in \text{EQM}_{NL}(\tau, G)$. *Then,* (c, y, k) *is incentive-compatible.*

Proof. Note first that the allocation (c, y, k) lies in the budget set of the agent. Now suppose the agent uses a mimicking strategy σ. He gets an allocation $(\hat{c}, \hat{y}, \hat{k})$, where

$$(\hat{c}, \hat{y}, \hat{k})(\theta^T, z^T) = (c, y, k)(\sigma(\theta^T, z^T), z^T).$$

The range of σ implies that $\sigma(\theta^T, z^T) \in \Theta^T$ for all (θ^T, z^T). Hence, we know that

$$
\begin{aligned}
c_t(\sigma(\theta^T, z^T), z^T) &+ k_{t+1}(\sigma(\theta^T, z^T), z^T) \\
&+ \tau_t((w_s(z^T)y_s(\sigma(\theta^T, z^T), z^T)_{s=1}^t, \\
&\quad\quad r_t(z^T)k_t(\sigma(\theta^T, z^T), z^t)) \\
&\leqslant (1 - \delta + r_t(z^T))k_t(\sigma(\theta^T, z^T), z^T) \\
&\quad\quad + w_t(z^T)y_t(\sigma(\theta^T, z^T), z^T) \\
&\quad\quad\quad\quad\quad\quad\quad \text{for all } t, (\theta^T, z^T).
\end{aligned}
$$

It follows that the allocation $(\hat{c}, \hat{y}, \hat{k})$ is in the budget set of the agent. Since (c, y, k) is an equilibrium, we can conclude that (c, y, k) provides at least as much *ex ante* utility to the agent as $(\hat{c}, \hat{y}, \hat{k})$. Hence, for any σ,

$$
V(\sigma_{TT}; c, y) \geqslant V(\sigma; c, y),
$$

and so (c, y, k) is incentive-compatible. $\quad\quad\square$

The key to this proposition is that taxes are only a function of an agent's choice of (y, k), and not his true θ. When faced with this kind of tax schedule, an agent with skill θ^T is free to choose the same allocation (c, y, k) as an agent with alternative skill history $\theta^{T\prime}$. It follows that a tax equilibrium outcome must be robust to any possible mimicking strategy, and so must be incentive-compatible.

4.3 Building an Optimal Tax System

The definition of the constraint set in the maximization problem (4.2) is overly abstract for the problem to be of use. In the Ramsey problem, we were able to show that the set of allocations that lie in $E(\tau_k, \tau_l)$ for

some (τ_k, τ_l) is defined by a simple set of equality constraints. We were then able to apply Lagrangian methods to solve the resulting constrained optimization
problem and characterize the optimal τ.

With nonlinear taxes, proposition 4.1 only characterizes a *superset* of implementable allocations. For
this reason, we follow a different approach with the
maximization problem (4.2) than we did in chapter 2
with the Ramsey problem. We have shown that the set
of incentive-compatible allocations is larger than the
set of tax equilibrium outcomes. Let IF(G) be the set
of incentive-feasible allocations, given G, and consider
the social planner's problem:

$$\max_{c,y,k} \sum_{z^T \in Z^T} \sum_{\theta^T \in \Theta^T} \left[\pi_\Theta(\theta^T \mid z^T)\pi_Z(z^T) \right.$$
$$\left. \times \left[u(c_t(\theta^T, z^T)) - v\left(\frac{y_t(\theta^T, z^T)}{\theta_t} \right) \right] \beta^{t-1} \right]$$
$$(4.3)$$

s.t. $(c, y, k) \in$ IF(G).

Suppose that (c^*, y^*, k^*) solves this problem. If we
can construct τ and k' such that (c^*, y^*, k') is in
$\text{EQM}_{\text{NL}}(\tau, G)$, then τ is necessarily an optimal tax. The
goal of this section is to describe one of the many
such τ.

4.3.1   The Static Case

In this subsection, I re-create an old result in public finance, and show how we can find such a τ in static settings. Suppose that $T = 1$ and Z is a singleton, so that
we have a static economy with no aggregate shocks.
Suppose (c^*, y^*) solves the planner's problem (4.3). I
claim that c^* depends on θ_1 only through y^*. To see

the truth of this claim, suppose by way of contradiction that $y^*(\theta_1) = y^*(\theta_1')$ and $c^*(\theta_1)$ is larger than $c^*(\theta_1')$. Then

$$u(c^*(\theta_1)) - v\left(\frac{y^*(\theta_1)}{\theta_1'}\right) > u(c^*(\theta_1')) - v\left(\frac{y^*(\theta_1')}{\theta_1'}\right)$$

and so (c^*, y^*) is not incentive-compatible.

This logic implies that there exists a strictly increasing function $\hat{c} : \bigcup_{\theta_1 \in \Theta}\{y^*(\theta_1)\} \to R_+$ such that

$$c^*(\theta_1) = \hat{c}(y^*(\theta_1)).$$

The function $\hat{c}$ has a finite domain, given by the range of possible effective labors in the optimal allocation. In order to build a realistic tax schedule, which allows agents to choose from an interval of possible effective labors, it is useful to extend the domain of $\hat{c}$ to all $y \geqslant \min_{\theta_1} y^*(\theta_1)$. For such y, define

$$\hat{c}(y) \equiv \max_{y' \leqslant y} \hat{c}(y')$$

$$\text{s.t. } y' \in \bigcup_{\theta_1 \in \Theta} \{y^*(\theta_1)\}.$$

Let $w = F_Y(\overline{K}_1, \sum_{\theta_1 \in \Theta} \pi_\Theta(\theta_1) y^*(\theta_1))$ be the marginal product of effective labor in the optimal allocation, and define a tax schedule τ as a function of labor income e so that

$$\tau(e) = e + (1 - \delta + r)\overline{K}_1 - \hat{c}(e/w)$$

$$\text{if } e \geqslant \min \bigcup_{\theta_1 \in \Theta} \{wy^*(\theta_1)\}$$

$$= 2e + (1 - \delta + r)\overline{K}_1$$

$$\text{if } e < \min \bigcup_{\theta_1 \in \Theta} \{wy^*(\theta_1)\}.$$

Here, r is the marginal product of capital, calculated using the optimal effective labor allocation y^*. (I abstract from the tax on capital income. In this setting, this tax is equivalent to an intercept term in the labor tax schedule.)

I claim that $(c^*, y^*) \in \mathrm{EQM}_{\mathrm{NL}}(\tau, G)$. Given the tax schedule τ, an individual with skill θ_1^* faces a choice problem of the form

$$\max_{(c,y)\in R_+^2} u(c) - v(y/\theta_1^*)$$

$$\text{s.t. } c \leqslant wy - \tau(wy) + (1 - \delta + r)\overline{K}_1$$

$$c \geqslant 0,$$

$$\bar{y} - y \geqslant 0,$$

$$y \geqslant 0.$$

It is budget-infeasible for the agent to choose $y' < \min \bigcup_{\theta_1 \in \Theta} \{y^*(\theta_1)\}$ because his taxes then exceed his income. Suppose instead that the agent chooses $y' \geqslant \min \bigcup_{\theta_1 \in \Theta} \{y^*(\theta_1)\}$, where $y' \notin \bigcup_{\theta_1 \in \Theta} \{y^*(\theta_1)\}$, and sets $c = wy' - \tau(wy') + (1 - \delta + r)\overline{K}_1$. Then, the agent can get the same consumption and work no more if he chooses y rather than y', where

$$y = \max_{\tilde{y} \leqslant y'} \tilde{y}$$

$$\text{s.t. } \tilde{y} \in \bigcup_{\theta_1 \in \Theta} \{y^*(\theta_1)\}.$$

Hence, there is no loss in generality in restricting attention to choices of $y \in \bigcup_{\theta_1 \in \Theta} \{y^*(\theta_1)\}$.

We also know that, because (c^*, y^*) is incentive-compatible,

$$u(wy^*(\theta_1^*) + (1 - \delta + r)k_1 - \tau(wy^*(\theta_1^*)))$$
$$- v(y^*(\theta_1^*)/\theta_1^*)$$
$$= u(c^*(\theta_1^*)) - v(y^*(\theta_1^*)/\theta_1^*)$$

$$\geqslant u(c^*(\theta_1)) - v(y^*(\theta_1)/\theta_1^*) \quad \text{for all } \theta_1$$
$$= u(wy^*(\theta_1) + (1 - \delta + r)k_1 - \tau(wy^*(\theta_1)))$$
$$- v(y^*(\theta_1)/\theta_1^*) \quad \text{for all } \theta_1$$

and so it follows that $(c^*(\theta_1^*), y^*(\theta_1^*))$ solves the individual's choice problem. We can conclude that indeed $(c^*, y^*) \in \text{EQM}_{\text{NL}}(\tau, G)$.

In this way, we can take any solution to the planner's problem (4.3) in the static setting, and use it to construct an optimal tax schedule. The tax schedule is designed so that after-tax earnings are a right-continuous step function of earnings themselves. The jumps in the step function take place at points in the set $\bigcup_{\theta_1 \in \Theta}\{wy^*(\theta_1)\}$. These jump discontinuities disappear if Θ is an interval, as opposed to a finite set as we have assumed.

4.3.2 The Need for Capital Income Taxes

In the static setting, there was no way for agents to accumulate capital and hence no room for capital income taxes. We turn to the issue of how to construct optimal tax schedules in dynamic settings. We focus first on the following question. Suppose (c^*, y^*, k^*) is a solution to (4.3), and we want to find (τ, G) such that (c^*, y^*, k') is in $\text{EQM}_{\text{NL}}(\tau, G)$. How would such a τ need to treat capital income?

Here, the lessons of chapter 3 about the intertemporal characteristics of Pareto optima with private information are crucial. Theorem 3.1 proved that, in a setting without aggregate shocks, a Pareto optimal allocation satisfied a "reciprocal" Euler equation, but not a standard Euler equation. This result can be extended to our setting with aggregate shocks.

Theorem 4.2. *Suppose* (c^*, y^*, k^*) *is a solution to the planner's problem (4.3) such that* $c_t^*(\theta^T, z^T) > 0$ *and* $c_{t+1}^*(\theta^T, z^T) > 0$ *for all* (θ^T, z^T). *Let* (K_{t+1}^*, Y_{t+1}^*) *be per-capita capital and effective labor in period* $(t + 1)$. *Then, for any* $\bar{z}^T$ *in* Z^T *such that* $K_{t+1}^*(\bar{z}^T) > 0$, *there exists* $\lambda_{t+1} : Z^T \rightarrow R_+$ *such that* λ_{t+1} *is* z^{t+1}-*measurable and*

$$\lambda_{t+1}(z^T)$$
$$= \frac{\beta\{E\{1/u'(c_{t+1}^*) \mid \theta^t = \bar{\theta}^t, z^{t+1} = (\bar{z}^t, z_{t+1})\}\}^{-1}}{u'(c_t^*(\bar{\theta}^T, \bar{z}^T))}$$

$$\text{for all } \bar{\theta}^T \text{ in } \Theta^T$$
$$\text{(4.4)}$$

and

$$1 = E\{\lambda_{t+1}(1 - \delta + F_k(K_{t+1}^*, Y_{t+1}^*)) \mid z^t = \bar{z}^t\}. \quad (4.5)$$

Proof. See the technical notes at the end of the chapter.   □

The programming problem (4.3) has both feasibility constraints and incentive constraints. The function λ represents the ratio of the multipliers on the history $(\bar{z}^t, z_{t+1})$ feasibility constraint and the history $\bar{z}^t$ feasibility constraint (normalized by the conditional probability of z_{t+1}). In this sense, λ represents the planner's marginal rate of substitution between consumption in history $\bar{z}^t$ and history $(\bar{z}^t, z_{t+1})$. With this interpretation, (4.5) is simply the planner's Euler equation for capital accumulation.

The expression (4.4) ties the planner's marginal rate of substitution to individual-level consumption. The numerator is the cross-sectional harmonic mean of individual marginal utilities, conditional on aggregate history $(\bar{z}^t, z_{t+1})$ and private history $\bar{\theta}^t$. (Implicitly, the expectation is summed over realizations of θ_{t+1}.) The denominator is simply marginal utility in aggregate history $\bar{z}^t$ and private history $\bar{\theta}^t$. Note that both the numerator and denominator may depend on $\bar{\theta}^t$, but their ratio does not.

These two equations are a direct generalization of the reciprocal Euler equation in theorem 3.1. Suppose Z is a singleton. Then, λ^{-1} is a constant that simultaneously equals

$$(1 - \delta + F_k(K^*_{t+1}, Y^*_{t+1}))$$

and

$$\beta^{-1} u'(c^*_t(\bar{\theta}^T, \bar{z}^T)) E\left\{ \frac{1}{u'(c^*_{t+1})} \;\middle|\; \theta^t = \bar{\theta}^t \right\}.$$

Combining these two delivers the reciprocal Euler equation, with $(1 - \delta + F_k(K^*_{t+1}, Y^*_{t+1}))$ playing the role of the gross rate of return.

This theorem is a characterization of optimal quantities. However, it provides important information about any tax system τ such that an optimal allocation $(c^*, y^*, k^*) \in \text{EQM}_{\text{NL}}(\tau, G)$. Suppose (c^*, y^*, k^*) solves (4.3). Suppose too that the incentive problem is such that the optimal c^*_{t+1} depends on the current realization of θ_{t+1}, so that

$$\text{Var}(u'(c^*_{t+1}) \mid \theta^t = \bar{\theta}^t, z^{t+1} = \bar{z}^{t+1}) > 0.$$

Then, we can apply Jensen's inequality to (4.4) conclude that

$$\lambda(\bar{z}_{t+1}) < \beta \frac{E\{u'(c^*_{t+1}) \mid \theta^t = \bar{\theta}^t, z^{t+1} = \bar{z}^{t+1}\}}{u'(c^*_t(\bar{\theta}^T, \bar{z}^T))}.$$

If we substitute into (4.5), we obtain

$$u'(c_t^*(\bar{\theta}^T, \bar{z}^T))$$
$$< \beta E\{u'(c_{t+1}^*)(1 - \delta + F_k(K_{t+1}^*, Y_{t+1}^*)) \mid$$
$$\theta^t = \bar{\theta}^t, z^t = \bar{z}^t\}.$$
$$(4.6)$$

The wedge in (4.6) immediately tells us that capital must be taxed in period $(t + 1)$. Suppose that, on the contrary, $(c^*, y^*, k') \in \text{EQM}_{\text{NL}}(\tau, G)$, and τ_{t+1} is independent of k_{t+1}. Then, the individual's Euler equation for capital accumulation will imply that

$$u'(c_t^*(\bar{\theta}^T, \bar{z}^T))$$
$$\geqslant \beta E\{u'(c_{t+1}^*)(1 - \delta + F_k(K_{t+1}^*, Y_{t+1}^*)) \mid$$
$$\theta^t = \bar{\theta}^t, z^t = \bar{z}^t\},$$
$$(4.7)$$

which contradicts (4.6). If τ implements a socially optimal allocation in which incentives matter at some date, then it is not possible for capital tax rates to equal zero in period $(t + 1)$.

This result about the need for capital income taxes contrasts with the conclusion that we obtained in chapter 2. (It is true that in chapter 2 we had no aggregate shocks. But the distinction between (4.6) and (4.7) exists even if Z is a singleton, so that there are no aggregate shocks.) We found there that the Ramsey approach says that capital income tax rates are optimally set to zero after period 2 if u is of the power form. The key difference here is that agents with a lot of capital in period $(t + 1)$ are hard to motivate via incentives in period $(t + 1)$. It is therefore optimal to deter capital accumulation in some fashion. In what follows, we figure out how best to do so.

4.3.3 How *Not* to Design Optimal Capital Income Taxes

We now know that if we are to construct a tax schedule that implements a given socially optimal allocation, that schedule must feature nonzero capital taxes. I next turn to the question of how to structure these capital income taxes. The typical approach in public finance is to set these taxes equal to the wedges in the social optimum. This approach, originally due to Pigou, makes the first-order conditions in the individual's problem line up with those in the planner's problem. In this subsection, I show in the context of a prototypical example that this approach does not always work.[2]

The example has two periods, with no shocks in period 1, and two equally likely possible realizations of skills in period 2. Specifically, let $u(c) = \ln(c)$, $v(l) = l^2/2$, and $\beta = 1$. Suppose too that $T = 2$, $\Theta = \{0, 1\}$, $Z = \{1\}$ (so that there are no aggregate shocks), $F(K, Y) = rK + wY$, and $\delta = 1$. As well, suppose $v(l) = l^2/2$, and $\pi_\Theta(1, 1) = \pi_\Theta(1, 0) = 1/2$. Set $G = 0$. Just for the purposes of this example, let (c_{2i}, y_{2i}) denote consumption and effective labor when $\theta = i$. Then, we can rewrite the planner's problem (4.3) as

$$\max_{c_1, c_{21}, c_{20}, y_1, y_{21}, K_2} \ln(c_1) - \tfrac{1}{2}y_1^2 + \tfrac{1}{2}\ln(c_{21})$$
$$- \tfrac{1}{4}y_{21}^2 + \tfrac{1}{2}\ln(c_{20})$$
$$\text{s.t. } c_1 + K_2 = rK_1 + wy_1$$
$$\tfrac{1}{2}c_{21} + \tfrac{1}{2}c_{20} = rK_2 + \tfrac{1}{2}wy_{21},$$

---

[2] The example closely resembles ones in Albanesi and Sleet (2006) and Golosov and Tsyvinski (2006).

$$\ln(c_{21}) - \tfrac{1}{2} y_{21}^2 \geq \ln(c_{20}),$$
$$c_{21}, c_{20}, y_{21}, K_2, y_1 \geq 0.$$

(In this statement of the problem, I have set $y_{20} = 0$, as would be true in a social optimum.) The solution to this problem must satisfy the following first-order conditions:

$$c_1^* + K_2^* = rK_1 + w y_1^*, \tag{4.8}$$

$$\tfrac{1}{2} c_{21}^* + \tfrac{1}{2} c_{20}^* = rK_2^* + \tfrac{1}{2} w y_{21}^*, \tag{4.9}$$

$$\ln(c_{21}^*) - \tfrac{1}{2} y_{21}^{*2} = \ln(c_{20}^*), \tag{4.10}$$

$$1/c_1^* = r/[0.5 c_{21}^* + 0.5 c_{20}^*], \tag{4.11}$$

$$w/c_{21}^* = y_{21}^*, \tag{4.12}$$

$$y_1^* = w/c_1^*. \tag{4.13}$$

Note that (4.10) implies that in the social optimum the highly skilled agent is indifferent between acting high-skilled and acting low-skilled. This indifference is necessary to provide the maximal insurance against skill risk.

As argued above, this optimal allocation can only emerge as an equilibrium outcome if the agent faces nonzero capital income taxes. Consider a tax system τ such that if an agent has capital holdings k_2 at the beginning of period 2 and effective labor y_2 in period 2, then he pays period 2 taxes $\tau^k r k_2 + \tau^y (w y_2)$. Given this tax system, an equilibrium in this economy is a specification of $(\hat{c}_1, \hat{c}_{21}, \hat{c}_{20}, \hat{y}_1, \hat{y}_{21}, \hat{k}_2)$ such that it solves

$$\max_{c_1, y_1, c_{21}, c_{20}, y_{21}, k_2} \ln(c_1) - \tfrac{1}{2} y_1^2 + \tfrac{1}{2} \ln(c_{21})$$
$$+ \tfrac{1}{2} \ln(c_{20}) - \tfrac{1}{4} y_{21}^2$$
$$\text{s.t. } c_1 + k_2 = r k_1 + w y_1,$$

$$c_{21} = rk_2 + wy_{21} - \tau^k rk_2 - \tau^y(wy_{21}),$$
$$c_{20} = rk_2 - \tau^k rk_2 - \tau^y(0),$$
$$k_2, c_{21}, c_{20}, y_{21}, y_1 \geqslant 0$$

and markets clear

$$\hat{c}_1 + \hat{k}_2 = rk_1 + w\hat{y}_1,$$
$$\tfrac{1}{2}\hat{c}_{21} + \tfrac{1}{2}\hat{c}_{20} = r\hat{k}_2 + \tfrac{1}{2}w\hat{y}_{21}.$$

Note that in equilibrium, $\tau^k r\hat{k}_2 + 0.5\tau^y(w\hat{y}_{21}) + 0.5\tau^y(0) = 0$, so that the government's budget is balanced in period 2.

Suppose that (c^*, y^*, k^*) is a socially optimal allocation in which $y_{21}^* > 0$, and suppose too that (c^*, y^*, k^*) is an equilibrium given τ. Then, the capital tax τ^k is such that the agent is marginally indifferent between saving a little more or a little less:

$$1/c_1^* = (1 - \tau^k)r[0.5/c_{21}^* + 0.5/c_{20}^*]. \qquad (4.14)$$

From (4.11), we know that $\tau^k > 0$. This tax system follows the Pigouvian prescription of aligning the agent's and society's first-order conditions.

However, despite this alignment, there is an intrinsic contradiction between (c^*, y^*, k^*) being an equilibrium and its being socially optimal. If (c^*, y^*, k^*) is an equilibrium given τ, the agent prefers (y_{21}^*, k_2^*) to all other choices of (y_{21}, k_2). Consider two alternative specifications of (y_{21}, k_2):

$$\text{Shirk:} \qquad (0, k_2^*),$$
$$\text{Shirk and save:} \qquad (0, k_2^* + \varepsilon).$$

Suppose the agent uses the shirk-and-save strategy $k_2 = k_2^* + \varepsilon$ and $y_{21} = 0$. His utility gain from this plan, relative to that provided by the shirk strategy of setting $y_{21} = 0$ and $k_2 = k_2^*$, is given by

$$\ln(c_1^* - \varepsilon) + \ln(c_{20}^* + r\varepsilon - \tau^k r\varepsilon) - \ln(c_1^*) - \ln c_{20}^*.$$

For ε small, this utility difference is well-approximated by

$$-\varepsilon/c_1^* + r(1 - \tau^k)\varepsilon/c_{20}^*.$$

Because $c_{20}^* < c_{21}^*$, the utility difference is larger than

$$-\varepsilon/c_1^* + r(1 - \tau^k)\varepsilon[0.5/c_{21}^* + 0.5/c_{20}^*],$$

which, by (4.14), equals zero. The shirk-and-save strategy makes the agent strictly better off relative to the shirking strategy.

We also know from (4.10) that the agent is indifferent between shirking and not shirking (that is, setting $y_{21} = y_{21}^*$ and $k_2 = k_2^*$). Hence, the shirk-and-save strategy makes the agent strictly better off relative to choosing the socially optimal (y_{21}^*, k_2^*). The socially optimal allocation is not an equilibrium.

Intuitively, we can think of the agent as choosing two continuous variables: savings and the probability of shirking (rather than working). We have designed the tax system so that the agent's first-order conditions (4.10) and (4.11) with respect to these continuous variables are aligned with society's first-order conditions. However, the agent's objective is not jointly concave with respect to these two decision variables. For this reason, even though the tax system deters shirking and deters saving viewed as separate decisions, it fails to stop agents from using the *joint* or *double* deviation of saving too much and then shirking.

4.3.4 An Optimal Capital Income Tax System: Two-Period Example

The above implementation uses a linear tax on capital income, which is set equal to the intertemporal wedge in the social optimum. This wedge is calculated *ex ante*, and so puts equal weight on both possible outcomes. However, at date 2, the agent has the ability to decide which outcome actually takes place. His choices actually determine the probability distribution of consumption in period 2. Thus, if he chooses to shirk with probability p when his skill level is 1, then his consumption equals c_{21}^* with probability $(1 - p)/2$ and equals c_{20}^* with probability $(p/2 + 1/2)$. The tax needs to keep the individual at the right savings level for any of these possible distributions of consumption in period 2.

One simple way that we can achieve this goal is to set the capital income tax rate equal to the *ex post* wedge, not the *ex ante* wedge. Given a socially optimal allocation (c^*, y^*), I define the following tax system:

$$\tau(rk_2, wy_2) = \tau_H^k rk_2 + \tau_H^y \quad \text{if } wy_2 > 0 \qquad (4.15)$$
$$= \tau_L^k rk_2 + \tau_L^y \quad \text{if } wy_2 = 0.$$

In this system, I pick the coefficients $(\tau_H^k, \tau_H^y, \tau_L^k, \tau_L^y)$ so that

$$\tau_H^k = 1 - \frac{1/c_1^*}{r/c_{21}^*}, \qquad (4.16)$$

$$\tau_L^k = 1 - \frac{1/c_1^*}{r/c_{20}^*}, \qquad (4.17)$$

$$\tau_H^y = y_{21}^* - c_{21}^* + (1 - \tau_H^k)rk_2^*, \qquad (4.18)$$

$$\tau_L^y = -c_{20}^* + (1 - \tau_L^k)rk_2^*. \qquad (4.19)$$

Under this tax system, the agent's *ex post* Euler equations for capital accumulation,

$$(1 - \tau_H^k)r/c_{21}^* = 1/c_1^*, \tag{4.20}$$

$$(1 - \tau_L^k)r/c_{20}^* = 1/c_1^*, \tag{4.21}$$

are both satisfied.

My claim is that the socially optimal allocation (c^*, y^*, k^*) is individually optimal, given this tax system. This claim can be justified in two parts. Suppose that the agent chooses $y_{21} > 0$. Then, given an arbitrary choice of (y_1, k_2), his consumptions are equal to

$$c_1 = wy_1 - k_2 + rk_1,$$
$$c_{21} = w(y_{21} - y_{21}^*) + (1 - \tau_H^k)r(k_2 - k_2^*) + c_{21}^*,$$
$$c_{20} = (1 - \tau_L^k)r(k_2 - k_2^*) + c_{20}^*.$$

The agent's derived utility is a concave function of (y_1, y_{21}, k_2), and so his optimal choice is the unique solution to the first-order conditions:

$$1/c_1 = wy_1,$$
$$1/c_{21} = wy_{21},$$
$$1/c_1 = r[0.5(1 - \tau_H^k)/c_{21} + 0.5(1 - \tau_L^k)/c_{20}].$$

It is readily shown that these first-order conditions are satisfied by the socially optimal allocation. It follows that, conditional on a positive specification of y_{21}, the agent's optimal choice is to set $y_1 = y_1^*$, $y_{21} = y_{21}^*$, and $k_2 = k_2^*$.

Now suppose the agent chooses $y_{21} = 0$. Given an arbitrary choice of (y_1, k_2), his consumptions are given by

$$c_1 = wy_1 - k_2 + rk_1,$$

$$c_{21} = (1 - \tau_L^k)r(k_2 - k_2^*) + c_{20}^*,$$
$$c_{20} = (1 - \tau_L^k)r(k_2 - k_2^*) + c_{20}^*.$$

Again, the agent's utility function is concave as a function of (y_1, k_2). His optimal choice must solve the first-order conditions:

$$1/c_1 = wy_1,$$
$$1/c_1 = (1 - \tau_L^k)r[0.5/c_{21} + 0.5/c_{20}].$$

It is optimal for the agent to set $y_1 = y_1^*$ and $k_2 = k_2^*$.

This discussion implies that there is no loss in discarding all elements of the agent's budget set except the two elements implied by setting $y_1 = y_1^*$, $k_2 = k_2^*$, and $y_{21} \in \{y_{21}^*, 0\}$. Because (c^*, y^*) is incentive-compatible, we know that the agent weakly prefers the former choice of y_{21}. It follows that (c^*, y^*, k^*) is in $\text{EQM}_{\text{NL}}(\tau, G)$.

We have successfully designed an optimal tax system for this two-period example economy. Note that while capital accumulation decisions are made in period 1, tax rates on capital brought into period 2 depend on the agent's effective labor in period 2. This dependence ensures that agents make the right capital accumulation decisions, regardless of how much they work in period 2.

4.3.5 A Generally Optimal Tax System: Description

The tax system in the previous subsection applies only to a simple example. In this subsection, I describe how to construct an optimal tax system in a wide class of environments; I justify its validity in the next subsection. The basic principle is the same as in the prior subsection: we set capital income tax rates equal to *ex post* wedges, not *ex ante* wedges. However, we first need to deal with an important subtlety.

In a solution (c^*, y^*, k^*) to (4.3), allocations depend on θ. In the optimal tax problem (4.2), taxes only depend on choice variables like y and k. In words, tax systems do not ask agents for direct reports about their skill shocks. Instead, tax systems condition agents' payments on their decisions about economic variables like labor income and capital income. This difference creates a potential problem: optimal consumption c_t^* may be different across two realizations of skill histories θ^t, even though the histories of labor income are not different. Then, it will be challenging to implement (c^*, y^*, k^*) using a tax system that depends only on $(w_s y_s)_{s=1}^t$ and $r_t k_t$.

To guard against this problem, I make the following assumption. Given a solution (c^*, y^*, k^*) to the planner's problem (4.3), define DOM_T to be a subset of $[0, \bar{y}]^T \times Z^T$ such that (y^T, z^T) is in DOM_T if and only if $y^T = y^*(\theta^T, z^T)$ for some θ^T in Θ^T. In words, (y^T, z^T) is in DOM_T if in the socially optimal allocation, there exists some type in Θ^T that receives the effective labor history y^T when the public history is z^T. I then make the following assumption.

Assumption 4.3. *For any solution (c^*, y^*, k^*) to the planner's problem (4.3), there is a function $\hat{c}^*$ such that*

$$\hat{c}^* : \text{DOM}_T \to R_+^T \tag{4.22}$$

$$\hat{c}_t^* \text{ is } (y^t, z^t)\text{-measurable,} \tag{4.23}$$

$$c^*(\theta^T, z^T) = \hat{c}^*(y^*(\theta^T, z^T), z^T) \quad \text{for all } (\theta^T, z^T). \tag{4.24}$$

We saw in section 4.3.1 that in a static setting assumption 4.3 is satisfied for any incentive-compatible allocation (not just optimal ones). However, in a dynamic setting, an agent's realization of θ provides information about both his *current* skills and his *future* skills. In a socially optimal allocation, a surprisingly large realization of current skills leads to higher consumption and more effective labor. Consumption and effective labor covary positively across agents as in the static case. In contrast, information in period t that generates upward revisions in forecasts of *future* skills lead the planner to reward the agent with more consumption and more leisure in period t. Thus, information about future skills induces a negative covariance between current consumption and current effective labor.

It is then no longer obvious that current consumption depends on current and past skills only through current and past effective labor. However, it is easy to prove that assumption 4.3 is satisfied as well when skill shocks are i.i.d., because the agent receives no information about his future skills. There is no similar proof for what happens when skill shocks are mean-reverting. However, it is intuitively plausible that the effect of information about future skills is outweighed by the effect of information about current skills. This intuition would suggest that assumption 4.3 continues to be valid when skills are mean-reverting. (This intuition is further supported by the fact that when skills are fixed over time, it is optimal for consumption and effective labor to covary positively in period 1.)

Matters are different if skills are actually an explosive process in the sense that a high current level of skills implies that the future growth rate of skills is high. In this case, the above intuition suggests that assumption 4.3 may be violated. Kocherlakota (2005) presents an example of this kind.

Given an optimal allocation (c^*, y^*, k^*) that satisfies assumption 4.3, I next construct the details of the tax system that implements an optimal allocation (c^*, y^*, k') as an equilibrium. As in the prior subsection, I use a linear tax on capital income. However, the tax *rate* in period t is a function of both current and past labor incomes; we set the tax rate equal to *ex post* wedges. I first define the tax system for elements of DOM_T, and then extend its domain to include all of $[0, \bar{y}]^T \times Z^T$.

More specifically, given the optimal allocation

$$(c^*, y^*, k^*),$$

we know from theorem 4.2 that there exists $\lambda_{t+1}^* : Z^{t+1} \to R_+$ such that

$$\lambda_{t+1}^* = \beta [E(u'(c_{t+1}^*)^{-1} \mid \theta^t, z^{t+1})]^{-1} / u'(c_t^*). \quad (4.25)$$

Let

$$\text{MPK}_t^*(z^T) = F_k(K_t^*(z^T), Y_t^*(z^T), z_t)$$

be the marginal product of capital in history z^t. Define the capital income tax rate $\tau_{t+1}^k : \text{DOM}_T \to R$ so that

$$
\begin{aligned}
\frac{\beta u'(\hat{c}_{t+1}^*(y^T, z^T))}{u'(\hat{c}_t^*(y^T, z^T))} & \\
\times \{1 - \delta + (1 - \tau_{t+1}^k(y^T, z^T)) & \text{MPK}_{t+1}^*(z^T)\} \\
= \lambda_{t+1}^*(z^T)(1 - \delta + & \text{MPK}_{t+1}^*(z^T)) \quad (4.26)
\end{aligned}
$$

for (y^T, z^T) in DOM_T. In this way, the capital income tax rate is defined so that the *ex post* intertemporal Euler equation is satisfied with equality at each date.[3]

---

[3] In this system, all asset income is taxed at the same rate. Albanesi (2006) shows that in a world with idiosyncratic entrepreneurial risk, it may be optimal to tax different types of asset income at different rates.

Next, I describe the labor tax code. In the static case, we simply defined labor taxes to be the difference between labor income and consumption. In the dynamic case, we operate somewhat similarly, but we have to be careful in our treatment of asset holdings. First, define

$$\text{MPL}_t^*(z^t) \equiv F_y(K_t^*(z^{t-1}), Y_t^*(z^t), z_t) \qquad (4.27)$$

to be the marginal product of effective labor. Then, let $(\psi^*, \hat{k}^*) : \text{DOM}_T \rightarrow R^T \times R_+^{T+1}$, $(\psi_t^*, \hat{k}_t^*)$ (y^t, z^t)-measurable, be defined so that

$$\hat{c}_t^*(y^T, z^T) + \hat{k}_{t+1}^*(y^T, z^T)$$
$$= (1 - \delta + \text{MPK}_t^*(z^T)(1 - \tau_t^k(y^T, z^T)))\hat{k}_t^*(y^T, z^T)$$
$$+ \text{MPL}_t^*(z^T)y_t - \psi_t^*(y^T, z^T),$$
$$(4.28)$$

$$\sum_{\theta^T \in \Theta^T} \pi(\theta^T \mid z^T)\hat{k}_{t+1}^*(y^*(\theta^T, z^T), z^T)$$
$$= K_t^*(z^T) \quad \text{for all } z^T, \qquad (4.29)$$

$$\hat{k}_1^* = K_1^*, \qquad (4.30)$$

$$\hat{k}_{T+1}^*(y^T, z^T) = 0 \quad \text{for all } (y^T, z^T), \qquad (4.31)$$

for all t and for all (y^T, z^T) in DOM_T. The function ψ^* describes the labor taxes, given that the agent chooses an effective labor sequence in DOM_T. The function $\hat{k}^*$ describes the agent's capital holdings so as to satisfy the flow budget constraint. The restriction (4.29) requires individual capital holdings to aggregate to the optimal level of per-capita capital.

It is easy to see that given (c^*, y^*, k^*), there exists a $(\psi, \hat{k}^*)$ that satisfies (4.28)–(4.31). For example, set $\hat{k}_t(y^T, z^T) = K_t^*(z^T)$, where K^* is per-capita capital in the optimal allocation (c^*, y^*, k^*), and define

$$\psi_t^*(y^T, z^T)$$
$$= -\hat{c}_t^*(y^T, z^T) - \hat{k}_{t+1}^*(y^T, z^T)$$
$$+ (1 - \delta + \text{MPK}_t^*(z^T)(1 - \tau_t^k(y^T, z^T)))$$
$$\times \hat{k}_t^*(y^T, z^T)$$
$$+ \text{MPL}_t^*(z^T)y_t. \qquad (4.32)$$

Then, $(\psi, \hat{k})$ satisfies (4.28)–(4.31).

We have now defined both labor and capital taxes for (y^T, z^T) in DOM_T. However, we also need to describe taxes when the agent chooses an effective labor sequence *not* in DOM_T. In doing so, we need to ensure that the extended tax schedules specify period t taxes that are measurable with respect to (y^t, z^t). To this end, define DOM_t to be a subset of $[0, \bar{y}]^T \times Z^T$ such that (y^T, z^T) is in DOM_t if and only if there exists $(\hat{y}^T, \hat{z}^T)$ in DOM_T with the property that $(\hat{y}^t, \hat{z}^t) = (y^t, z^T)$. DOM_t contains all (y^T, z^T) that, as of period t, are consistent with the agent's using the effective labor strategy y^*.

It is straightforward to extend the domain of ψ^* and τ^k to DOM_t. For each (y^T, z^T) in DOM_t, let $\Phi(y^T, z^T)$ be an element of DOM_T so that $\Phi^t(y^T, z^T) = (y^t, z^t)$. Define

$$\psi_{\text{ext},t}^*(y^T, z^T) = \psi_t^*(\Phi(y^T, z^T))$$
$$\text{for all } (y^T, z^T) \text{ in } \text{DOM}_t,$$
$$\tau_{\text{ext},t+1}^{k*}(y^T, z^T) = \tau_{t+1}^k(\Phi(y^T, z^T))$$
$$\text{for all } (y^T, z^T) \text{ in } \text{DOM}_t.$$

Clearly, $\psi_{\text{ext},t}^*$ is (y^t, z^t)-measurable and $\tau_{\text{ext},t+1}^{k*}$ is (y^{t+1}, z^{t+1})-measurable. Then, define ψ^{**} : $R_+^T \times$

$Z^T \to R^T$ by

$$\psi_t^{**}(y^T, z^T) = \psi_{\text{ext},t}^*(y^T, z^T)$$
$$\text{if } (y^T, z^T) \text{ is in DOM}_t \qquad (4.33)$$
$$= 2y_t w_t(z^T)$$
$$\text{for any } (y^T, z^T) \text{ not in DOM}_t$$

and define $\tau^{k**} : R_+^T \times Z^T \to R^T$ by

$$\tau_{t+1}^{k**}(y^T, z^T) = \tau_{\text{ext},t+1}^{k*}(y^T, z^T)$$
$$\text{if } (y^T, z^T) \text{ is in DOM}_t$$
$$= 1 - (\delta - 1)/\text{MPK}_{t+1}^*(z^T)$$
$$\text{if } (y^T, z^T) \text{ is not in DOM}_t.$$

As is made clear in the next subsection, the taxes when (y^T, z^T) is outside of DOM$_t$ are sufficient to make budget-infeasible any effective labor sequences that lie outside of DOM$_T$.

Finally, we can combine these two pieces together to form the overall system. Let e_t denote labor earnings $(w_t y_t)$ in period t and Γ_t denote capital income $(r_t k_t)$ in period t. Then the overall tax system is $\tau = (\tau_t)_{t=1}^T$, where $\tau_t : R_+^t \times R_+ \times Z^t \to R$ is defined by

$$\tau_t(e^t, \Gamma_t, z^t) = \tau_t^{k**}((e_s/\text{MPL}_s^*(z^T))_{s=1}^t, z^t)\Gamma_t$$
$$+ \psi_t^{**}((e_s/\text{MPL}_s^*(z^T))_{s=1}^t, z^t).$$
$$(4.34)$$

If Θ is finite (as we have assumed), this tax system has a number of discontinuities. Only a finite number of labor income histories are consistent with social optimality, and so all other labor income histories result in draconian penalties. If Θ is instead an interval, the sets DOM$_t$ will be intervals too, and the discontinuities in the tax system will vanish.

4.3.6 A Generally Optimal Tax System: Justification

In the previous subsection, I described a tax system. In this subsection, I show explicitly that $(c^*, y^*, k') \in \text{EQM}_{\text{NL}}(\tau, G)$, where

$$k'_t(\theta^T, z^T) = \hat{k}^*_t(y^*(\theta^T, z^T), z^T) \quad \text{for all } (\theta^T, z^T)$$

and in this way show that τ is in fact a solution to the optimal tax problem (4.2).

4.3.6.1 *Optimal Consumption-Savings Decisions*

Suppose that the agent chooses an effective labor strategy y such that $y(\theta^T, z^T)$ is not in DOM_T for some (θ^T, z^T). Then, at some date, he loses all of his wealth and his taxes become twice as large as his income. It follows that the agent cannot afford to pay his taxes if he uses such a strategy. Hence, an effective labor strategy is budget-feasible only if $y(\theta^T, z^T)$ is in DOM_T for all (θ^T, z^T).

Fix an effective labor strategy $y' : \Theta^T \times Z^T \to R_+$ such that $y'(\theta^T, z^T) \in \text{DOM}_T$ for all elements of $\Theta^T \times Z^T$. What are the agent's strategies for consumption and capital, given y'? I claim that the agent chooses

$$c'_t(\theta^T, z^T) = \hat{c}^*(y'(\theta^T, z^T), z^T), \tag{4.35}$$

$$k'_t(\theta^T, z^T) = \hat{k}^*(y'(\theta^T, z^T), z^T). \tag{4.36}$$

In words, agents' consumption-savings decisions are fully determined by their effective labor strategy y'.

To justify this claim, we can first verify the intertemporal Euler equation. Define

$$R^k_{t+1}(y^T, z^T) = (1 - \delta + \text{MPK}^*_{t+1}(z^T)(1 - \tau^k_{t+1}(y^T, z^T))$$

to be the after-tax return on capital, as a function of the agent's effective labor y^T and the aggregate shock history z^T. Note that

$$
E\left\{ \frac{\beta u'(c'_{t+1}(\theta^T, z^T))R^k_{t+1}(y'(\theta^T, z^T), z^T)}{u'(c'_t(\theta^T, z^T))} \; \Big| \right.
$$

$$
\left. (\theta^t, z^t) = (\bar{\theta}^t, \bar{z}^t) \right\}
$$

$$
= E\{\lambda^*_{t+1}(z^T)(1 - \delta + \mathrm{MPK}^*_{t+1}(z^T)) \mid
$$

$$
\theta^t = \bar{\theta}^t, \; z^t = \bar{z}^t\}
$$

$$
(4.37)
$$

because of the *ex post* definition of τ^k_{t+1} in (4.26). Both λ^*_{t+1} and MPK^*_{t+1} depend only on aggregate shocks, and so θ^t is useless in predicting $\lambda^*_{t+1}(1 - \delta + \mathrm{MPK}^*_{t+1})$, given z^t. Hence, the right-hand side of this expression becomes

$$
E\{\lambda^*_{t+1}(z^T)(1 - \delta + \mathrm{MPK}^*_{t+1}(z^T)) \mid z^t = \bar{z}^t\},
$$

which equals 1 according to theorem 4.2. It is simple (but tedious) to verify that k' satisfies the flow budget constraints (4.28), given c' and y'. Since (c', k') satisfies both the budget constraints and intertemporal Euler equations, it is individually optimal given the choice of y'.

4.3.6.2 Optimal Labor Choices

We have designed the tax system so that agents will only choose effective labor strategies which result in sequences in DOM_T. Let y' be any effective labor strategy other than y^* such that $(y'(\theta^T, z^T), z^T)$ is in DOM_T for all (θ^T, z^T). This range restriction means that the observed sequences of effective labor choices are all consistent with different realizations of θ^T. We can define

$$
\sigma : \Theta^T \times Z^T \to \Theta^T
$$

so that

$$y'(\theta^T, z^T) = y^*(\sigma(\theta^T, z^T), z^T)$$

for all (θ^T, z^T) and σ_t is (θ^t, z^t)-measurable for all t. We know from the previous subsection that this choice y' of an effective labor strategy implies that the agent's consumption is

$$c'(\theta^T, z^T) = \hat{c}^*(y^*(\sigma(\theta^T, z^T), z^T), z^T)$$
$$\text{for all } (\theta^T, z^T),$$

which equals $c^*(\sigma(\theta^T, z^T), z^T)$.

This argument implies that the tax system τ defined in (4.34) has the property that varying effective labor strategies in the agent's budget set is exactly equivalent to his varying mimicking strategies in the incentive constraint. Since (c^*, y^*) is incentive-compatible, we know that σ_{TT} (that is, not pretending to be anyone else) is the best mimicking strategy available. It follows that the agent's optimal choice from his budget set is (c^*, y^*, k').

4.4 Properties of the Optimal Tax System

We now know how to find a solution to the optimal tax problem (4.2).[4] First, find a solution (c^*, y^*, k^*) to the planner's problem (4.3). Second, if that solution satisfies assumption 4.3, we use the recipe (4.34) to find an optimal tax system. This connection allows us to exploit the results in chapter 3 to understand the properties of the optimal tax system (4.34).

---

[4] Section 4.3 describes only one class of the many possible optimal tax systems. Correspondingly, this section describes the properties of only the tax systems set forth in section 4.3.

4.4.1 Purely Redistributive Capital Income Taxes

In this section, we show that the period t expectation of the capital income tax rate in period $(t + 1)$ is zero. We also show that this result implies that capital income tax raises no aggregate revenue.

Recall that the capital income tax rate τ_{t+1}^k is defined in (4.26) so as to satisfy

$$\frac{\beta u'(\hat{c}_{t+1}^*(y^T, z^T))}{u'(\hat{c}_t^*(y^T, z^T))}$$
$$\times \{1 - \delta + (1 - \tau_{t+1}^k(y^T, z^T))\text{MPK}_{t+1}^*(z^T)\}$$
$$= \lambda_{t+1}^*(z^T)(1 - \delta + \text{MPK}_{t+1}^*(z^T)). \quad (4.38)$$

This tax is defined for all possible labor income histories. We can define equilibrium capital income tax rates as a function of skills themselves:

$$\hat{\tau}_{t+1}^k(\theta^T, z^T) = \tau_{t+1}^k(y^*(\theta^T, z^T), z^T)$$
$$\text{for all } (\theta^T, z^T), \quad (4.39)$$

which implies that

$$(1 - \hat{\tau}_{t+1}^k)$$
$$= \frac{\beta^{-1}\lambda_{t+1}^*(1 - \delta + \text{MPK}_{t+1}^*)u'(c_{t+1}^*)^{-1}u'(c_t^*)}{\text{MPK}_{t+1}^*}$$
$$- \frac{1 - \delta}{\text{MPK}_{t+1}^*}.$$

Theorem 4.2 implies that

$$\lambda_{t+1}^*(\bar{z}^T)u'(c_t^*(\bar{\theta}^T, \bar{z}^T))$$
$$\times E\{\beta^{-1}u'(c_{t+1}^*)^{-1} \mid \theta^t = \bar{\theta}^t, z^{t+1} = \bar{z}^{t+1}\} = 1.$$
$$(4.40)$$

Hence, if we take the expectation of the after-tax rate, conditional on (θ^t, z^{t+1}) equalling $(\bar{\theta}^t, \bar{z}^{t+1})$, we get 1. It follows that

$$E\{\hat{\tau}^k_{t+1} \mid \theta^t = \bar{\theta}^t, z^{t+1} = \bar{z}^{t+1}\} = 0.$$

Thus, when an investor buys more capital at date t, his expected tax rate in period $(t+1)$ is zero, conditional on any realization of the aggregate state in that period.

Who pays the higher tax? This is also easy to see. Conditional on (θ^t, z^{t+1}), the variance in the wealth tax rate derives from the dependence of $u'(c^*_{t+1})^{-1}$ on θ_{t+1}. The after-tax rate $(1 - \hat{\tau}^k_{t+1})$ is surprisingly high for agents with a surprisingly high $1/u'(c^*_{t+1})$, that is, a high c^*_{t+1}.

There is a second, slightly more subtle, implication: under the optimal system, wealth taxes are purely redistributional. Suppose (c^*, y^*, k') is in $\text{EQM}_{\text{NL}}(\tau, G)$. At any date, all agents with the same history θ^t take the same capital holdings k' into period $(t+1)$. Some of these agents will end up facing a high tax rate on the income from their holdings. Some will get a subsidy. However, from the law of large numbers, the cross-sectional average tax rate across these agents equals the expected tax rate, and so equals 0. Since the tax is linear, the net collections from these agents with the same level of capital holdings will be zero.

Hence, in any public history z^t, regardless of the level of government purchases, the government's total capital income tax collections are zero. Note that the redistribution is somewhat counterintuitive. The government takes from those agents with surprisingly low consumption in period $(t+1)$ and gives to those agents with surprisingly high consumption in period $(t+1)$. This high tax rate on capital income for unexpectedly poor people deters agents from over-accumulating capital from period t to period $(t + 1)$, and then working less in period $(t+1)$. In this fashion, the tax system is able to provide better incentives to agents to work and generates more output for all to share.

Recall that socially optimal allocations feature a wedge between tomorrow's marginal value of capital and today's, so that if (c^*, y^*, k^*) solves (4.3), and $u'(c^*_{t+1})$ is a nondegenerate function of θ_{t+1}, then

$$u'(c^*_t(\theta^T, z^T))$$
$$< \beta E\{u'(c^*_{t+1})(1 - \delta + F_k(K^*_{t+1}, Y^*_{t+1})) \mid$$
$$\theta^t = \bar{\theta}^t, \ z^t = \bar{z}^t\}.$$
$$(4.41)$$

How does a tax system with *zero* average taxes generate this wedge? The answer lies in *risk*. When an agent buys an extra unit of capital under the optimal tax system, he gets taxed at a high rate when his consumption is low. The tax system introduces a positive covariance between agents' consumptions and their after-tax rates of return. Capital is a worse hedge against idiosyncratic consumption risk than it would be in the absence of taxes. In this fashion, the tax system creates the wedge present in (4.41).

4.4.2 Long-Run Capital Income Taxes

Under the Ramsey approach, capital income taxes are zero after period 2 if u is of the power form (proposition 2.3). This result is not true of solutions to the nonlinear tax problem (4.2). However, it is also true under the Ramsey approach that for more general utility functions, capital income taxes converge to zero over time (proposition 2.4). In this section, I consider an infinite horizon version of the optimal tax problem (4.2), and evaluate whether the zero long-run capital income tax characterization applies to solutions to the nonlinear tax problem. I restrict attention to the case in which Z is a singleton.

Suppose that (c^*, y^*, k^*) solves an infinite horizon version of (4.2), and $\lim_{t \to \infty} E[1/u'(c_t^*)]$ converges to a finite positive limit. Then, theorem 4.2 (the reciprocal Euler equation with capital) implies that

$$1 = \lim_{t \to \infty} \beta(1 - \delta + \mathrm{MPK}_{t+1}^*).$$

It follows from the Martingale Convergence Theorem (theorem 3.2) that in a solution (c^*, y^*, k^*) to (4.3), $\lim_{t \to \infty} 1/u'(c_t^*(\theta^\infty))$ is finite for almost all θ^∞. We can use these results about optimal *quantities* to derive implications for the long-run behavior of *capital income taxes*.

When Z is a singleton, capital income tax rates τ_{t+1}^{k*} satisfy

$$\frac{\beta(1 - \delta + (1 - \hat{\tau}_{t+1}^k(\theta^\infty))\mathrm{MPK}_{t+1}^*)}{u'(c_t^*(\theta^\infty))} = \frac{1}{u'(c_{t+1}^*(\theta^\infty))}$$
$$(4.42)$$

for all θ^∞ in Θ^∞. If we subtract

$$\frac{\beta(1 - \delta + \mathrm{MPK}_{t+1}^*)}{u'(c_t^*(\theta^\infty))}$$

from both sides, and then take limits with respect to t, we obtain

$$\lim_{t \to \infty} \frac{\beta\hat{\tau}_{t+1}^k(\theta^\infty)\mathrm{MPK}_{t+1}^*}{u'(c_t^*(\theta^\infty))}$$
$$= \lim_{t \to \infty} \left[\frac{1}{u'(c_t^*(\theta^\infty))} - \frac{1}{u'(c_{t+1}^*(\theta^\infty))} \right]. \quad (4.43)$$

For almost all θ^∞, $1/u'(c_t^*(\theta^\infty))$ converges to a finite limit as t goes to infinity. For any such θ^∞, the right-hand side converges to zero, and so, for almost all

θ^∞,

$$\lim_{t \to \infty} \frac{\beta \hat{\tau}_{t+1}^k(\theta^\infty) \text{MPK}_{t+1}^*}{u'(c_t^*(\theta^\infty))} = 0. \qquad (4.44)$$

There are now two possibilities. If

$$\lim_{t \to \infty} \frac{1}{u'(c_t^*(\theta^\infty))}$$

is positive for a given sample path θ^∞, then the long-run capital income tax rate ($\lim_{t \to \infty} \hat{\tau}_{t+1}^k(\theta^\infty)$) is 0 for that sample path. To understand this case, consider example 1 in section 3.7.2. In that example, skill shocks are i.i.d. over time, $v'(0) > 0$, and $v'(\bar{y}) < \infty$. In that case, in optimal allocations, agents either got so wealthy that they did not produce anymore, or they got so poor that they always produced $\bar{y}$. In both cases, the incentive problem vanishes in the limit, and so it is optimal to set long-run capital income taxes to zero.

In contrast, consider example 2 in section 3.7.3. In that example, skill shocks are i.i.d. over time, and $v'(\bar{y}) = \infty$. Then, $c_t^*(\theta^\infty)$ converges to zero (immiseration) along at least some sample paths. For such sample paths, (4.44) does not pin down the long-run capital income tax rate, and it may well be positive.

4.4.3 Indeterminacy of Labor Income Taxes and Government Debt

The nature of optimal allocations tells us a lot about the structure of capital income taxes. However, the optimal allocation also imposes tight restrictions on the present value of lifetime taxes, as a function of y^T. It is easiest to see this when Z is a singleton, so that there are no aggregate shocks. Then, the capital tax rate is set so that the *ex post* Euler equation holds for all y^T in DOM_T:

$$u'(\hat{c}_t^*(y^T))$$
$$= \beta u'(\hat{c}_{t+1}^*(y^T))(1 - \delta + \text{MPK}_{t+1}^*(1 - \tau_{t+1}^k(y^T)).$$
$$(4.45)$$

Now multiply each flow budget constraint (4.28) by $\beta^{t-1}u'(\hat{c}_t^*(y^T))$, and add them over t. Because of (4.45), the capital terms cancel, and we get the following present value restriction:

$$\sum_{t=1}^{T} \beta^{t-1}u'(\hat{c}_t^*(y^T))\psi_t^*(y^T)$$

$$= \sum_{t=1}^{T} \beta^{t-1}u'(\hat{c}_t^*(y^T))\{\text{MPL}_t^* y_t - \hat{c}_t^*(y^T)\}$$
$$+ u'(\hat{c}_1^*(y^T))(1 - \delta + \text{MPK}_1^*)\bar{K}_1 \quad (4.46)$$

for all y^T in DOM_T. This present value formula uses the individual's own shadow interest rate, evaluated at the socially optimal c^*. The present value of the difference between earned income and consumption is on the right-hand side of (4.46). This difference depends only on socially optimal quantities (c^*, y^*). The present value of labor income taxes collected is on the left-hand side of (4.46). Just as in the static case, but now in present value terms, the gap between income and consumption in the socially optimal allocation equals labor income taxes for every y^T in DOM_T.

However, this present value restriction says little about the timing of tax collections; indeed, there is a large set of labor income tax schedules and individual capital holdings (ψ^*, k') such that $(c^*, y^*, k') \in$

$\text{EQM}_{\text{NL}}(\tau, G)$. For example, suppose $T = 2$, but people only earn labor income in period 1 (which implies in turn that optimal capital taxes are zero for everyone). Half of the people are high-skilled and half are low-skilled. Suppose one optimal tax system is to tax agents with high income \$10,000 in period 1 to buy public goods, and not tax agents with low income. Then, we can construct another optimal tax system by taxing high-income agents \$5,000 in period 1, and \$5,000$(1 + r)$ in period 2, while taxing low-income agents \$5,000 in period 1 and then giving them \$5,000$(1 + r)$ in period 2. This tax system is also optimal, because the present value of the tax burden for each possible income sequence is kept the same. But individual-capital holdings in equilibrium change (high-income agents hold more capital under the second system, while low-income agents hold less).

In the class of optimal tax systems that we have considered, we have imposed the restriction that

$$\sum_{\theta^T \in \Theta^T} \pi(\theta^T) \hat{k}_{t+1}^*(y^*(\theta^T)) = K_t^*. \tag{4.47}$$

This restriction ensures that the total wealth of private agents at each date equals the total wealth of society. The government never has any debt or assets. However, using the reasoning in the above paragraph, it is possible to construct optimal tax systems with alternative streams of government debt. For example, suppose as in the above paragraph that we have an optimal tax system which taxes high-income agents \$10,000 in period 1 and does not tax low-income agents. Suppose we lower the taxes of high-income agents to \$1,000 in period 1 and raise them to \$9,000$(1 + r)$ in period 2. This new tax system is still optimal, because the present value of taxes has

remained unchanged for all agents. However, the total taxes collected in period 1 is only $500 per capita
instead of $5,000. If the government is to continue to
spend $5,000 per person in period 1, it must borrow
$4,500 per high-skilled agent.

In this way, even though taxes are distortionary, a
given optimal allocation is consistent with a host of
processes for government debt. The main idea is that
if taxes in a given period are allowed to depend on past
realizations of individual income, then we can change
the timing of tax collections in arbitrary ways without
affecting individual choices. In this fashion, we obtain
an *individual-level* version of Ricardian equivalence,
which eliminates any notion of an optimal debt plan
for the government (Bassetto and Kocherlakota 2004).

This irrelevance result can be used to provide a
simple tight relationship between an optimal allocation and the set of optimal labor income tax schedules. We have seen that any optimal ψ^* must satisfy
(4.46). Suppose conversely that $\psi^* : \text{DOM}_T \to R^T$, ψ_t^*
y^t-measurable for all t, satisfies (4.46). Define

$$\hat{k}_{t+1}^*(y^T)$$

$$= \left(\beta^{1-t} u'(\hat{c}_t^*(y^T))^{-1} \sum_{s=t+1}^{T} \beta^{s-1} u'(\hat{c}_s^*(y^T)) \right.$$

$$\left. \times \{ \text{MPL}_s^* y_s + \hat{c}_s^*(y^T) + \psi_s^*(y^T) \} \right).$$

$$(4.48)$$

It is simple to show that $(\psi^*, \hat{k}^*)$ satisfies the agent's
flow budget constraint (4.28). This capital holdings
process may not satisfy (4.47), but this restriction
arises only because we are imposing period-by-period
government budget balance. It follows that if the government can freely borrow and lend, the restriction

(4.46) completely describes the set of all possible labor income tax schedules as a function of y^T in DOM_T.

4.4.4 A Social Security Implementation

The United States government keeps track of almost every worker's complete history of labor earnings. In (4.2), we allow both labor and capital income taxes to depend on this rich record at every date. Such dependence is certainly technologically feasible, but it is not a feature of the current tax code. In this subsection, I describe a particular optimal tax system that more closely resembles the dependence that we observe in the current tax system. Again, I focus on the case in which Z is a singleton; the discussion closely follows that in Grochulski and Kocherlakota (2008).

We have seen that if (c^*, y^*, k^*) is optimal, then any labor income tax schedule ψ^* that satisfies (4.46) is optimal. Until now, we have been assuming that all elements of Θ^T have positive probability. Suppose instead that there exists some period $S < T$ such that $\theta_t = 0$ for all $t > S$, so that agents retire after date S. We know that c_t^* is θ^S-measurable for any $t \geqslant S$.

Now, define the following labor income tax schedule:

$$\psi_t'(y^t) = \alpha y_t, \qquad \text{where } 0 < \alpha < 1, \ t \leqslant S,$$
$$\psi_t'(y^S) = -\gamma(y^S), \quad \text{where } t > S,$$
$$\gamma(y^S) > 0 \text{ for all } y^S.$$

This tax schedule levies a flat tax α on labor income until retirement. Then, after retirement, agents receive a transfer that depends on their history of labor incomes. The structure of this tax plan closely resembles the current social security system. We can readily set the constant α and the function γ so that the

present value of net taxes collected equals the present
value of the difference between labor incomes and
consumptions:

$$\sum_{t=1}^{S} \beta^{t-1} u'((\hat{c}_t^*(y^S))) \alpha y_s$$

$$- \sum_{t=S+1}^{T} \beta^{t-1} u'((\hat{c}_t^*(y^S))) \gamma(y_S)$$

$$= \sum_{t=1}^{T} \beta^{t-1} u'((\hat{c}_t^*(y^S))) \{ \text{MPL}_t^* y_t - \hat{c}_t^*(y^S) \}$$

$$+ u'(\hat{c}^*(y^S))(1 - \delta + \text{MPK}_1^*) \bar{K}_1 \quad (4.49)$$

for all y^S. In this tax system, all desired insurance
is accomplished via the dependence of social security
transfers on the history of labor incomes. Agents with
high labor income realizations, who have paid a lot
into the system, will get back disproportionately less.

There are two ways in which this tax system differs from the current one in structure. First, in the
proposed system, people are able to borrow against
their social security payments. Such loans are not
currently legally enforceable. Second, while labor income taxes at date t are functions only of labor income at that date, capital income taxes as defined in
(4.39) necessarily depend on the full history of labor
incomes.

The general point is that optimal social insurance
can be accomplished in many ways other than the tax
code itself. There is little history dependence in the
current United States tax system except in social security. Yet, even this small amount of history dependence is enough to achieve desirable outcomes, as long
as agents can borrow against their future transfers.

4.4.5 Optimal Monetary Policy

As discussed in chapter 2, the nominal interest rate set by the Federal Reserve is essentially a tax on the liquidity services provided by money. Following da Costa and Werning (2008), we can use the Mirrleesian approach of this chapter to understand how this tax should be set over time.

There are many ways to model the liquidity services that agents derive from money relative to other assets. One simple way is to assume, as Lucas and Stokey (1987) do, that there are cash and credit goods. Agents can use money to buy either of these goods, but cannot use credit or bonds to buy cash goods. Assume that agents' momentary utility functions take the form

$$u(c_{cash}, c_{credit}) - v(l),$$

where c_{cash} is the consumption of cash goods, c_{credit} is the consumption of credit goods, and l is labor. Preferences are additively separable between consumption goods and labor. However, u need not be homothetic, so that cash goods may be luxuries or necessities or neither.

For the moment, I will ignore money and think about the government as facing an optimal commodity taxation problem. Suppose that cash goods can be transformed one-for-one into credit goods, and vice versa. Suppose too that the government taxes cash goods at a rate equal to R and does not tax the credit goods. It uses the proceeds for lump-sum redistribution or for government purchases. It is simple to show that the government could make all agents better off relative to this system. Suppose agents with labor income y have after-tax labor income $y - \tau(y)$. These agents choose consumption goods and credit goods so as to solve

$$\max_{c_{\text{cash}}, c_{\text{credit}}} u(c_{\text{cash}}, c_{\text{credit}})$$

$$\text{s.t. } c_{\text{cash}}(1 + R) + c_{\text{credit}} = y - \tau(y).$$

Let $(c_{\text{cash}}, c_{\text{credit}})(y)$ solve this problem, and $U^*(y)$ be the associated maximized utility. Now define $\tau'(y)$ so that $U^*(y)$ is also the maximized value of this problem:

$$\max_{c_{\text{cash}}, c_{\text{credit}}} u(c_{\text{cash}}, c_{\text{credit}})$$

$$\text{s.t. } c_{\text{cash}} + c_{\text{credit}} = y - \tau'(y).$$

In this problem, the tax rate R on cash goods has been lowered to zero. Because this distortion has been removed, we know that $\tau'(y)$ is larger than $\tau(y)$. Without affecting incentives ($U^*(y)$ is unchanged), the government can collect more tax revenue via a tax on labor income than by taxing cash goods.

This logic is an example of a general message of optimal taxation theory. The tax on cash goods distorts both cash/credit good purchases and labor supply decisions. This double distortion is inefficient. The government can collect more revenue by eliminating the distortion between cash and credit goods, and raising taxes on labor supply. In cash–credit models of money, this same logic implies that an optimal monetary policy is to set the nominal interest rate to be zero. More generally, in *any* monetary model, money is an intermediate input. Taxing this intermediate input is a form of double taxation that is suboptimal.[5]

---

[5] This discussion de-emphasizes the role of price rigidities. Correia et al. (2008) show that even if the government is restricted to using linear taxes, it can use correctly timed sales taxes to undo the impact of price rigidities. This power does not disappear if taxes are allowed to be nonlinear.

4.5 Remarks about the Optimal System

In this section, I briefly discuss some additional aspects of the optimal system.

4.5.1 Linear versus Nonlinear Capital Income Taxes

In the optimal system described above, capital income taxes are linear. One consequence of this restriction is that in the optimal system, agents' taxes only depend on past activities through the record of their past labor incomes. More generally, a tax system could use an agent's capital holdings as a source of information about his past labor income choices. Such tax systems are necessarily nonlinear in capital income. Albanesi and Sleet (2006) describe such an optimal system for the case in which skill shocks are i.i.d. over time. One advantage of their system over the one described here is that period t taxes are functions only of current variables.

4.5.2 Tax Arbitrages

The tax on capital income is a linear function of capital income itself. However, agents with different labor incomes do not face the same marginal capital income tax rate. As a consequence, the tax system still admits tax arbitrages, that is, intertemporal trades that would be gainful if done behind the back of the tax authority. For example, suppose that there are two agents A and B. Both hold capital in period $(t - 1)$, but agent A faces no labor income risk from period t onward while B does. Then, agent B should give agent A his capital in period $(t - 1)$ in exchange for receiving a risk-free repayment in period t. This trade allows agent B to avoid the tax risk that the optimal system imposes on him.[6]

This trade is but one of many possible arbitrages. However, I do not view these arbitrage opportunities as big flaws in the proposed system. All of these arbitrages are intrinsically intertemporal, and so they necessarily depend on an element of enforcement. (For example, in the above transaction, agent B relies on agent A to repay a loan.) But such loans are specifically designed to cheat the tax authorities, and so it is difficult to see how they would actually be enforced.

4.5.3   Private Sector Insurance

There are two distinct kinds of private information: adverse selection and moral hazard. Adverse selection refers to private information that exists at the time of signing a contract. Moral hazard refers to private information that arises during the course of a contract. In the model that I describe in this chapter, the government's problem maximizes the objective of a representative agent. Hence, all of the private information takes the form of moral hazard.

As Prescott and Townsend (1984) emphasize, there is no role for government intervention when agents are faced with moral hazard. This general point takes the following form in our model. There could be a date 0 market, in which firms compete to hire workers. The firms would offer contracts that would fully specify compensation (consumption) as a function of current and past effective labors. The firms would either ban

---

[6] Golosov and Tsyvinski (2007) explore the properties of optimal capital income taxes under the constraint that the tax system must be free of these kinds of arbitrages.

or monitor all asset trades on the part of their workers. The contracts would be full-commitment, in the sense that neither party could tear up the contract, and the contract could not be renegotiated even if it were in the best interests of both parties to do so. This competitive market would result in socially optimal insurance. If $G > 0$, then the government could supplement the market with a date 0 lump-sum tax on all consumers of sufficient size to fund all future government purchases.

In principle, this purely private sector arrangement works fine. However, the contracts require a great deal of commitment on the part of both workers and firms. In reality, of course, workers can quit their jobs anytime in the United States. Even employers offer only limited amounts of commitment. It is certainly difficult for firms to default on contracts with a given worker. However, firms can readily renege on contracts with a group of workers, by shutting down divisions or closing down completely. Given this background, there is a role for a tax system that provides insurance against large skill shocks that lead to unemployment, job-to-job transitions, or long-term disability.

Having said that, the model does exaggerate the role for government. There is strong evidence that firms do provide insurance against productivity shocks for workers (see Guiso et al. 2005). and the model completely dispenses with this role for the private sector. We do need intermediate analyses of optimal taxation that entertain a role for both private and public sectors in insuring workers against skill risk. (Chetty and Saez (2008) provide a useful first step in this direction in a static context.) It is a reasonable conjecture that, unless firms have a great deal of ability to monitor asset transactions, it will be necessary for the government to employ the kinds of asset income taxes that are described in this chapter.

4.5.4 The Ramsey Approach in Heterogeneous Agent Economies

There is a host of work that analyzes optimal taxation of labor and capital incomes in heterogeneous agent economies, given that the taxes satisfy various functional form restrictions. In an early influential contribution, Aiyagari (1995) assumes that taxes are linear functions of current capital and labor incomes. He finds that long-run optimal capital income taxes are positive when agents face uninsurable skills that evolve stochastically over time. Intuitively, agents tend to over-accumulate capital for precautionary savings reasons, and need to be taxed to deter this effect. Aiyagari's model assumes away income effects on labor supply, which lie at the heart of the discussion of taxation in this chapter. More recently, several authors have studied the properties of optimal taxes in which agents have fixed heterogeneous attributes over time. Saez (2002) studies the properties of optimal affine taxes on capital income, assuming that people are initially heterogeneous in wealth (not skills). Werning (2007) analyzes the properties of optimal affine taxes on labor income and capital income, when idiosyncratic shocks are fixed at their period 1 realizations.[7] These authors emphasize that affine tax systems (which allow for exemptions via intercept terms) can offer considerable improvement over linear ones.

---

[7] He also analyzes the properties of optimal taxes when one relaxes the restriction of affineness.

In an ambitious quantitative exercise, Conesa, Kitao, and Krueger (CKK) (Conesa et al. 2009) consider an overlapping-generations economy in which agents are born with distinct life-cycle profiles of skills. The government can use nonlinear taxes on current labor income, as long as the tax schedule lies in a particular finite-dimensional class of functions. However, all tax systems are age-independent and must exhibit separability between capital and labor incomes. CKK find that the optimal capital income tax rate is large and positive.

All of these papers are fundamentally flawed because their analyses hinge critically on unrealistic functional form restrictions. Contrary to Aiyagari and others, all governments use nonlinear and, indeed, nonaffine tax schedules. CKK do allow for nonaffine tax schedules. However, they require that taxes cannot be conditioned on age.[8] It is hard to understand what the motivation for this restriction might be. Age is clearly an observable and immutable characteristic. (Indeed, in the United States, transfers are explicitly conditioned on age (via social security).) Unfortunately, this unrealistic restriction matters a great deal for CKK's results. In their model, if the government can condition labor income taxes on age, then the optimal capital income tax rate is in fact near zero.

In this chapter, we have also imposed a functional form restriction: governments cannot condition taxes on agents' skills. This restriction is overly strong, because governments do receive a steady stream of signals about an individual's skills over the course

---

[8] See also Gorry and Oberfield (2008). Weinzierl (2008) shows that there are large welfare gains from conditioning taxes on current labor income and age as opposed to current labor income alone.

of that person's lifetime. Optimally designed taxes should condition on variables like height (Mankiw and Weinzierl 2008) or educational attainment that are correlated with skills. However, the failure of the current *suboptimal* tax system to condition on all relevant public information does not invalidate the characterizations of *optimal* taxes that we derived in this chapter. Our key assumption is only that it is impossible to condition taxes on all variables that both affect labor productivity and are known to the individual. It is this privacy of information about at least some aspects of earnings ability that lies at the heart of the Mirrlees approach.

4.6 Summary

In a world with evolving skill risk, optimal labor income taxes trade off insurance versus incentives. To resolve this trade-off optimally, capital income taxes must be nonzero at any finite date. Without such taxes, agents will be left with an incentive to over-accumulate capital from one period to the next and under-work in the later period.

I allow the government to contemplate a rich set of tax instruments, and so there are many optimal systems. I focus on systems in which capital income taxes are linear and the capital income tax rate is designed to equate *ex post* private and social marginal rates of transformation. In this kind of system, aggregate capital income tax revenues are always zero. The key to the system is tax risk: agents face a high capital income tax rate when their consumption is low, and this deters them from accumulating capital.

I reach more limited conclusions about the structure of other kinds of macroeconomic policy. Within the proposed class of tax systems, the present value of optimal labor income taxes is pinned down as a function of a person's labor incomes over his lifetime. However, the timing of collection of these taxes (and government debt) is not determined. I show that we can exploit this indeterminacy to construct an optimal tax system that is a relatively minor modification of the current social security system.

4.7 Technical Notes

These notes provide a proof of theorem 4.2 and a brief discussion about allowing agents to have private information about aggregate shocks.

4.7.1 Proof of Theorem 4.2

The proof is similar to the proof of theorem 3.1. I consider a class of perturbations to a putative optimum. The perturbations work the same as in the earlier proof: I raise period t utility from consumption by $\delta_t(\theta^t)$ and then lower period $(t + 1)$ utility by $\delta_{t+1}(\theta^t, z_{t+1})$, so that the discounted gain/loss is the same for all θ^{t+1}. I then optimize over this class of perturbed allocations.

Suppose (c^*, y^*, k^*) solves (4.3). Fix $\bar{z}^t$. Suppose $c_t^*(\theta^t, \bar{z}^t) > 0$ for all θ^t in Θ^t, $c_{t+1}^*(\theta^{t+1}, \bar{z}^t, z_{t+1}) > 0$ for all θ^{t+1} in Θ^{t+1} and all z_{t+1} in Z, and $K_{t+1}^*(\bar{z}^t) > 0$. (In this proof, I write c_t^* as a function of (θ^t, z^t), because it is measurable with respect to those variables; similarly, I write K_{t+1} as a function of z^t, not z^T.) Consider c' that satisfies

$$u(c_t'(\theta^t, \bar{z}^t)) = u(c_t^*(\theta^t, \bar{z}^t)) + \delta_t(\theta^t) \quad \forall \theta^t \in \Theta^t,$$
$$(4.50)$$

$$u(c'_{t+1}(\theta^{t+1}, \bar{z}^t, z_{t+1}))$$
$$= u(c^*_{t+1}(\theta^{t+1}, \bar{z}^t, z_{t+1})) + \delta_{t+1}(\theta^t, z_{t+1})$$
$$\forall (\theta^{t+1}, z_{t+1}) \in \Theta^{t+1} \times Z, \quad (4.51)$$

where

$$\beta \sum_{z_{t+1}} \delta_{t+1}(\theta^t, z_{t+1}) \pi_Z(z_{t+1} \mid \bar{z}^t) + \delta_t(\theta^t) = \Delta. \quad (4.52)$$

Our first step is to show that (c', y^*, k^*) is incentive-compatible. Suppose the agent uses a mimicking strategy σ. He gets extra expected utility

$$V(\sigma; c', y^*) - V(\sigma; c^*, y^*)$$
$$= \sum_{z_{t+1} \in Z} \pi_Z(\bar{z}^t, z_{t+1}) \sum_{\theta^{t+1} \in \Theta^{t+1}} [\pi_\Theta(\theta^{t+1} \mid \bar{z}^t, z_{t+1})$$
$$\times \{(u(c'_t(\sigma^t(\theta^t, \bar{z}^t), \bar{z}^t))$$
$$+ \beta u(c'_{t+1}(\sigma^{t+1}(\theta^{t+1}, \bar{z}^t, z_{t+1}), \bar{z}^t, z_{t+1})))\}]$$
$$- \sum_{z_{t+1} \in Z} \pi_Z(\bar{z}^t, z_{t+1}) \sum_{\theta^{t+1} \in \Theta^{t+1}} [\pi_\Theta(\theta^{t+1} \mid \bar{z}^t, z_{t+1})$$
$$\times \{(u(c^*_t(\sigma^t(\theta^t, \bar{z}^t), \bar{z}^t))$$
$$+ \beta u(c^*_{t+1}(\sigma^{t+1}(\theta^{t+1}, \bar{z}^t, z_{t+1}), \bar{z}^t, z_{t+1})))\}]$$

from c' relative to c^*. We can rewrite the difference in expected utility as

$$V(\sigma; c', y^*) - V(\sigma; c^*, y^*)$$
$$= \pi_Z(\bar{z}^t) \sum_{\theta^t \in \Theta^t} \pi_\Theta(\theta^t \mid \bar{z}^t) \delta_t(\sigma^t(\theta^t, \bar{z}^t))$$
$$+ \pi_Z(\bar{z}^t) \beta \sum_{z_{t+1} \in Z} \sum_{\theta^{t+1} \in \Theta^{t+1}} [\pi_\Theta(\theta^{t+1} \mid \bar{z}^t, z_{t+1})$$
$$\times \pi_Z(z_{t+1} \mid \bar{z}^t) \delta_{t+1}(\sigma^t(\theta^t, \bar{z}^t), z_{t+1})].$$

By (4.1), we know

$$\sum_{\theta_{t+1}} \pi_\Theta(\theta^t, \theta_{t+1} \mid \bar{z}^t, z_{t+1}) = \pi_\Theta(\theta^t \mid \bar{z}^t).$$

Hence, we can rewrite the difference again as

$$
\begin{aligned}
V(\sigma; c', y^*) &- V(\sigma; c^*, y^*) \\
&= \pi_Z(\bar{z}^t) \sum_{\theta^t \in \Theta^t} \pi_\Theta(\theta^t \mid \bar{z}^t) \delta_t(\sigma^t(\theta^t, \bar{z}^t)) \\
&\quad + \pi_Z(\bar{z}^t) \beta \sum_{z_{t+1} \in Z} \sum_{\theta^t \in \Theta^t} \pi_\Theta(\theta^t \mid \bar{z}^t) \pi_Z(z_{t+1} \mid \bar{z}^t) \\
&\quad\quad\quad\quad\quad\quad\quad\quad \times \delta_{t+1}(\sigma^t(\theta^t, \bar{z}^t), z_{t+1}) \\
&= \pi_Z(\bar{z}^t) \sum_{\theta^t \in \Theta^t} \pi_\Theta(\theta^t \mid \bar{z}^t) \delta_t(\sigma^t(\theta^t, \bar{z}^t)) \\
&\quad - \pi_Z(\bar{z}^t) \sum_{\theta^t \in \Theta^t} \pi_\Theta(\theta^t \mid \bar{z}^t) \delta_t(\sigma^t(\theta^t, \bar{z}^t)) + \Delta \\
&= \Delta.
\end{aligned}
$$

It follows that the ranking of mimicking strategies is the same under (c', y^*) as under (c^*, y^*).

Given this result, $(0, 0, 0, c_t^*, c_{t+1}^*, K_{t+1}^*)$ must solve the following problem:

$$\max_{\Delta, \delta_t, \delta_{t+1}, c_t', c_{t+1}', K_{t+1}'} \Delta$$

s.t. $u(c_t'(\theta^t, \bar{z}^t)) = u(c_t^*(\theta^t, \bar{z}^t)) + \delta_t(\theta^t)$

$$\text{for all } \theta^t \text{ in } \Theta^t,$$

$$
\begin{aligned}
u(c_{t+1}'(\theta^{t+1}, \bar{z}^t, z_{t+1})) \\
= u(c_{t+1}^*(\theta^{t+1}, \bar{z}^t, z_{t+1})) + \delta_{t+1}(\theta^t, z_{t+1})
\end{aligned}
$$

$$\text{for all } \theta^t \text{ in } \Theta^t \text{ and } z_{t+1} \text{ in } Z,$$

$$\beta \sum_{z_{t+1}} \delta_{t+1}(\theta^t, z_{t+1}) \pi_Z(z_{t+1} \mid \bar{z}^t) = \Delta - \delta_t(\theta^t)$$

$$\text{for all } \theta^t \text{ in } \Theta^t,$$

$$\sum_{\theta^t \in \Theta^t} \pi_\Theta(\theta^t \mid \bar{z}^t) c_t'(\theta^t, \bar{z}^t) + K_{t+1}'$$

$$= \sum_{\theta^t \in \Theta^t} \pi_\Theta(\theta^t \mid \bar{z}^t) c_t^*(\theta^t, \bar{z}^t) + K_{t+1}^*(\bar{z}^t),$$

$$\sum_{\theta^{t+1} \in \Theta^{t+1}} \pi_\Theta(\theta^{t+1} \mid \bar{z}^t, z_{t+1}) c_{t+1}'(\theta^{t+1}, \bar{z}^t, z_{t+1})$$

$$- F(K_{t+1}', Y_{t+1}^*(\bar{z}^t), z_{t+1}) - (1 - \delta) K_{t+1}'$$

$$= -K_{t+2}^*(\bar{z}^t, z_{t+1}) - G_{t+1}(\bar{z}^t, z_{t+1})$$

$$\text{for all } z_{t+1} \text{ in } Z,$$

$$c_t'(\theta^t, \bar{z}^t), \ c_{t+1}'(\theta^{t+1}, \bar{z}^t, z_{t+1}), \ K_{t+1}' \geqslant 0$$

$$\text{for all } \theta^{t+1} \text{ in } \Theta^{t+1} \text{ and all } z_{t+1} \text{ in } Z.$$

The first-order necessary conditions to this problem imply that

$$u'(c_t^*(\theta^t, \bar{z}^t)) \eta_t(\theta^t) = \pi_\Theta(\theta^t \mid \bar{z}^t) \xi_t, \qquad (4.53)$$

$$\eta_{t+1}(\theta^{t+1}, z_{t+1}) u'(c_{t+1}^*(\theta^{t+1}, z_{t+1}))$$

$$= \pi_\Theta(\theta^{t+1} \mid \bar{z}^t, z_{t+1}) \xi_{t+1}(z_{t+1}), \quad (4.54)$$

$$\beta \pi_Z(z_{t+1} \mid \bar{z}^t) \eta_t(\theta^t) = \sum_{\theta_{t+1} \in \Theta} \eta_{t+1}(\theta^{t+1}, z_{t+1}),$$

$$(4.55)$$

$$\xi_t = \sum_{z_{t+1}} (1 - \delta + F_{k,t+1}(\bar{z}^t, z_{t+1})) \xi_{t+1}(z_{t+1}), \quad (4.56)$$

where η_t is the multiplier on the first set of constraints, η_{t+1} is the multiplier on the second set of constraints, ξ_t is the multiplier on the first feasibility constraint, and ξ_{t+1} is the multiplier on the z_{t+1} feasibility constraints. We can substitute out η_t and η_{t+1}

to get

$$
\frac{\beta \pi_Z(z_{t+1} \mid \bar{z}^t) \pi_\Theta(\theta^t \mid \bar{z}^t) \xi_t}{u'(c_t^*(\theta^t, \bar{z}^t))}
$$

$$
= \sum_{\theta_{t+1} \in \Theta} \frac{\pi_\Theta(\theta^t, \theta_{t+1} \mid \bar{z}^t, z_{t+1}) \xi_{t+1}(z_{t+1})}{u'(c_{t+1}^*(\theta^t, \theta_{t+1}, \bar{z}^t, z_{t+1}))}
$$

$$
\forall \theta^t \in \Theta^t, \ z_{t+1} \in Z.
$$

(4.57)

Define $\lambda(z_{t+1}) \equiv \pi_Z(z_{t+1} \mid \bar{z}^t)^{-1} \xi_{t+1}(z_{t+1}) / \xi_t$. We can then solve for λ to be

$$
\lambda(z_{t+1})
$$

$$
= \Bigg[\sum_{\theta_{t+1} \in \Theta} \frac{\pi_\Theta(\theta^t, \theta_{t+1} \mid \bar{z}^t, z_{t+1})}{\pi_\Theta(\theta^t \mid \bar{z}^t)}
$$

$$
\times \frac{u'(c_t^*(\theta^t, \bar{z}^t))}{u'(c_{t+1}^*(\theta^t, \theta_{t+1}, \bar{z}^t, z_{t+1}))} \Bigg]^{-1}.
$$

(4.58)

By assumption (4.1), we know that π_Θ is such that $\pi_\Theta(\theta^t \mid \bar{z}^t, z_{t+1})$ is independent of z_{t+1}. Hence,

$$
\pi_\Theta(\theta^t \mid \bar{z}^t, z_{t+1}) = \pi_\Theta(\theta^t \mid \bar{z}^t) \quad \text{for all } z_{t+1} \text{ in } Z,
$$

(4.59)

and so

$$
\frac{\pi_\Theta(\theta^t, \theta_{t+1} \mid \bar{z}^t, z_{t+1})}{\pi_\Theta(\theta^t \mid \bar{z}^t)} = \frac{\pi_\Theta(\theta^t, \theta_{t+1} \mid \bar{z}^t, z_{t+1})}{\pi_\Theta(\theta^t \mid \bar{z}^t, z_{t+1})}
$$

$$
= \pi_\Theta(\theta_{t+1} \mid \theta^t, \bar{z}^t, z_{t+1}).
$$

(4.60)

It follows that

$$
\lambda(z_{t+1}) = \frac{E\{1/u'(c_{t+1}^*) \mid \theta^t, \bar{z}^t, z_{t+1}\}}{u'(c_t^*(\theta^t, \bar{z}^t))} \quad \text{for all } \theta^t, z_{t+1}
$$

(4.61)

and using (4.56) and the definition of λ_{t+1} we get

$$1 = E\{\lambda_{t+1}(1 - \delta + F_{K,t+1}) \mid \bar{z}^t\}, \qquad (4.62)$$

which proves the theorem.

4.7.2 Private Information about Aggregates?

In this chapter, I impose the restriction (4.1) that $(z_{t+1}, \ldots, z_T)$ is independent of θ^t, conditional on z^t. This restriction implies that all agents have common information about current and future aggregates. Relaxing this assumption is certainly desirable, but it raises some intriguing subtleties.

Suppose, for example, that $T = 2$, that $Z = \{z_H, z_L\}$, and that $\pi_Z(z_i, z_H) = \pi_Z(z_i, z_L) = 1/4$ for any i. As well, suppose that $\Theta = \{\theta_L, \theta_H\}$ and that, for any $i \in \{H, L\}$,

$$\pi_\Theta(\theta_j, \theta_j \mid z_i, z_j) = 0.97 \quad \text{for } j \in \{H, L\},$$
$$\pi_\Theta(\theta_k, \theta_m \mid z_i, z_j) = 0.01 \quad \text{for } j \in \{H, L\}$$
$$\text{and } (k, m) \neq (j, j).$$

Here, there are two possible joint distributions. One joint distribution puts a lot of weight on all agents being high-skilled in both periods, while the other joint distribution puts a lot of weight on all agents being low-skilled in both periods.

The period 1 realization of z is uninformative. In this sense, agents receive no information in period 1 about the current cross-sectional distribution of θs, other than their own realization of θ. However, the agents' period 1 allocations of c and y necessarily depend on the joint distribution of θs, because of the feasibility constraint. This connection introduces a subtle feedback from the allocation of resources to the agent's period 1 information about the period 2 joint distribution of skills. This information has the possibility to affect the agent's incentives in period 2.

It follows that to design a socially optimal allocation, a planner must take into account the allocation's effect on the agents' information. For example, it is possible that, as in Townsend (1988), an optimal allocation will feature random consumption (as a way of hiding information about the future). We can avoid this "information leakage" issue in economies with a unit measure of agents by imposing the assumption (4.1) on the shocks. In a finite-agent economy, agents' skill realizations always give them private information about the joint distribution of skills in the population. This feature makes *all* finite-agent economies hard to analyze.

References

Aiyagari, S. R. 1995. Optimal capital income taxation with incomplete markets, borrowing constraints, and constant discounting. *Journal of Political Economy* 103: 1158–75.

Albanesi, S. 2006. Optimal taxation of entrepreneurial capital with private information. Working Paper, Columbia University.

Albanesi, S., and C. Sleet. 2006. Dynamic optimal taxation with private information. *Review of Economic Studies* 73:1–30.

Bassetto, M., and N. Kocherlakota. 2004. On the irrelevance of government debt when taxes are distortionary. *Journal of Monetary Economics* 51:299–304.

Chetty, R., and E. Saez. 2008. Optimal taxation and social insurance with endogenous private insurance. NBER Working Paper 14403.

Conesa, J.-C., S. Kitao, and D. Krueger. 2009. Taxing capital? Not a bad idea after all! *American Economic Review* 90:25–48.

Correia, I., J.-P. Nicolini, and P. Teles. 2008. Optimal fiscal and monetary policy: equivalence results. *Journal of Political Economy* 116:141–70.

da Costa, C., and I. Werning. 2008. On the optimality of the Friedman rule with heterogeneous agents and nonlinear income taxation. *Journal of Political Economy* 116:82–112.

Golosov, M., and A. Tsyvinski. 2007. Optimal taxation with endogenous insurance markets. *Quarterly Journal of Economics* 122:487–534.

Gorry, C. A., and E. Oberfield. 2008. Optimal taxation over the life cycle. Working Paper, University of Chicago.

Grochulski, B., and N. Kocherlakota. 2008. Nonseparable preferences and optimal social security systems. Working Paper, University of Minnesota.

Guiso, L., L. Pistaferri, and F. Schivardi. 2005. Insurance within the firm. *Journal of Political Economy* 113:1054–87.

Kocherlakota, N. 2005. Zero expected wealth taxes: a Mirrlees approach to dynamic optimal taxation. *Econometrica* 73:1587–621.

Lucas, R. E., Jr., and N. L. Stokey. 1987. Money and interest in a cash-in-advance economy. *Econometrica* 55:491–513.

Mankiw, N. G., and M. Weinzierl. 2008. The optimal taxation of height: a case study of utilitarian income redistribution. Working Paper, Harvard University.

Prescott, E., and R. Townsend. 1984. Pareto optima and competitive equilibria with adverse selection and moral hazard. *Econometrica* 52:21–46.

Saez, E. 2002. Optimal progressive capital income taxes in the infinite horizon model. NBER Working Paper 9046.

Townsend, R. 1988. Information constrained insurance: the revelation principle extended. *Journal of Monetary Economics* 21:411–50.

Weinzierl, M. 2008. The surprising power of age-dependent taxes. Working Paper, Harvard University.

Werning, I. 2007. Optimal fiscal policy with redistribution. *Quarterly Journal of Economics* 122:955–67.

5

Optimal Intergenerational Taxation

Chapter 4 described an optimal tax system given the presence of skill risk within a fixed cohort of individuals. The taxation of wealth plays a critical role in this system. In this chapter, we turn to the issue of how taxes should be structured in the presence of *intergenerational* transmission of skills and assets. We will be especially interested in how governments should set bequest taxes[1] in this setting. The answer to this question is far from clear. Optimal taxes trade off incentives against insurance, and bequests affect this trade-off in a number of ways. On the one hand, bequests create adverse incentive effects on their recipients. They also create undue risk for children, by linking their outcomes to those of their parents. These considerations suggest that bequests should be taxed. On the other hand, bequests provide a way to motivate parents to work harder.

In this chapter, we extend the Mirrleesian tools developed in chapters 3 and 4 to resolve these issues. This extension builds heavily on the work of Phelan (2006) and Farhi and Werning (2007, forthcoming). A

---

[1] Throughout this chapter, bequests can really be any form of parent-to-child transfers.

key element of the analysis is a simple point: in an intergenerational context, a generic Pareto optimal allocation puts weight on the currently alive and those yet to be born. It follows that even if parents care about their children and other descendants, a planner necessarily cares even more about those children and descendants. This disconnect between the objectives of the society and its member individuals has important consequences for the structure of optimal bequest taxes.[2]

5.1 An Intergenerational Tax Problem

In this section, I describe a canonical intergenerational taxation problem. I begin by constructing an infinite horizon model with a unit measure of *dynasties*. A dynasty lasts forever, and consists of a sequence of finitely lived people who are altruistically linked. A newborn agent's skills are random, given his ancestors' skills. The government's problem is how to design a tax system that insures people against this prenatal skill risk, while still providing incentives to them to produce output.

5.1.1 Dynastic Environment

In this section, I describe an infinite horizon model with a unit measure of dynasties. In each dynasty, only one person is alive at each date. At the beginning of each period t, the existing dynasty representative dies. He is immediately replaced by a newborn dynasty member, who lives for that period, and then

---

[2] See Amador et al. (2006) for a related analysis of optimal social insurance when agents have hyperbolic preferences and stochastic tastes.

dies at the beginning of the next. In its mathematics, the model closely resembles the model that we studied in chapter 3. However, its economics is quite different.

An agent born in period t has utility

$$u(c_t) - v(l_t) + \beta V_{t+1}, \quad 0 < \beta < 1,$$

where c_t is the agent's consumption, l_t is his effort, and V_{t+1} is the utility of the dynasty member born in period $(t + 1)$. As before, u', $-u''$, v', and v'' are all positive. This utility function resembles the utility functions that we used in earlier chapters. However, β is now the agent's *altruism* factor toward his descendants, not his discount factor.

I abstract from aggregate shocks and government purchases, and I restrict attention to the case in which a dynasty's skills are Markov. Specifically, Nature draws a skill θ_t from a finite set Θ for the newborn agent in date $t > 1$, so that conditional on the history θ^{t-1}, the probability of θ_t is given by $\mu(\theta_t \mid \theta_{t-1})$. These draws are i.i.d. across dynasties with the same history θ^{t-1}. I assume full support, so that at each date $\mu(\theta_t \mid \theta_{t-1}) > 0$ for all θ_t, θ_{t-1} in Θ^2. Also, I assume that a law of large numbers applies, so that the fraction of dynasties with skill history θ^t is equal to the *ex ante* probability $\pi(\theta^t) = \mu(\theta_t \mid \theta_{t-1}) \cdots \mu(\theta_2 \mid \theta_1)\pi(\theta_1)$, where π is the probability density function of Nature's period 1 draw of θ_1.

As before, an agent with skill θ_t can generate effective labor according to the production function

$$y_t = \theta_t l_t.$$

All dynasties in the economy are initially endowed with $\overline{K}_1$ units of capital. Then, an allocation is a mapping $(c, y, k) = (c_t, y_t, k_{t+1})_{t=1}^{\infty}$ such that

$$c_t : \quad \Theta^t \to R_+,$$
$$y_t : \quad \Theta^t \to [0, \bar{y}],$$
$$k_{t+1} : \quad \Theta^t \to R_+.$$

(Note that in this chapter, as opposed to chapters 3 and 4, I write allocations in period t as a function of θ^t.) Let $F(K, Y)$ be an aggregate production function such that F is homogeneous of degree 1 in its first two arguments, and suppose capital depreciates at rate δ from one period to the next. Then, a feasible allocation must satisfy

$$C_t + K_{t+1} \leqslant (1 - \delta)K_t + F(K_t, Y_t) \quad \text{for all } t,$$
$$K_1 \leqslant \overline{K}_1,$$

where

$$C_t \equiv \sum_{\theta^t \in \Theta^t} \pi(\theta^t) c_t(\theta^t),$$
$$Y_t \equiv \sum_{\theta^t \in \Theta^t} \pi(\theta^t) y_t(\theta^t),$$
$$K_{t+1} \equiv \sum_{\theta^t \in \Theta^t} \pi(\theta^t) k_{t+1}(\theta^t)$$

represent per-capita consumption, effective labor, and capital respectively.

5.1.2 Dynastic Equilibrium with Taxes

At each date t, a new dynasty member is born. Hence, a dynasty's asset holdings in a given period t can be interpreted as being the bequest received by that newborn dynasty member. With this interpretation, we can set up a canonical taxation problem that will allow us to analyze optimal bequest taxation.

Suppose that there is a large number of identical firms. The firms rent capital and hire effective labor from the agents, taking wages w_t and rental rates r_t as given in period t. At each date t, agents can lease capital to the firms and provide effective labor to the firms. They can also trade one-period government debt and capital with one another.

Before period 1, the government commits to a tax schedule. A tax schedule specifies tax collections in period t as a function of current and past labor incomes for the dynasties, and also the bequest received in period t. Thus, a tax schedule is a sequence of mappings $(\tau_t)_{t=1}^{\infty}$ such that $\tau_t : R_+^t \times R_+ \to R$. Given τ, and sequences w and r for wages and rents respectively, the dynasty solves the problem:

$$\max_{c,y,k,b} \sum_{t=1}^{\infty} \sum_{\theta^t \in \Theta^t} \pi(\theta^t) \beta^{t-1} [u(c_t(\theta^t)) - v(y_t(\theta^t)/\theta_t)]$$

$$(5.1)$$

$$\text{s.t. } c_t(\theta^t) + k_{t+1}(\theta^t) + b_{t+1}(\theta^t)$$
$$+ \tau_t((w_s y_s(\theta^s))_{s=1}^t, k_t(\theta^{t-1}) + b_t(\theta^{t-1}))$$
$$\leqslant (1 - \delta + r_t)\{k_t(\theta^{t-1}) + b_t(\theta^{t-1})\}$$
$$+ w_t y_t(\theta^t) \quad \text{for all } (t, \theta^t),$$

$$(c_t, y_t, k_{t+1} + b_{t+1}, \bar{y} - y_t)$$

is nonnegative for all t, θ^t,

$$k_1 \leqslant \overline{K}_1, \quad b_1 = 0.$$

Here, k represents the dynasty's holdings of capital and b represents the dynasty's holdings of government debt. I impose the restriction that bequests $(k + b)$ are nonnegative.

I assume that the initial dynast solves the choice problem for all descendants. However, this is without loss of generality, because the initial dynast's objective function is increasing in the utilities of all descendants. This "pure" altruism means that the initial dynast's plan is time-consistent, in the sense that no descendant would choose to deviate from it.

The formulation of (5.1) assumes that a decision-maker at date t knows the entire history θ^t (his parents' skills, grandparents' skills, etc.). However, it is not essential that the agent have this much information. The agent at date t does need to know the recorded history $(w_s y_s)_{s=1}^{t-1}$ of labor incomes, because this information potentially influences his taxes and those of his future descendants. However, θ is Markov, and so the history of skills θ^{t-1} plays no role in forecasting future realizations of θ. There would be no loss in generality if we were to restrict an agent at time t to condition his decisions only on θ_t and $(w_s y_s)_{s=1}^{t-1}$ rather than θ^{t-1}.

The government also commits at the beginning of period 1 to a sequence of government debts $(B_t)_{t=2}^\infty$. Then, given a government's policy (τ, B), an equilibrium in this economy is an allocation (c, y, k) and prices (r, w) such that (c, y, k) solves the agent's problem given (τ, r, w) and markets clear in every date and history:

$$C_t + K_{t+1} = (1 - \delta)K_t + F(K_t, Y_t) \quad \text{for all } t,$$

$$\sum_{\theta^t \in \Theta^t} \pi(\theta^t) b_t(\theta^t) = B_t,$$

$$K_1 = \overline{K}_1.$$

If (c, y, k) is an equilibrium given a policy (τ, B), then I write that (c, y, k) is in $\text{EQM}_{\text{DYN}}(\tau, B)$. (Here, "DYN" stands for dynasty.)

In this dynastic model, I explicitly allow for government assets. Bequests are implicitly and realistically restricted to be nonnegative, because of the lower bound on individual asset holdings. Hence, government assets and debt can potentially play a large role in intergenerational wealth transmission. (In contrast, individuals faced no borrowing constraint in the model of chapter 4, and so government assets ended up being irrelevant.) In addition, the government taxes the stock of bequests rather than the flow of income from capital. Other than that, there is little formal difference between the setup in chapter 4 and this dynastic one.

One patently unrealistic feature of the tax schedules in this setting is that they condition on a dynasty's entire past of labor incomes. For now, I retain this assumption. In chapter 6, I show how *optimal* labor income tax schedules need only condition on a low-dimensional summary statistic of the past.

5.1.3 A Novel Government Objective

The big impact of the dynastic model is on the nature of the social objective. At each date, a new group of agents is born. A generic Pareto optimal allocation puts weight on all of these agents. We consider a particular weighting scheme, and assume that the government seeks to maximize the objective function

$$\sum_{t=1}^{\infty} \rho^{t-1} \sum_{\theta^t \in \Theta^t} \pi(\theta^t) V_t(\theta^t)$$

for some choice of ρ, where $0 < \rho < 1$. Recall here that V_t is the utility of agents born in period t. In this objective, the planner treats all dynasties equally. The planner weights future agents less, but does put weight on those future agents.

This objective is interesting because the planner puts weight on agents newly born in period t in two ways. The first is indirect: the planner cares about the newborn agents' ancestors and the ancestors cared about the newborn agents. The second is direct: the planner puts weight ρ^t on the newborn agents. To see this more clearly, it is useful to unfold it in terms of the underlying flow utilities $u(c_t) - v(l_t)$. Recall that

$$V_t = u(c_t) - v(l_t) + \beta V_{t+1}.$$

Then

$$
\begin{aligned}
V_1 &+ \rho V_2 + \rho^2 V_3 + \cdots \\
&= u(c_1) - v(l_1) + (\rho + \beta)V_2 + \rho^2 V_3 + \cdots \\
&= u(c_1) - v(l_1) + (\rho + \beta)(u(c_2) - v(l_2) + \beta V_3) \\
&\quad + \rho^2 V_3 + \cdots \\
&= u(c_1) - v(l_1) + (\rho + \beta)(u(c_2) - v(l_2)) \\
&\quad + (\beta^2 + \rho\beta + \rho^2)V_3 + \cdots \\
&= \sum_{t=1}^{\infty} \hat{\rho}_t(\rho)[u(c_t) - v(l_t)] + \lim_{t \to \infty} \hat{\rho}_t V_t,
\end{aligned}
$$

where

$$\hat{\rho}_1(\rho) = 1 \quad \text{and} \quad \hat{\rho}_t(\rho) = \frac{\rho^t - \beta^t}{\rho - \beta}.$$

It is simple to prove that if u and v are bounded, then $\lim_{t \to \infty} \hat{\rho}_t V_t$ is zero. Hence, the planner's objective is

$$\sum_{t=1}^{\infty} \hat{\rho}_t(\rho)[u(c_t) - v(l_t)].$$

What is interesting in this objective is that the planner is *always* more patient than the dynasty is. That is,

$$\frac{\hat{\rho}_{t+1}(\rho)}{\hat{\rho}_t(\rho)} = \beta + \frac{\rho^t}{\hat{\rho}_t(\rho)} > \beta.$$

Intuitively, the planner always puts more weight on a newborn than his ancestors did, because of the presence of the ρ^t term.

5.1.4 Government's Problem

With this objective in hand, we can define the government's optimization problem to be

$$\max_{(c,y,k,\tau,K^g)} \sum_{t=1}^{\infty} \sum_{\theta^t \in \Theta^t} \hat{\rho}_t(\rho)\pi(\theta^t)$$
$$\times \left\{ u(c_t(\theta^T)) - v\left(\frac{y_t(\theta^T)}{\theta_t}\right) \right\} \quad (5.2)$$
$$\text{s.t. } (c,y,k) \in \text{EQM}_{\text{DYN}}(\tau,B).$$

We need to convert this abstract problem into one that is more manageable. We proceed as in chapter 4. Taxes are not directly based on skills, but instead are based only on histories of labor incomes. Hence, as in chapter 4, any tax-equilibrium outcome must be incentive-compatible given privacy of information about θ. Put another way, if $(c,y,k) \in \text{EQM}_{\text{DYN}}(\tau,B)$, (c,y) must satisfy the incentive constraint:

$$\sum_{t=1}^{\infty} \sum_{\theta^t \in \Theta^t} \pi(\theta^t)\left[u(c_t(\theta^t)) - v\left(\frac{y_t(\theta^t)}{\theta_t}\right)\right]\beta^{t-1}$$
$$\geqslant \sum_{t=1}^{\infty} \sum_{\theta^t \in \Theta^t} \pi(\theta^t)$$
$$\times \left[u(c_t(\sigma^t(\theta^t))) - v\left(\frac{y_t(\sigma^t(\theta^t))}{\theta_t}\right)\right]\beta^{t-1} \quad (5.3)$$

for any mimicking strategy $\sigma = (\sigma_t)_{t=1}^{\infty}$, where $\sigma_t :$ $\Theta^t \to \Theta$. (Again, because the initial dynast's utility is strictly increasing in the utility of his descendants, there is no loss in assuming that the initial dynast is the family member who chooses among possible mimicking strategies.) I call any (c, y) that satisfies (5.3) incentive-compatible.

We can then attack (5.2) as follows. Consider the following planner's problem:

$$\max_{(c,y,k)} \sum_{t=1}^{\infty} \sum_{\theta^t \in \Theta^t} \hat{\rho}_t(\rho) \pi(\theta^t) \left\{ u(c_t(\theta^t)) - v\left(\frac{y_t(\theta^t)}{\theta_t}\right) \right\},$$

(5.4)

$$K_1 \leqslant \overline{K}_1,$$

(c, y) is incentive-compatible,

(c, y, k) is feasible.

I refer to solutions to the problem (5.4), for any specification of ρ, as being *social optima*. Suppose (c^*, y^*, k^*) is a social optimum. We know that the set of (c, y, k) that lie in the constraint set of the planner's problem (5.4) is no smaller than the set of (c, y, k) that lie in the constraint set of the optimal tax problem (5.2). Hence, given a solution (c^*, y^*, k^*) to (5.4), if we can find (k', τ, B) such that $(c^*, y^*, k') \in$ $\text{EQM}_{\text{DYN}}(\tau, B)$, then the government tax-asset policy (τ, B) is an optimal one.

In this discussion, I have treated ρ as a fixed parameter. More correctly, different choices of ρ correspond to different Pareto optima. When ρ is near 1, we are essentially looking at a Pareto optimum that puts a lot of weight on future generations. When ρ is near 0, we are looking at a Pareto optimum that puts a lot of weight on the initial dynasts.

5.2 Another Reciprocal Euler Equation

In this section, I derive a necessary condition that a social optimum must satisfy. The necessary condition is a generalization of the reciprocal Euler equation originally derived in chapter 3.

5.2.1 Reciprocal Euler Equation: General Case

We can derive another version of the reciprocal Euler equation in this setting. Suppose (c^*, y^*, K^*) is a solution to (5.4). As we did in chapter 3, we can set up the following maximization problem[3]:

$$\max_{c_t', c_{t+1}', K_{t+1}', \Delta} \left(\hat{\rho}_t(\rho) \sum_{\theta^t \in \Theta^t} \pi(\theta^t) u(c_t'(\theta^t)) \right.$$

$$\left. + \hat{\rho}_{t+1}(\rho) \sum_{\theta^{t+1} \in \Theta^{t+1}} \pi(\theta^{t+1}) u(c_{t+1}'(\theta^{t+1})) \right)$$

$$(5.5)$$

$$\text{s.t. } u(c_t'(\theta^t)) + \beta u(c_{t+1}'(\theta^{t+1}))$$

$$= \Delta + u(c_t^*(\theta^t))$$

$$+ \beta u(c_{t+1}^*(\theta^{t+1})) \quad \forall \theta^{t+1}, \quad (5.6)$$

$$\sum_{\theta^t \in \Theta^t} \pi(\theta^t) c_t'(\theta^t) + K_{t+1}' = \sum_{\theta^t \in \Theta^t} \pi(\theta^t) c_t^*(\theta^t) + K_{t+1}^*,$$

$$(5.7)$$

$$\sum_{\theta^{t+1} \in \Theta^{t+1}} \pi(\theta^{t+1}) c_{t+1}'(\theta^{t+1})$$

$$- \sum_{\theta^{t+1} \in \Theta^{t+1}} \pi(\theta^{t+1}) c_{t+1}^*(\theta^{t+1})$$

---

[3] Sleet and Yeltekin (2006) use a similar problem to analyze sustainable equilibrium outcomes when a government can repeatedly choose tax systems over time.

$$= (1 - \delta)K'_{t+1} + F(K'_{t+1}, Y^*_{t+1})$$
$$- (1 - \delta)K^*_{t+1} - F(K^*_{t+1}, Y^*_{t+1}). \qquad (5.8)$$

The constraint set to this problem is essentially identical to that in the maximization problem (3.19) that we used to derive the reciprocal Euler equation in chapter 3. The constraint set includes a set of possible perturbations (c', K') to consumption and capital for the planner. The first constraint (5.6) ensures that (c', y^*) is incentive-compatible, because c' is formed by adding a constant Δ to the utility that the dynasty gets along any path θ^{t+1}. The latter constraints (5.7) and (5.8) ensure that the perturbations are feasible. However, the planner's objective (5.5) is not simply Δ, as it was in problem (3.19). The different objective reflects the fact that in this dynastic setting, the planner's discount factor $\hat{\rho}_{t+1}/\hat{\rho}$ is different from β.

The constraint set in the above problem is smaller than that in (5.4) but contains the socially optimal allocation (c^*, y^*, K^*). Hence, setting $c'_t = c^*_t$, $c'_{t+1} = c^*_{t+1}$, $K'_{t+1} = K^*_{t+1}$, and $\Delta = 0$ satisfies the first-order necessary conditions. These take the form of a reciprocal Euler equation

$$\frac{1}{u'(c^*_t(\theta^t))}$$
$$= \beta^{-1}(1 - \delta + \text{MPK}^*_{t+1})^{-1} \sum_{\theta_{t+1} \in \Theta} \frac{\mu(\theta_{t+1} \mid \theta_t)}{u'(c^*_{t+1}(\theta^{t+1}))}$$
$$+ \left(1 - \frac{\hat{\rho}_{t+1}(\rho)\beta^{-1}}{\hat{\rho}_t(\rho)}\right) \sum_{\theta^t \in \Theta} \pi(\theta^t) \left[\frac{1}{u'(c^*_t(\theta^t))}\right],$$
$$(5.9)$$

where $\text{MPK}^*_{t+1} \equiv F_K(K^*_{t+1}, Y^*_{t+1})$. (I derive these first-order necessary conditions in the technical notes at the end of this chapter.)

To understand the intuition behind (5.9), it is useful to break it into two pieces. First, by taking unconditional expectations of both sides, we obtain

$$E\left\{\frac{1}{u'(c_{t+1}^*)}\right\}$$
$$= \frac{\hat{\rho}_{t+1}(\rho)}{\hat{\rho}_t(\rho)}(1 - \delta + \mathrm{MPK}_{t+1}^*)E\left\{\frac{1}{u'(c_t^*)}\right\}. \quad (5.10)$$

Recall that $1/u'(c)$ is the marginal cost to the planner of providing more momentary utility to an agent. The restriction (5.10) is an Euler equation that says that the planner allocates resources over time so that the discounted average marginal cost in period $(t + 1)$ is equal to the average marginal cost in period t. This restriction is governed solely by the planner's discount factor (not by the dynasty's altruism factor).

Next, if we multiply (5.9) through by

$$\beta(1 - \delta + \mathrm{MPK}_{t+1}^*)$$

and then add it to (5.10), we obtain

$$\left\{E_t\frac{1}{u'(c_{t+1}^*)} - E\frac{1}{u'(c_{t+1}^*)}\right\}$$
$$= \beta(1 - \delta + \mathrm{MPK}_{t+1}^*)\left\{\frac{1}{u'(c_t^*)} - E\frac{1}{u'(c_t^*)}\right\}. \quad (5.11)$$

This equation (5.11) imposes an intertemporal restriction on the deviation of $1/u'(c_t^*)$ from its mean $E[1/u'(c_t^*)]$. These deviations exist in a socially optimal allocation as an optimal response to the incentive problem. The condition (5.11) says that it is optimal to smooth the marginal cost of these deviations over time. This smoothing is governed by the dynasty's own altruism factor β, because it is this factor that enters the incentive constraints.

5.2.2 Special Cases of the Reciprocal Euler Equation

In this subsection, we build intuition into the reciprocal Euler equation (5.9) by examining several special cases.

Suppose first that $\rho = 0$. This means that the planner puts no extra weight on children, beyond the weight imposed by the initial dynast. Then

$$\left(1 - \frac{\hat{\rho}_{t+1}\beta^{-1}}{\hat{\rho}_t}\right) = 0$$

and we return to the original reciprocal Euler equation. If $\rho > 0$, then the original reciprocal equation does not hold. Instead, we obtain

$$\frac{1}{u'(c_t^*(\theta^t))}$$
$$< \beta^{-1}(1 - \delta + \text{MPK}_{t+1}^*)^{-1} \sum_{\theta^{t+1} \geqslant \theta^t} \frac{\mu(\theta_{t+1} \mid \theta_t)}{u'(c_{t+1}^*(\theta^{t+1}))}$$

or

$$u'(c_t^*(\theta^t))$$
$$> \beta(1 - \delta + \text{MPK}_{t+1}^*)\left\{ \sum_{\theta^{t+1} \geqslant \theta^t} \frac{\mu(\theta_{t+1} \mid \theta_t)}{u'(c_{t+1}^*(\theta^{t+1}))} \right\}^{-1}$$

because the planner puts more weight on the future than in the long-lived agent case.

The case in which $\theta_t = \theta_1$ for all t (so that skills are constant over time for a dynasty) is especially interesting. Then

$$\frac{1}{u'(c_t^*(\theta_1))} = \beta^{-1}(1 - \delta + \text{MPK}_{t+1}^*)^{-1}\frac{1}{u'(c_{t+1}^*(\theta_1))}$$
$$+ \left(1 - \frac{\hat{\rho}_{t+1}\beta^{-1}}{\hat{\rho}_t}\right)E\left[\frac{1}{u'(c_t)}\right].$$

In this case, we can conclude that

$$u'(c_t^*(\theta_1)) > \beta(1 - \delta + \text{MPK}_{t+1}^*)u'(c_{t+1}^*(\theta_1)).$$

In this fixed skill case, an agent would like to borrow from their children. This makes sense, because the planner systematically puts more weight on descendants than individuals themselves do.

5.3 Properties of Socially Optimal Allocations

In a socially optimal allocation, when an agent is privately informed about his skill level, c_t^* typically depends on θ_t. This dependence is necessary to elicit higher output from the highly skilled agents. It is possible to use the reciprocal Euler equation (5.9) to learn a great deal about the dependence of consumption on current and past skill realizations of the dynasty's members.

In chapter 3, we established three critical properties of Pareto optimal allocations with private information in the nondynastic model ($\rho = 0$). The first property is that allocations are history dependent. The second property is that there is an intertemporal wedge between current consumption and future consumption. Finally, if $\beta R = 1$, Pareto optimal allocations feature growing inequality and zero mobility in the long run. In this section, we assess to what extent these properties are true of socially optimal allocations in the dynastic model.

5.3.1 History Dependence

Recall that if (c^*, y^*, K^*) is socially optimal in the dynastic setting, it must satisfy the restriction

$$\left\{ E_t \frac{1}{u'(c_{t+1}^*)} - E\frac{1}{u'(c_{t+1}^*)} \right\}$$

$$= \beta(1 - \delta + \text{MPK}_{t+1}^*) \left\{ \frac{1}{u'(c_t^*)} - E\frac{1}{u'(c_t^*)} \right\}. \quad (5.12)$$

In words, this equation says that if an agent's $1/u'(c_t^*)$ is larger than its mean over all agents, then we should expect $1/u'(c_{t+1}^*)$ to be larger than its mean too. Intuitively, suppose it is socially optimal to reward a parent with higher than average consumption in period t. Because u is concave, and because the parent is altruistic, it is optimal to smooth this extra reward over the parent's current consumption and the consumptions of his descendants. This smoothing may well not be one-for-one. Indeed, if β is small relative to $(1 - \delta + \text{MPK}_{t+1}^*)$, the left-hand side will be a small fraction of the right-hand side; the parent receives most of his rewards during his lifetime.

This simple result has an important consequence. It is socially optimal for children's opportunities to depend on the performance of their parents. This dependence is an optimal way to provide incentives to the parents, given that they care about their children. As we shall see, the strength of this dependence is influenced by the relative size of the planner's discount factor ρ to the parents' altruism factor β.

5.3.2 Intertemporal Wedge

Recall that if (c^*, y^*, K^*) is socially optimal in the dynastic setting, then

$$\frac{1}{u'(c_t^*)} = \beta^{-1}(1 - \delta + \text{MPK}_{t+1}^*)^{-1} E_t \frac{1}{u'(c_{t+1}^*)}$$
$$+ \left(1 - \frac{\hat{\rho}_{t+1}(\rho)\beta^{-1}}{\hat{\rho}_t(\rho)}\right) E\left\{\frac{1}{u'(c_t^*)}\right\}.$$

If $\rho = 0$, then this restriction collapses to the now-familiar reciprocal Euler equation:

$$\frac{1}{u'(c_t^*)} = \beta^{-1}(1 - \delta + \text{MPK}_{t+1}^*)^{-1} E_t \frac{1}{u'(c_{t+1}^*)}.$$

This Euler equation implies that if $\text{Var}_t(u'(c_{t+1}^*)) > 0$, so that children's consumption is a nontrivial function of their realized skills in period $(t + 1)$, then

$$u'(c_t^*) < \beta(1 - \delta + \text{MPK}_{t+1}^*) E_t u'(c_{t+1}^*).$$

It is an optimal response to an incentive problem in period $(t + 1)$ for the (discounted) expected marginal utility of period $(t + 1)$ consumption to exceed period t marginal utility.

However, if $\rho > 0$, then this result disappears. We know that if $\rho > 0$, then

$$\frac{\hat{\rho}_{t+1}(\rho)\beta^{-1}}{\hat{\rho}_t(\rho)} > 1$$

because the planner's discount factor exceeds the parent's altruism factor. Hence, we can conclude that

$$\frac{1}{u'(c_t^*)} < \beta^{-1}(1 - \delta + \text{MPK}_{t+1}^*)^{-1} E_t \frac{1}{u'(c_{t+1}^*)} \quad (5.13)$$

or

$$u'(c_t^*) > \beta(1 - \delta + \text{MPK}_{t+1}^*)\left\{E_t \frac{1}{u'(c_{t+1}^*)}\right\}^{-1}. \quad (5.14)$$

The planner puts more weight on children than parents do and so it is socially optimal for $u'(c_t^*)$ to be relatively high. This extra weight on $u'(c_t^*)$ may or may not undo the extra weight on $u'(c_{t+1}^*)$ generated by the incentive effect.

5.3.3 Long-Run Planner's Discount Factor and Long-Run Allocations

The long-run properties of socially optimal allocations hinge critically on the discount factor of the planner between date t and date $(t + 1)$. This discount factor can be written as

$$\frac{\hat{\rho}_{t+1}(\rho)}{\hat{\rho}_t(\rho)} = \frac{\rho^{t+1} - \beta^{t+1}}{\rho^t - \beta^t}. \tag{5.15}$$

What happens to this expression as t converges to infinity? We can rewrite it as

$$\lim_{t \to \infty} \frac{\hat{\rho}_{t+1}(\rho)}{\hat{\rho}_t(\rho)} = \lim_{t \to \infty} \frac{\rho - \beta^{t+1}/\rho^t}{1 - \beta^t/\rho^t}. \tag{5.16}$$

This limit depends on the relative sizes of β (a fundamental parameter of the environment) and ρ (a parameter that indexes various socially optimal allocations). If $\rho > \beta$, then β^t/ρ^t converges to zero and so

$$\lim_{t \to \infty} \frac{\hat{\rho}_{t+1}(\rho)}{\hat{\rho}_t(\rho)} = \rho. \tag{5.17}$$

If $\beta \geqslant \rho$, then we can apply L'Hôpital's rule to find that

$$\lim_{t \to \infty} \frac{\hat{\rho}_{t+1}(\rho)}{\hat{\rho}_t(\rho)} = \beta. \tag{5.18}$$

We can conclude that

$$\lim_{t \to \infty} \frac{\hat{\rho}_{t+1}(\rho)}{\hat{\rho}_t(\rho)} = \max(\rho, \beta).$$

Now suppose that (c^*, y^*, K^*) is socially optimal and that $\lim_{t \to \infty} E\{1/u'(c_t^*)\}$ is a finite positive number. We know that, for all t,

$$E\left\{\frac{1}{u'(c_{t+1}^*)}\right\} = \frac{\hat{\rho}_{t+1}(\rho)}{\hat{\rho}_t(\rho)}(1 - \delta + \mathrm{MPK}_{t+1}^*)E\left\{\frac{1}{u'(c_t^*)}\right\}.$$

It follows that in the long run, the marginal gross rate of return on capital is given by the reciprocal of the planner's discount factor

$$\lim_{t \to \infty}(1 - \delta + \mathrm{MPK}_{t+1}^*) = \frac{1}{\max(\rho, \beta)}.$$

The reciprocal Euler equation (5.9) then implies that, in the long run,

$$\frac{1}{u'(c_{t+1}^*)} = \frac{\beta/\max(\rho, \beta)}{u'(c_t^*)} + \left(1 - \frac{\beta}{\max(\rho, \beta)}\right)E\left[\frac{1}{u'(c_t^*)}\right] + \xi_{t+1},$$

(5.19)

where ξ_{t+1} is a martingale difference.

The three components of the right-hand side of (5.19) have simple interpretations. The first piece represents the planner's desire to smooth rewards over time. This need for smoothing is small if the parent's altruism factor β is small relative to ρ, and disappears if $\beta = 0$. The second piece represents the planner's desire to insure future children against the risk of having relatively unskilled parents. This gets large if ρ is large relative to β. Finally, the martingale difference ξ_{t+1} arises from the planner's need to provide incentives in period $(t + 1)$.

If $\rho \leqslant \beta$, then the long-run properties of social optima in this dynastic model are the same as those in the model with long-lived agents. The reciprocal of marginal utility follows a martingale. As long as ξ_{t+1} is nondegenerate, inequality grows over time. Eventually, because of the martingale convergence theorem, we know that consumption becomes immobile. Note that this result means that the (conditional) variance of the incremental shocks ξ_{t+1} must be shrinking along every sample path. In this sense, incentive effects have to vanish in the long run.

In contrast, suppose that $\rho > \beta$. Now, individual $1/u'(c_t^*)$ is mean-reverting (because $\beta/\max(\rho, \beta) < 1$). Intuitively, the high value of ρ means that the planner cares more about ensuring equality of opportunity for newborns than about smoothing rewards to their parents. There are now two opposing forces. As before, the incentive effect ξ_{t+1} tends to increase inequality over time. However, the transmission of past shocks is now less one-for-one, and this makes inequality shrink over time. This tension between the (inequality-increasing) incentive effect and (inequality-decreasing) imperfect transmission means that there may be a long-run limiting cross-sectional distribution of consumption with nontrivial incentive effects.

5.4 Optimal Bequest Taxation

We now move to mapping our characterizations of socially optimal allocations into characterizations of optimal taxes. Suppose (c^*, y^*, k^*) is a socially optimal allocation such that

$$y^{*t}(\theta^t) = y^{*t}(\theta^{t'}) \quad \Longrightarrow \quad c_t^*(\theta^t) = c_t^*(\theta^{t'})$$

for all $(t, \theta^t, \theta^{t'})$. Then, as in chapter 4, we can build an optimal tax system τ such that $(c^*, y^*, k') \in$

EQM(τ, B) for some (k', B). This optimal tax system is a nonlinear function of a current dynast's labor income, his ancestors' labor incomes, and the current dynast's inheritance. To avoid repetition, I will not go over that construction in detail. Instead, I will focus on the properties of the optimal bequest taxes intrinsic in that system.

In chapter 4, we constructed optimal wealth taxes by setting tax rates so as to satisfy *ex post* Euler equations. In this setting, wealth is equivalent to bequests. So, we can design optimal bequest taxes in the same way. If τ^*_{t+1} is the tax rate on the bequest inherited by the agent born in period $(t + 1)$, the tax rate should satisfy

$$\beta(1 - \tau^*_{t+1}(\theta^{t+1}))\frac{u'(c^*_{t+1}(\theta^{t+1}))}{u'(c^*_t(\theta^t))}(1 - \delta + \text{MPK}^*_{t+1}) = 1$$

(5.20)

for all θ^{t+1}.

5.4.1 Regressive *Ex Post* Bequest Taxes

Bequest taxes satisfy *ex post* Euler equations, and so, when a person receives an inheritance, his bequest tax depends on his labor income. In particular, (5.20) implies that the bequest tax rate equals:

$$\tau^*_{t+1}(\theta^{t+1}) = 1 - \frac{\beta^{-1}(1 - \delta + \text{MPK}^*_{t+1})^{-1}u'(c^*_t(\theta^t))}{u'(c^*_{t+1}(\theta^{t+1}))}.$$

The tax rate is a decreasing function of c^*_{t+1}. Hence, conditional on a parent's consumption c^*_t, surprisingly low-consumption descendants face a high tax rate on their bequests. This tax deters a double deviation in which parents leave a large bequest to a child, and then that child shirks.

5.4.2 Expected Bequest Tax Rates

When we calculated expected wealth tax rates in the long-lived agent case, they were zero. When we calculate expected bequest taxes, we obtain

$$E\{\tau_{t+1}^*(\theta^{t+1}) \mid \theta^t\}$$
$$= 1 - \beta^{-1}(1 - \delta + \text{MPK}_{t+1}^*)^{-1}u'(c_t^*(\theta^t))$$
$$\times E\left\{\frac{1}{u'(c_{t+1}^*(\theta^{t+1}))} \ \Big| \ \theta^t\right\}$$
$$= \left(1 - \frac{\hat{\rho}_{t+1}\beta^{-1}}{\hat{\rho}_t}\right)u'(c_t^*(\theta^t))E\left[\frac{1}{u'(c_t^*)}\right].$$

Because the planner puts more weight on the future, the term in brackets is negative. Expected tax rates on bequests are always negative: the planner subsidizes bequests. Why is this? The planner likes children more than parents do.

Note that this has nothing to do with private information. In fact, if Θ is a singleton, we still get a subsidy. This subsidy is exactly the Pigouvian subsidy,

$$\left(1 - \frac{\hat{\rho}_{t+1}\beta^{-1}}{\hat{\rho}_t}\right),$$

which corrects the gap between private incentives and social ones.

5.4.3 Parents' Skills and Subsidies

Consider again the expression

$$E\{\tau_{t+1}(\theta^{t+1}) \mid \theta^t\}$$
$$= \left(1 - \frac{\hat{\rho}_{t+1}\beta^{-1}}{\hat{\rho}_t}\right)u'(c_t^*(\theta^t))E\left[\frac{1}{u'(c_t)}\right].$$

The absolute value of this expression is decreasing in c_t^*. Consumption-poor parents are subsidized at a higher rate than consumption-rich parents.

Again, the Pigouvian subsidy is a useful benchmark. Suppose

$$u'(c_t^*(\theta^t)) > \left\{ E\left[\frac{1}{u'(c_t^*)} \right] \right\}^{-1}. \qquad (5.21)$$

These consumption-poor agents are subsidized more than the Pigouvian subsidy. If

$$u'(c_t^*(\theta^t)) < \left\{ E\left[\frac{1}{u'(c_t^*)} \right] \right\}^{-1}, \qquad (5.22)$$

these consumption-rich agents are subsidized less than the Pigouvian subsidy. Note that

$$E(\mathrm{MU}_t)E\{1/\mathrm{MU}_t\} = 1 - \mathrm{Cov}(\mathrm{MU}_t, 1/\mathrm{MU}_t)$$
$$> 1$$

and so

$$E\{\tau_{t+1}(\theta^{t+1})\} > \left(1 - \frac{\hat{\rho}_{t+1}\beta^{-1}}{\hat{\rho}_t} \right).$$

The overall average subsidy rate is less than the Pigouvian subsidy.

Intuitively, the planner's extra weight in his discount factor is given by

$$\frac{\rho^t}{\hat{\rho}_t}. \qquad (5.23)$$

The extra weight in his rate of time preference is given by

$$\left[\frac{\hat{\rho}_t}{\rho_t u'(c_t^*(\theta^t))} \right]^{-1}. \qquad (5.24)$$

The planner is more patient than all households. But he is especially more patient than poor households.

5.4.4 Long-Run Bequest Taxes

We earlier identified three properties of bequest taxes. First, surprisingly low-skilled children face higher bequest tax rates. Second, for any parent, the expected bequest tax rate is negative. Third, low-consumption parents face higher expected bequest subsidy rates. What happens to these properties in the long run?

If $\beta < \rho$, they all survive, because the limiting planner discount factor is larger than β. But if $\beta \geqslant \rho$, then the limiting planner discount factor equals β. In this case, the first property survives because

$$\tau_{t+1}^*(\theta^{t+1}) = 1 - \frac{\beta^{-1}(1 - \delta + \mathrm{MPK}_{t+1}^*)^{-1}u'(c_t^*(\theta^t))}{u'(c_{t+1}^*(\theta^{t+1}))}$$
(5.25)

still implies that taxes are a decreasing function of c_{t+1}^*. However, the other two properties vanish. Recall expected bequest tax rates are equal to

$$E\{\tau_{t+1}(\theta^{t+1}) \mid \theta^t\}$$
$$= \left(1 - \frac{\hat{\rho}_{t+1}\beta^{-1}}{\hat{\rho}_t}\right)u'(c_t^*(\theta^t))E\left[\frac{1}{u'(c_t^*)}\right]$$

and this becomes zero in the limit if $\beta \geqslant \rho$.

Thus, the long-run expected bequest tax rates vary across social optima, depending on the value of ρ. If the social optimum is one in which the planner puts a lot of weight on future generations, we get long-run subsidies. If it is one in which the planner's extra weight on descendants vanishes, then we get long-run zero bequest taxes, which are regressive *ex post*.

5.5 Summary

Generically, a social planner's objective puts weight on all individuals both born and unborn. Hence, even if parents care about their children, societies necessarily care even more. Even without any incentive considerations, it is good social policy to *subsidize* bequests not *tax* them.

Incentives introduce two key features into the structure of bequest taxes. Bequest subsidies introduce more inequality (that is, prenatal risk) for the next generation. To control this force, it is optimal to subsidize bequests from poor parents at a higher rate than the bequests from rich parents. In addition, bequest subsidies introduce adverse incentive effects for the recipients, because rich children will not work as hard. It is optimal to control this effect by subsidizing at a lower rate the bequests received by children who produce less. In this way, incentive effects generate a subtle interaction between the outcomes of parents, the outcomes of children, and the size of bequest subsidies.

The degree of long-run immobility varies across Pareto optimal allocations. If the planner's discount factor is low, then (as in the immortal agent case) the martingale convergence theorem implies that consumption is immobile in the long run. If the planner's discount factor is high, then $1/u'(c)$ is mean-reverting, and so consumption need not be immobile. The cross-generational mobility of wealth or consumption is not informative about the optimality or suboptimality of intergenerational insurance.

5.6 Technical Notes

In this section, I provide a proof of the intergenerational reciprocal Euler equation. Recall that if (c^*, y^*, k^*) is an optimal allocation, then

$$(c_t^*, c_{t+1}^*, K_{t+1}^*, 0)$$

solves the problem (5.5):

$$\max_{c_t', c_{t+1}', K_{t+1}', \Delta} \hat{\rho}_t(\rho) \sum_{\theta^t \in \Theta^t} \pi(\theta^t) u(c_t'(\theta^t))$$

$$+ \hat{\rho}_{t+1}(\rho) \sum_{\theta^{t+1} \in \Theta^{t+1}} \pi(\theta^{t+1}) u(c_{t+1}'(\theta^{t+1}))$$

s.t. $u(c_t'(\theta^t)) + \beta u(c_{t+1}'(\theta^{t+1}))$

$$= \Delta + u(c_t^*(\theta^t)) + \beta u(c_{t+1}^*(\theta^{t+1})) \quad \forall \theta^{t+1},$$
$$(5.26)$$

$$\sum_{\theta^t \in \Theta^t} \pi(\theta^t) c_t'(\theta^t) + K_{t+1}' = \sum_{\theta^t \in \Theta^t} \mu(\theta^t) c_t^*(\theta^t) + K_{t+1}^*,$$
$$(5.27)$$

$$\sum_{\theta^{t+1} \in \Theta^{t+1}} \pi(\theta^{t+1}) c_{t+1}'(\theta^{t+1})$$

$$- \sum_{\theta^{t+1} \in \Theta^{t+1}} \pi(\theta^{t+1}) c_{t+1}^*(\theta^{t+1})$$

$$= (1 - \delta) K_{t+1}' + F(K_{t+1}', Y_{t+1}^*)$$
$$- (1 - \delta) K_{t+1}^* - F(K_{t+1}^*, Y_{t+1}^*). \quad (5.28)$$

Let η_{t+1} be the multiplier on the first constraint (5.26), and $(\lambda_t, \lambda_{t+1})$ be the multipliers on the latter two constraints (5.27), (5.28). The first-order conditions for this problem are

$$\hat{\rho}_t(\rho) \pi(\theta^t) u'(c_t^*(\theta^t))$$

$$= u'(c_t^*(\theta^t)) \sum_{\theta^{t+1} \geq \theta^t} \eta_{t+1}(\theta^{t+1}) + \lambda_t \pi(\theta^t), \quad (5.29)$$

$$\hat{\rho}_{t+1}(\rho)\pi(\theta^{t+1})u'(c^*_{t+1}(\theta^{t+1}))$$
$$= \beta u'(c^*_{t+1}(\theta^{t+1}))\eta_{t+1}(\theta^{t+1}) + \lambda_{t+1}\pi(\theta^{t+1}),$$
$$\text{(5.30)}$$

$$\lambda_t = \lambda_{t+1}(1 - \delta + \text{MPK}^*_{K,t+1}), \tag{5.31}$$

$$\sum_{\theta^{t+1}} \eta_{t+1}(\theta^{t+1}) = 0. \tag{5.32}$$

If we solve out for η_{t+1} using (5.30), and plug into (5.29), we obtain

$$\hat{\rho}_t(\rho) = \beta^{-1}\hat{\rho}_{t+1}(\rho)$$
$$- \beta^{-1} \sum_{\theta^{t+1} \geqslant \theta^t} \frac{\lambda_{t+1}\mu(\theta_{t+1} \mid \theta_t)}{u'(c^*_{t+1}(\theta^{t+1}))}$$
$$+ \frac{\lambda_t}{u'(c^*_t(\theta^t))}. \tag{5.33}$$

At the same time, if we sum (5.29) over θ^t, and use (5.32), we get

$$0 = \hat{\rho}_t(\rho) - \sum_{\theta^t} \frac{\lambda_t\pi(\theta^t)}{u'(c^*_t(\theta^t))}.$$

Combining these two equations gives

$$\sum_{\theta^t} \frac{\pi(\theta^t)}{u'(c^*_t(\theta^t))}$$
$$= \beta^{-1}\hat{\rho}_{t+1}(\rho)\lambda_t^{-1}$$
$$- \beta^{-1}\lambda_{t+1}\lambda_t^{-1}E\left[\frac{1}{u'(c^*_{t+1}) \mid \theta^t}\right]$$
$$+ \frac{1}{u'(c^*_t(\theta^t))}. \tag{5.34}$$

Rearranging and solving for λ_t, we get

$$
\frac{1}{u'(c_t^*(\theta^t))}
$$
$$
= \beta^{-1}(1 - \delta + \text{MPK}_{t+1}^*)^{-1} E\left[\frac{1}{u'(c_{t+1}^*)} \;\middle|\; \theta^t \right]
$$
$$
+ \left(1 - \frac{\beta^{-1}\hat{\rho}_{t+1}(\rho)}{\hat{\rho}_t(\rho)}\right) \sum_{\theta^t} \frac{\pi(\theta^t)}{u'(c_t^*(\theta^t))},
$$

which proves the proposition.

References

Amador, M., G.-M. Angeletos, and I. Werning. 2006. Commitment vs. flexibility. *Econometrica* 74:365–96.

Farhi, E., and I. Werning. 2007. Inequality and social discounting. *Journal of Political Economy* 115:365–402.

———. Forthcoming. Progressive estate taxation. *Quarterly Journal of Economics*.

Sleet, C., and S. Yeltekin. 2006. Credibility and endogenous social discounting. *Review of Economic Dynamics* 9:410–37.

6

Quantitative Analysis: Methods and Results

The preceding chapters provide qualitative characterizations of optimal tax systems. These characterizations are robust, in the sense in that they are
applicable for a wide class of shock processes and
preferences, but partial. I now take up a different question. Suppose we have a quantitative specification of
primitives (preferences, technology, and the law of
motion of shocks) for a particular economy. How do
we translate this information about primitives into a
complete specification of an optimal tax system for
this economy?

The analysis in chapters 4 and 5 is key to answer-
ing this question. That discussion shows how we can
convert an optimal allocation of resources into an optimal tax system, and allows us to focus on a more basic question: given a specification of primitives in the
economy, how do we solve for an optimal allocation of
resources? In most cases of interest, we cannot answer
this question analytically. Instead, we must *compute*
numerical approximations to its answer. The big difficulty is that optimal allocations generally depend on
the entire history of past realizations of skill shocks.
We can only hope to make progress if we somehow
make this dependence manageable.

In this chapter, I consider two possible ways to do so. The first approach is to figure out a method to summarize the dependence of the optimal allocation on the past via a relatively low-dimensional summary statistic. I use the work of Spear and Srivastava (1987) to show how this can be done when skill shocks are i.i.d. I then extend their analysis using the method of Fernandes and Phelan (2000) to include the case in which skills follow a Markov chain.[1]

The second approach is to assume that agents live for a small number of (lengthy) periods, and that the space of possible skill realizations is small. Under these assumptions, the planner's problem becomes a nonlinear optimization problem with a small number of controls. I show how this approach can be used to great effect in an infinite-horizon overlapping-generations economy, as long as the agents themselves are finitely lived.

6.1 Immortal Agents in an Open Economy

In this section, I discuss how to make the social planner's problem recursive with respect to a low-dimensional state, given an exogenous interest rate. The baseline model is essentially an infinite horizon version of the setup in chapter 3. There is a unit

---

[1] Battaglini and Coate (2008) consider an economy in which agents are risk-neutral and skills evolve according to a Markov chain with a two-point support. They provide an explicit characterization of optimal labor income taxes in this environment. (Asset income taxes play no role because preferences are linear in consumption.) They find that labor income taxes should be zero for any agent who is currently or was ever highly skilled in the past. We shall see in section 6.2 that this sharp result disappears when we use a more plausible parameterization of preferences.

measure of infinitely lived agents. The agents have preferences of the form

$$\sum_{t=1}^{\infty} \beta^{t-1}[u(c_t) - v(l_t)], \quad 0 < \beta < 1,$$

where c_t is period t consumption and l_t is period t effort. Let θ_t be the agent's skill at date t, where θ_t is an element of a finite set Θ. An agent with skill θ_t can produce $y_t = \theta_t l_t$ units of consumption. Skills evolve stochastically so that the probability of any sequence $\theta^t = (\theta_1, \ldots, \theta_t)$ in Θ^t is positive.

An allocation (c, y) is a sequence of mappings $(c_t, y_t)_{t=1}^{\infty}$, so that $(c_t, y_t) : \Theta^t \to R_+^2$. At each date, an agent's output y_t is observable. However, his skill and effort decision are private information, and so the agent can employ any mimicking strategy $\sigma = (\sigma_t)_{t=1}^{\infty}$, where $\sigma_t : \Theta^t \to \Theta$. Let Σ be the set of all such strategies. Then, (c, y) is incentive-compatible (IC) if and only if

$$E \sum_{t=1}^{\infty} \beta^{t-1} \left\{ u(c_t(\theta^t)) - v\left(\frac{y_t(\theta^t)}{\theta_t}\right) \right\}$$

$$\geqslant E \sum_{t=1}^{\infty} \beta^{t-1} \left\{ u(c_t(\sigma^t(\theta^t))) - v\left(\frac{y_t(\sigma_t(\theta^t))}{\theta_t}\right) \right\}$$

$$\text{for all } \sigma \in \Sigma.$$
$$(6.1)$$

We assume that the economy is an open one, with an exogenous gross interest rate $R = \beta^{-1}$. The planner's problem is to choose a specification of (c, y) so as to maximize *ex ante* utility, subject to an intertemporal societal budget constraint and subject to (c, y) being incentive-compatible:

$$\max_{c,y} E \sum_{t=1}^{\infty} \beta^{t-1} \left[u(c_t) - v\left(\frac{y_t}{\theta_t}\right) \right] \qquad (6.2)$$

$$\text{s.t. } E \sum_{t=1}^{\infty} \beta^{t-1}[y_t - c_t] \geq 0,$$

$$(c, y) \text{ is IC,}$$

$$y_t(\theta^t), c_t(\theta^t) \geq 0 \quad \text{for all } \theta^t \in \Theta^t.$$

In the following sections, we study how to make this problem computationally feasible if θ is i.i.d., and, more generally, if θ is Markov.

6.1.1 I.I.D. Skills

In this section, I suppose that θ_t is i.i.d. over time. Under this assumption about skills, Spear and Srivastava (1987) demonstrate that the solution $(c^*, y^*)(\theta^t)$ depends on θ^{t-1} only through the continuation (sometimes called *promised*) utility that the agent has at date t. In this way, they make the problem (6.2) recursive in a useful fashion.

To understand their argument, consider an optimal allocation (c^*, y^*) and fix a skill history $\bar{\theta}^t$. Define the continuation allocation $(c'_s(\theta^s), y'_s(\theta^s))_{s=1}^{\infty}$ by $c'_s(\theta^s) = c^*_{t+s}(\bar{\theta}^t, \theta^s)$ and $y'_s(\theta^s) = y^*_{t+s}(\bar{\theta}^t, \theta^s)$, and define $U^*_t(\bar{\theta}^t; c^*, y^*)$ to be the continuation utility of the agents with history $\bar{\theta}^t$:

$$U^*_t(\bar{\theta}^t; c^*, y^*)$$

$$= E\left[\sum_{s=1}^{\infty} \beta^{s-1} \left\{ u(c^*_{t+s}(\theta^{t+s})) - v\left(\frac{y^*_{t+s}(\theta^{t+s})}{\theta_{t+s}}\right) \right\} \Bigg| \right.$$

$$\left. \theta^t = \bar{\theta}^t \right].$$

The continuation allocation (c', y') is obviously incentive-compatible. Spear and Srivastava's key insight is much stronger: this continuation allocation is actually the least costly incentive-compatible allocation among all of those that provide utility $U_t^*(\bar{\theta}^t; c^*, y^*)$ to the agents.

We can establish this result by contradiction. Suppose that we can find an incentive compatible allocation (c'', y'') such that

$$E\left\{ \sum_{s=1}^{\infty} \beta^{s-1}\left[u(c_s''(\theta^s)) - v\left(\frac{y_s''(\theta^s)}{\theta_s}\right) \right] \right\}$$
$$= U_t^*(\bar{\theta}^t; c^*, y^*) \quad (6.3)$$

but

$$E\left\{ \sum_{s=1}^{\infty} \beta^{s-1}[c_s''(\theta^s) - y_s''(\theta^s)] \right\}$$
$$< E\left\{ \sum_{s=1}^{\infty} \beta^{s-1}[c_s'(\theta^s) - y_s'(\theta^s)] \right\}. \quad (6.4)$$

Then, by substituting (c'', y'') for (c', y') as a continuation allocation, we can construct a better allocation than (c^*, y^*). Define (c^{**}, y^{**}) to be an allocation so that

$$c^{**} = c^*, \qquad y^{**} = y^* \quad (6.5)$$

except

$$c_{t+s}^{**}(\bar{\theta}^t, \theta_{t+1}^{t+s}) = c_s''(\bar{\theta}^t, \theta_{t+1}^{t+s}),$$
$$y_{t+s}^{**}(\bar{\theta}^t, \theta_{t+1}^{t+s}) = y_s''(\bar{\theta}^t, \theta_{t+1}^{t+s}),$$

where $\theta_{t+1}^{t+s} = (\theta_{t+1}, \theta_{t+2}, \ldots, \theta_{t+s})$. This new allocation (c^{**}, y^{**}) is cheaper than (c^*, y^*) and provides the same *ex ante* utility as (c^*, y^*). Hence, the new allocation is superior to (c^*, y^*) as long as (c^{**}, y^{**})

is in fact incentive-compatible. Checking the incentive-compatibility of (c^{**}, y^{**}) is, however, nontrivial, because substituting in a new continuation allocation in this fashion could change a person's incentives to mimic other agents in *earlier* periods.

It is here that the i.i.d. structure of θ plays a critical role. Suppose that an agent has true type $\theta^{t'}$, but has acted in periods 1 through t like his type is $\hat{\theta}^t$. This agent's continuation utility under the doubly starred allocation is

$$
U_t(\hat{\theta}^t, \theta^{t'}; c^{**}, y^{**})
$$

$$
= E\left[\sum_{s=1}^{\infty} \beta^{s-1}\left[u(c_{t+s}^{**}(\hat{\theta}^t, \theta_{t+1}^{t+s}))\right.\right.
$$

$$
\left.\left. - v\left(\frac{y_{t+s}^{**}(\hat{\theta}^t, \theta_{t+1}^{t+s})}{\theta_{t+s}}\right)\right]\,\middle|\,\theta^t = \theta^{t'}\right].
$$

$$(6.6)$$

The conditioning is irrelevant here, because θ_t is i.i.d. over time, and so the continuation utility is the same under (c^{**}, y^{**}) as under (c^*, y^*):

$$
U_t(\hat{\theta}^t, \theta^{t'}; c^{**}, y^{**}) = U_t(\hat{\theta}^t, \hat{\theta}^t; c^{**}, y^{**}) \quad (6.7)
$$

$$
= U_t(\hat{\theta}^t, \hat{\theta}^t; c^*, y^*) \quad (6.8)
$$

$$
= U_t(\hat{\theta}^t, \theta^{t'}; c^*, y^*). \quad (6.9)
$$

We can conclude that since the starred allocation is incentive-compatible, so is the doubly starred allocation (c^{**}, y^{**}).

We have shown that at any history, the continuation part of (c^*, y^*) is a minimal-cost incentive-compatible allocation among all those that provide the same continuation utility. This characterization of (c^*, y^*) implies it must satisfy the following functional equation. Let Domain be the set of *ex ante* utilities U such that there exists an incentive-compatible allocation (c, y) which satisfies

$$U = E\left\{\sum_{s=1}^{\infty} \beta^{s-1}\left[u(c_s) - v\left(\frac{y_s}{\theta_s}\right)\right]\right\}. \qquad (6.10)$$

Define the function C to be

$$C(U) = \min_{(c,y)} E\left\{\sum_{s=1}^{\infty} \beta^{s-1}[c_s - y_s]\right\} \qquad (6.11)$$

$$\text{s.t. } E\left\{\sum_{s=1}^{\infty} \beta^{s-1}\left[u(c_s) - v\left(\frac{y_s}{\theta_s}\right)\right]\right\} = U,$$

$$(c, y) \text{ is IC},$$

$$c, y \geq 0.$$

In words, $C(U)$ is the cost (in net present value terms) that needs to be paid by the planner in order to provide utility U to the agent. Then, the cost function C is a solution to the following functional equation:

$$C(U) = \min_{c,y,U'} \sum_{\theta \in \Theta} \pi(\theta)[c(\theta) - y(\theta) + \beta C(U'(\theta))]$$

$$(6.12)$$

$$\text{s.t. } u(c(\theta)) - v(y(\theta)/\theta) + \beta U'(\theta)$$
$$\geq u(c(\theta')) - v(y(\theta')/\theta) + \beta U'(\theta')$$
$$\text{for all } \theta, \theta',$$

$$\sum_{\theta} \pi(\theta)[u(c(\theta)) - v(y(\theta)/\theta) + \beta U'(\theta)] = U,$$

$$U'(\theta) \in \text{Domain} \quad \text{for all } \theta \text{ in } \Theta,$$

$$c(\theta), y(\theta) \geq 0 \quad \text{for all } \theta \text{ in } \Theta.$$

The functional equation (6.12) captures the following recursive procedure. After a history θ^{t-1} of skill shocks, the planner has to deliver some continuation utility U to the agent. To do so in an efficient (that is, cost-effective) fashion, he looks to minimize costs among all incentive-compatible allocations. These incentive-compatible allocations can be characterized by their specification of (c, y) and their specification of continuation utility U' as a function of the agent's skill realization θ in period t. Then, in the following period, the planner repeats the procedure (and so $C(U'(\theta))$ captures his continuation costs).

By Blackwell's Theorem, the right-hand side of (6.12) describes a contraction on the space of bounded functions that map from Domain into the real line. We can use standard dynamic programming arguments to conclude that C is the unique bounded solution to this functional equation.

One important subtlety is the Domain of U' in the above problem. As defined above, Domain includes any U' such that there is an incentive-compatible allocation that delivers initial utility U'. Suppose u is bounded from above and below by u^+ and u_+. Suppose too that v is bounded from above and below by v^+ and v_+. Then, utility is bounded from above and below by

$$U^+ = \frac{u^+ - v_+}{1 - \beta}, \tag{6.13}$$

$$U_+ = \frac{u_+ - v^+}{1 - \beta}. \tag{6.14}$$

Can we pick any U in this domain $[U_+, U^+]$? The answer is no, because it is typically *not* possible to find an incentive-compatible allocation that delivers the minimal level of consumption in every date and state, and also gets the agent to work as hard as possible in every period. The incentive-compatibility constraints impose restrictions on what the domain of U' is.

We can solve for Domain numerically using a simple recursive procedure.[2] Define a mapping T that maps intervals $[a, b]$ in the real line into intervals $[T_+(a, b), T^+(a, b)]$ in the real line as follows:

$$T_+(a, b)$$

$$= \min_{c, y, U'} \sum_\theta \pi(\theta)[u(c(\theta)) - v(y(\theta)/\theta) + \beta U'(\theta)]$$

(6.15)

$$\text{s.t. } u(c(\theta)) - v(y(\theta)/\theta) + \beta U'(\theta)$$
$$\geqslant u(c(\theta')) - v(y(\theta')/\theta) + \beta U'(\theta')$$

for all θ, θ',

$$c(\theta), y(\theta) \geqslant 0 \quad \text{for all } \theta,$$
$$U'(\theta) \in [a, b] \quad \text{for all } \theta,$$

$$T^+(a, b)$$

$$= \max_{c, y, U'} \sum_\theta \pi(\theta)[u(c(\theta)) - v(y(\theta)/\theta) + \beta U'(\theta)]$$

(6.16)

$$\text{s.t. } u(c(\theta)) - v(y(\theta)/\theta) + \beta U'(\theta)$$
$$\geqslant u(c(\theta')) - v(y(\theta')/\theta) + \beta U'(\theta')$$

for all θ, θ',

$$c(\theta), y(\theta) \geqslant 0 \quad \text{for all } \theta,$$
$$U'(\theta) \in [a, b] \quad \text{for all } \theta.$$

In words, T_+ (T^+) presumes that period $(t + 1)$ continuation utilities U' are in the set (a, b), and then

---

[2] In this description, I assume that Domain is an interval (as opposed to a disconnected subset of the real line). We can ensure that it is connected by allowing for stochastic allocations of output.

generates the lowest (highest) possible period t continuation utility. These operators are both monotone and continuous. We can start with a big interval that includes Domain (such as $[U_+, U^+]$). Then, beginning with that interval, we can iteratively apply T until we get convergence. The resulting interval is the domain of U' in (6.12).

This discussion has two major implications. The first concerns computation. We now have a tractable procedure to compute optimal allocations when θ_t is i.i.d. First, we iterate on T to find Domain. We iterate on the functional equation (6.12) to find C and policy functions (c^*, y^*, U'). We find the initial *ex ante* utility by looking for U_0 such that $C(U_0) = 0$. Given that U_0, we can roll the policy functions forward to construct an optimal allocation process.

The second implication concerns tax systems. The optimal tax systems described in chapters 4 and 5 depend potentially on the entire past history of skill realizations. But we know that if θ_t is i.i.d., optimal allocations are a time-invariant increasing function of a one-dimensional summary statistic. (In a finite horizon setting, the allocation must depend on a time-index and on this one-dimensional summary statistic.) Analogously, if θ_t is i.i.d. over time, we can restructure the optimal tax systems in chapters 4 and 5 so that they depend on the past only through a one-dimensional summary statistic.[3] This result is

---

[3] It is well-known that, for any n, there is a continuous function from $[0, 1]^n$ into $[0, 1]$. Given this result, it is always possible to devise a one-dimensional summary statistic for past histories of labor income, no matter how long they might be. However, these "space-filling" encodings of the past are necessarily nondifferentiable almost everywhere. Economically, this property implies that even small mistakes on the part of past agents may lead to large changes in future allocations.

especially important in the intergenerational context discussed in chapter 5. Instead of keeping track of the entire dynasty's labor income history, the tax system only needs to condition on a summary statistic (U).

6.1.2 Markov Skills

Assuming skills are i.i.d. over time is highly problematic. If we think of θ as being wages, the i.i.d. assumption implies that a person with a wage of $20 per hour is just as likely to earn $10 per hour next year as someone who currently earns $10 per hour. In reality, wages display a lot more persistence. To capture this persistence, in this section I suppose instead that θ_t is governed by a Markov chain. I attack this problem using methods originally due to Fernandes and Phelan (2000).[4] Unfortunately, the results are somewhat negative. In many familiar dynamic models (like real business cycle models), adding this kind of persistence adds one state variable (θ_t), because the state variable is useful in forecasting the future. However, as we shall see, a state variable that is both private information and Markov adds N states, where N is the number of possible realizations of the Markov chain. Like continuation utility itself, these additional states are continuous, not discrete, variables.

Suppose θ_1 is drawn from a probability density π^+ over a set $\Theta = \{\bar{\theta}_1, \ldots, \bar{\theta}_N\}$, and then θ_t evolves according to a transition probability density $\pi(\bar{\theta}_n \mid \bar{\theta}_m)$, which is positive for all m, n. Let (c^*, y^*) be an optimal allocation, and suppose an agent with history $\hat{\theta}^t$ has continuation utility $U_t^*(\hat{\theta}^t)$ in this optimal allocation. In the i.i.d. case, we showed that the continuation

---

[4] Zhang (2009) extends the method of Fernandes and Phelan (2000) to a continuous time setting in which skills have a two-point support.

allocation from this node must be the minimal-cost incentive-compatible allocation that delivers $U_t^*(\hat{\theta}^t)$. To make this argument, we exploited the fact that when θ_t is i.i.d., the continuation utility of a person with true history $\hat{\theta}^t$ who mimicked a person with history $\tilde{\theta}^t$ is given by

$$
\begin{aligned}
U_t(\tilde{\theta}^t, \hat{\theta}^t; c^*, y^*) & \\
= E\Bigg[\sum_{s=1}^{\infty} \beta^{s-1} \Bigg[& u(c_{t+s}^*(\tilde{\theta}^t, \theta_{t+1}^{t+s})) \\
& - v\left(\frac{y_{t+s}^*(\tilde{\theta}^t, \theta_{t+1}^{t+s})}{\theta_{t+s}} \right) \Bigg] \, \Bigg| \, \theta^t = \hat{\theta}^t \Bigg] \\
= U_t^*(\tilde{\theta}^t; c^*, y^*). & \hspace{3em} (6.17)
\end{aligned}
$$

This utility is independent of $\hat{\theta}^t$. This meant that we could stick in any continuation allocation (c, y) with the same continuation utility $U_t^*(\tilde{\theta}^t; c, y)$, without affecting the incentive to mimic another skill in prior periods.

But this argument no longer works if θ_t is Markov. In that case, $U_t(\tilde{\theta}^t, \hat{\theta}^t)$ depends on both $\hat{\theta}^t$ and the last true skill realization, $\hat{\theta}_t$. Another continuation allocation with the same $U_t^*(\hat{\theta}^t)$ will typically have a different $U_t(\hat{\theta}^t, \hat{\theta}^t)$. Plugging in such a continuation allocation may well generate a new allocation that is not incentive-compatible, because it might make lying optimal for an agent in period t. This means that the continuation allocation will typically *not* be the minimal-cost incentive-compatible allocation that delivers $U_t^*(\tilde{\theta}^t)$ and so our recursiveness argument no longer applies.

This issue implies that we have to change to a different solution method. Suppose (c^*, y^*) is optimal, and fix a history $\tilde{\theta}^t$. Let $U_t(\tilde{\theta}^t, \hat{\theta}_t)$ be the continuation utility for an agent who has acted as if he had a skill history $\tilde{\theta}^t$ but was actually a type $\hat{\theta}_t$ in period t. Pick any continuation allocation (c', y') such that

$$U_t(\hat{\theta}^t, \bar{\theta}_n)$$

$$= E\left[\sum_{s=1}^{\infty} \beta^{s-1}\left[u(c'_s(\theta^s)) - v\left(\frac{y'_s(\theta^s)}{\theta_s}\right)\right] \,\Big|\, \theta_0 = \bar{\theta}_n\right]$$

for all $\bar{\theta}_n$. Then, if we substitute in this continuation allocation, we know that the resulting overall allocation must be incentive-compatible.

This result suggests the following recursive approach. Define

$$C(\theta, U_{\bar{\theta}_1}, U_{\bar{\theta}_2}, \dots, U_{\bar{\theta}_N})$$

$$= \min_{c,y} E\left\{ \sum_{t=1}^{\infty} \beta^{t-1}[c_t(\theta^t) - y_t(\theta^t)] \,\Big|\, \theta_0 = \theta\right\}$$

s.t. (c, y) IC,

$$E\left\{ \sum_{t=1}^{\infty} \beta^{t-1}\left[u(c_t(\theta^t)) - v\left(\frac{y_t(\theta^t)}{\theta_t}\right)\right] \,\Big|\, \theta_0 = \bar{\theta}_n\right\}$$

$$= U_{\bar{\theta}_n} \quad \text{for all } n$$

to be the minimum cost of providing an incentive-compatible allocation which delivers utility $U_{\bar{\theta}_n}$ to each true skill $\bar{\theta}_n$, given that the agent has acted as if his skill realization was θ. Thus, θ captures the principal's beliefs about the agent's future draws of θ. The principal's beliefs are correct given that the agent responds optimally by not mimicking any other type. But the only way to ensure that a nonmimicking strategy is optimal is to keep track of the agent's utility for all other types.

At any node, we will not lose incentive-compatibility if we substitute in a continuation allocation that keeps continuation utility the same for all possible types. It follows that the cost function C must satisfy the functional equation

$$
C(\theta, U_{\bar{\theta}_1}, U_{\bar{\theta}_2}, \ldots, U_{\bar{\theta}_N})
$$
$$
= \min_{c,y,U'} \sum_{\bar{\theta}_n} \pi(\bar{\theta}_n \mid \theta)[c(\bar{\theta}_n) - y(\bar{\theta}_n)
$$
$$
+ \beta C(\bar{\theta}_n, (U'_{\bar{\theta}_k})_{k=1}^N(\bar{\theta}_n))]
$$
$$
\tag{6.18}
$$
$$
\text{s.t. } u(c(\bar{\theta}_n)) - v(y(\bar{\theta}_n)/\bar{\theta}_n) + \beta U'_{\bar{\theta}_n}(\bar{\theta}_n)
$$
$$
\geqslant u(c(\theta'_n)) - v(y(\theta'_n)/\bar{\theta}_n) + \beta U'_{\bar{\theta}_n}(\theta'_n)
$$
$$
\text{for all } \bar{\theta}_n, \theta'_n,
$$
$$
\tag{6.19}
$$
$$
\sum_{\bar{\theta}_n} \pi(\bar{\theta}_n \mid \bar{\theta}_m)\left[u(c(\bar{\theta}_n)) - v\left(\frac{y(\bar{\theta}_n)}{\bar{\theta}_n}\right) + \beta U'_{\bar{\theta}_n}(\bar{\theta}_n)\right]
$$
$$
= U_{\bar{\theta}_m}, \quad m = 1, \ldots, N,
$$
$$
c(\bar{\theta}_n), y(\bar{\theta}_n) \geqslant 0 \quad \text{for all } n, \tag{6.20}
$$
$$
U'(\bar{\theta}_n) \in \mathrm{DOM} \quad \text{for all } n. \tag{6.21}
$$

Here, the set DOM represents the set of possible continuation utility vectors associated with incentive-compatible allocations. Mathematically,

$$
(U_{\bar{\theta}_k})_{k=1}^N \in \mathrm{DOM}
$$

if and only if (c, y) is incentive-compatible and

$$
E\left\{ \sum_{t=1}^{\infty} \beta^{t-1}\left[u(c_t(\theta^t)) - v\left(\frac{y_t(\theta^t)}{\theta_t}\right)\right] \;\middle|\; \theta_0 = \bar{\theta}_k\right\}
$$
$$
= U_{\bar{\theta}_k}.
$$

The functional equation (6.18) captures the following procedure. For each $\bar{\theta}_n$, the planner picks a consumption, an output, and a *vector* of continuation utilities. The vector describes the continuation utility for every true type.

The policy functions to this functional equation govern the evolution of the optimal contract in periods 2 and thereafter. In period 1, the planner's problem works differently because he does not need to worry about ensuring incentive-compatibility in any prior period. The first-period draw of θ is governed by π^+. Then, in the first period, the planner's problem is

$$\max_{c_1, y_1, U'} \sum_{\bar{\theta}_n} \pi^+(\bar{\theta}_n)\left[u(c_1(\bar{\theta}_n)) \right.$$
$$\left. - v\left(\frac{y_1(\bar{\theta}_n)}{\bar{\theta}_n}\right) + \beta U'_{\bar{\theta}_n}(\bar{\theta}_n) \right]$$

$$(6.22)$$

$$\text{s.t. } u(c_1(\bar{\theta}_n)) - v(y_1(\bar{\theta}_n)/\bar{\theta}_n) + \beta U'_{\bar{\theta}_n}(\bar{\theta}_n)$$
$$\geqslant u(c_1(\theta'_n)) - v(y_1(\theta'_n)/\bar{\theta}_n) + \beta U'_{\bar{\theta}_n}(\theta'_n)$$
$$\text{for all } \bar{\theta}_n, \theta'_n,$$

$$\sum_{\bar{\theta}_n} \pi^+(\bar{\theta}_n)[c_1(\bar{\theta}_n) - y_1(\bar{\theta}_n)$$
$$+ \beta C(\bar{\theta}_n, (U'_{\bar{\theta}_k})_{k=1}^N(\bar{\theta}_n))] = 0,$$

$$c_1(\bar{\theta}_n), y_1(\bar{\theta}_n) \geqslant 0 \quad \text{for all } n,$$

$$U'(\bar{\theta}_n) \in \text{DOM} \quad \text{for all } n.$$

At this stage, if we know DOM, we can solve for the set of optimal allocations. We first find C using (6.18). (The right-hand side of this functional equation is a contraction operator on the space of bounded functions from $\Theta \times R^N$ into itself. Hence, if we know DOM, we can iterate on this functional equation to solve for C.)

Then, we solve for (c_1, y_1) using (6.22), and future consumption allocations using the policy functions from the minimization problem (6.18).

However, we still need to find the set DOM. We can find this set using an approach similar to what we used in the i.i.d. case. First, we define a mapping T that maps compact subsets of R^N into compact subsets of R^N as follows. A utility vector $(U_{\bar{\theta}_k})_{k=1}^N$ is in $T(B)$, where B is a compact subset of R^N, if there exists

$$(c(\bar{\theta}_n), y(\bar{\theta}_n), (U'_{\bar{\theta}_m})_{m=1}^N(\bar{\theta}_n))_{n=1}^N$$

such that

$$U_{\bar{\theta}_k} = \sum_{\bar{\theta}_n} \pi(\bar{\theta}_n \mid \bar{\theta}_k)[u(c(\bar{\theta}_n))$$
$$- v(y(\bar{\theta}_n)/\bar{\theta}_n) + \beta U'_{\bar{\theta}_n}(\bar{\theta}_n)],$$
$$\tag{6.23}$$

$$u(c(\bar{\theta}_n)) - v(y(\bar{\theta}_n)/\bar{\theta}_n) + \beta U'_{\bar{\theta}_n}(\bar{\theta}_n)$$
$$\geqslant u(c(\theta'_n)) - v(y(\theta'_n)/\bar{\theta}_n) + \beta U'_{\bar{\theta}_n}(\theta'_n)$$
$$\text{for all } \bar{\theta}_n, \theta'_n$$

$$\text{for all } \bar{\theta}_n, (U'_{\bar{\theta}_m})_{m=1}^N(\bar{\theta}_n) \in B.$$

What does T do? It translates a set of continuation utility vectors from period $(t+1)$ into a set of continuation utility vectors in period t. The domain of continuation utility vectors is a *fixed point* of T.

We can start with a very large B, which is known to contain the set of all possible continuation utility vectors, and iterate on T until we converge to some fixed point. This fixed point is the domain DOM of continuation utility vectors. Hence, we have a three-step procedure that works. We first iterate on T to find the set DOM of continuation utility vectors. Given DOM, we iterate on the functional equation (6.18) to find the cost function C. Finally, we use C to solve the period 1 problem.

Unfortunately, there are significant practical difficulties with steps 1 and 2. First, it is basically impossible to work with a set operator numerically. We need some way to describe the relevant sets in a more usable way. Thus, in the i.i.d. case, with a one-dimensional set, we described the relevant sets using endpoints. In the Markov case, when the sets are N-dimensional, it is much more difficult to know how to summarize the relevant information. At a minimum, we need some way to guarantee that DOM is convex. Generally, we do this by allowing for randomized allocations. Then, once we get to step 2, we need to find a fixed point of a functional equation, where the function maps $\Theta \times$ DOM into R. This nontrivial task is made more challenging by the fact that DOM is typically nonrectangular (i.e., it is *not* the Cartesian product of N intervals).

6.2   A Closed Overlapping Generations Economy

In this section, I study the properties of optimal taxes in a loosely calibrated infinite horizon overlapping-generations economy.[5] In the model, agents live for

---

[5] In a recent paper, Huggett and Parra (2009) construct optimal allocations in an overlapping-generations model economy, given that skills are fixed over time and are private information. They use this calculation to inform the construction of desirable tax reforms for a model economy in which skills can evolve stochastically over time. They find that the welfare gains of such a reform can be large.

In a remarkable and early contribution, Ordover and Phelps (1979) study optimal capital income taxation in an overlapping-generations setting.

three periods and work for the first two of these periods. Their skills when young have two possible realizations, and their skill growths into middle age also have two possible realizations. The distribution of skill growths are independent of their skill realizations when they are young. The agents are not altruistic toward their descendants. I calibrate the model, using recent evidence on the evolution of the cross-sectional distribution of wages over the life cycle.

It is straightforward to compute a highly accurate approximate solution for optimal taxes, given that the planner wishes to maximize long-run welfare. The main finding is that the optimal tax system provides more insurance to young low-skilled agents against future skill shocks than to young high-skilled agents.

6.2.1 Model Description

Time is discrete and is indexed by the natural numbers. At each date, a unit measure of agents is born. Agents live for three periods, and can work in the first two periods of their lives. Agents born at date t have the utility function

$$u(c_t^y) - v(l_t^y) + \beta[u(c_{t+1}^m) - v(l_{t+1}^m)] + \beta^2 u(c_{t+2}^o).$$

Here, c_t^y (l_t^y) represents the consumption (effort) of young agents at date t, c_t^m (l_t^m) is the consumption (effort) of middle-aged agents at date t, and c_t^o is the consumption of old agents at date t.

At date 1, there is also a unit measure of middle-aged agents who will live for two periods, but work only in period 1. They have the utility function

$$u(c_1^m) - v(l_1^m) + \beta u(c_2^o).$$

Finally, at date 1, there is a unit measure of old agents who will live for one period only. They do not work, and they prefer more consumption to less.

I assume that skill shocks are highly persistent. Specifically, half of the young agents born at date t have skills θ_H and the other half have skills θ_L. Half of the highly skilled young agents have skills $\theta_H \theta'_H$ when middle-aged, while the other half have skills $\theta_H \theta'_L$. Half of the low-skilled young agents have skills $\theta_L \theta'_H$ when middle-aged, while the other half have skills $\theta_L \theta'_L$. This specification means that logged skills have a unit root. Similarly, equal fractions of the middle-aged agents at date 1 have skills $\theta_i \theta'_j$, where $i, j \in \{H, L\}$.

All period 1 agents are endowed with K_1 units of capital per person. In this setting, an allocation is a specification of $(c_t^y, c_t^m, c_t^o, l_t^y, l_t^m, K_t)_{t=1}^{\infty}$ such that

$$K_t \in R_+, \qquad (6.24)$$

$$
\begin{aligned}
c_t^y : &\qquad \{\theta_H, \theta_L\} \rightarrow R_+, \quad t \geqslant 1, \\
c_t^m : &\quad \{\theta_H, \theta_L\} \times \{\theta'_H, \theta'_L\} \rightarrow R_+, \quad t \geqslant 2, \\
c_t^o : &\quad \{\theta_H, \theta_L\} \times \{\theta'_H, \theta'_L\} \rightarrow R_+, \quad t \geqslant 3, \\
l_t^y : &\qquad \{\theta_H, \theta_L\} \rightarrow R_+, \quad t \geqslant 1, \\
l_t^o : &\quad \{\theta_H, \theta_L\} \times \{\theta'_H, \theta'_L\} \rightarrow R_+, \quad t \geqslant 2,
\end{aligned}
$$

and

$$
\begin{aligned}
c_1^m : &\quad \{\theta_i \theta'_j\}_{i,j \in \{H,L\}} \rightarrow R_+, \qquad (6.25) \\
l_1^m : &\quad \{\theta_i \theta'_j\}_{i,j \in \{H,L\}} \rightarrow R_+, \\
c_2^o : &\quad \{\theta_i \theta'_j\}_{i,j \in \{H,L\}} \rightarrow R_+, \\
&\qquad c_1^o \in R_+.
\end{aligned}
$$

Society can combine effective labor and capital to generate consumption goods according to an aggregate production function F. Capital depreciates over time at rate δ, but it is possible to turn consumption goods one-for-one into capital and vice versa. This specification of technology implies that an allocation

$$(c_t^y, c_t^m, c_t^o, l_t^y, l_t^m, K_t)_{t=1}^\infty$$

is feasible if

$$C_t + K_{t+1} \leqslant (1 - \delta)K_t + F(K_t, Y_t), \quad t \geqslant 1, \quad (6.26)$$

$$C_1 = \sum_{i \in \{H,L\}} \frac{c_1^y(\theta_i)}{2} + \sum_{i,j \in \{H,L\}} \frac{c_1^m(\theta_i \theta_j')}{4} + c_1^o,$$

$$Y_1 = \sum_{i \in \{H,L\}} l_1^y(\theta_i)\theta_i + \sum_{i,j \in \{H,L\}} \frac{l_1^m(\theta_i \theta_j')\theta_i \theta_j'}{4},$$

$$C_2 = \sum_{i \in \{H,L\}} \frac{c_2^y(\theta_i)}{2} + \sum_{i,j \in \{H,L\}} \frac{c_2^m(\theta_i, \theta_j')}{4}$$
$$+ \sum_{i,j \in \{H,L\}} \frac{c_2^o(\theta_i \theta_j')}{4},$$

$$Y_2 = \sum_{i \in \{H,L\}} \frac{l_2^y(\theta_i)\theta_i}{2} + \sum_{i,j \in \{H,L\}} \frac{l_2^m(\theta_i, \theta_j')\theta_i \theta_j'}{4},$$

$$C_t = \sum_{i \in \{H,L\}} \frac{c_t^y(\theta_i)}{2} + \sum_{i,j \in \{H,L\}} \frac{c_t^m(\theta_i, \theta_j')}{4}$$
$$+ \sum_{i,j \in \{H,L\}} \frac{c_t^o(\theta_i, \theta_j')}{4}, \quad t \geqslant 3,$$

$$Y_t = \sum_{i \in \{H,L\}} \frac{l_t^y(\theta_i), \theta_i}{2}$$
$$+ \sum_{i,j \in \{H,L\}} \frac{l_t^m(\theta_i, \theta_j')\theta_i \theta_j'}{4}, \quad t \geqslant 3.$$

6.2.2   Model Calibration

I now turn to the calibration of the above model. In doing so, I immediately face a conflict between practicality and theoretical purity. In an abstract sense, the above analysis works for any notion of labor input. However, in a calibration, I must have information about elasticities that represent the response of labor input to changes in an agent's productivity or skill. There is an intrinsic conflict here: I need information about labor input and skills, even though the optimal tax problem presumes that the government is unable to condition taxes on either variable.

More concretely, I treat the labor input variable l as measuring *time* spent working. I assume that taxes can only be conditioned on earnings (the product of wages and hours). This approach allows me to exploit off-the-shelf estimates of the usual notions of elasticities to calculate optimal taxes. But it is silent about why the government is unable to base taxes on wages or hours.

I treat a period as if it consists of twenty years. Given these considerations, I set

$$u(c) = \ln(c), \qquad\qquad (6.27)$$
$$\beta = 0.98^{20},$$
$$\delta = 1 - 0.9^{20},$$
$$F(K, Y) = K^{0.3} Y^{0.7}.$$

These settings are twenty-year analogs of standard annual parameterizations used in calibrated business cycle models.

The elasticity of labor supply plays a critical role in determining optimal taxes. I set

$$v(l) = \frac{l^{1+1/\psi}}{1 + 1/\psi}.$$

For these isoelastic preferences, the parameter ψ represents the Frisch elasticity of labor supply. Microeconometric estimates of this parameter are typically low (around 0.1) while estimates based on aggregate data are higher (around 1). Accordingly, I consider three values for ψ (0.1, 0.5, and 1).

I calibrate the wage process as follows. I assume that, on average, individual wages grow by about 50% from youth to middle age. This specification is roughly consistent with figure 1 in Low (2005). To complete the calibration of the law of motion of θ, I use recent work by Heathcote et al. (2007). Using data from the CEX and the PSID, they find that the cross-sectional variance of logged wages at age 30 equals 0.25 and the cross-sectional variance of logged wages at age 50 equals 0.37 (see their figure 2).[6] Correspondingly, I set

$$\theta_H = \exp(0.5), \qquad\qquad (6.28)$$
$$\theta_L = \exp(-0.5),$$
$$\theta'_H = \exp(0.4 + \sqrt{0.12}),$$
$$\theta'_L = \exp(0.4 - \sqrt{0.12}).$$

This particular choice of parameters is not uncontroversial. However, it reflects three key well-established properties of wages that will prove important when we solve for optimal taxes. First, wages grow over the life cycle. Second, wages are highly persistent (here, logged wages have a unit root). Finally, much, but not all, of the uncertainty about individual wages is resolved early in one's life.

---

[6] These variances are actually the result of a filtering procedure described in footnote 37 of Heathcote et al.: "Effectively, we regress age/year observations for second moments on a full set of time-dummies and plot the residuals by age group, averaging across all cohorts. This is how the lines labeled 'Data' are constructed in Figures 2–4."

6.2.3   Computing Long-Run Optimal Allocations

In this section, I describe how to compute a particular Pareto optimal allocation, given that agents are privately informed about wages and hours. In the next section, I show how to map this allocation into an optimal tax schedule (much as we did in chapter 4).

In overlapping-generations economies, Pareto optima are distinguished by the relative weights of the various generations. As in Phelan (2006), I assume that the planner maximizes steady-state welfare. Given that assumption, the optimal capital–effective labor ratio (K/Y) satisfies the golden rule

$$\alpha K^{\alpha-1} Y^{1-\alpha} = \delta. \tag{6.29}$$

Note that (as is standard in overlapping-generations economies) the optimal capital–effective labor ratio is unrelated to agents' discount factors. We can denote this optimal capital–effective labor ratio by $k^* = (\delta/\alpha)^{1/(\alpha-1)}$.

In this simple setup, a mimicking strategy

$$\sigma = (\sigma_1, \sigma_2)$$

is a pair of mappings where

$$\sigma_1 : \qquad\qquad \{\theta_H, \theta_L\} \to \{\theta_H, \theta_L\}, \tag{6.30}$$
$$\sigma_2 : \quad \{\theta_H, \theta_L\} \times \{\theta'_H, \theta'_L\} \to \{\theta'_H, \theta'_L\}.$$

Let Σ be the set of all mimicking strategies, and define

$$W(c^y, c^m, c^o, l^y, l^m; \sigma)$$

$$= \sum_{(i,j)\in\{H,;L\}^2} \frac{1}{4}\bigg[u(c^y(\sigma_1(\theta_i)))$$

$$+ \beta u(c^m(\sigma_1(\theta_i), \sigma_2(\theta_i, \theta'_j)))$$

$$+ \beta^2 u(c^{\mathrm{o}}(\sigma_2(\theta_i, \theta_j'))) - v\left(\frac{l^{\mathrm{y}}(\sigma_1(\theta_i))\sigma_1(\theta_i)}{\theta_i}\right)$$

$$- \beta v\left(\frac{l^{\mathrm{m}}(\sigma_1(\theta_i), \sigma_2(\theta_i, \theta_j'))\sigma_1(\theta_i)\sigma_2(\theta_i, \theta_j')}{\theta_i \theta_j'}\right)\Bigg].$$

$$(6.31)$$

Then, socially optimal allocations of consumption and effort solve the planner's problem

$$\max_{c^{\mathrm{y}}, c^{\mathrm{m}}, c^{\mathrm{o}}, l^{\mathrm{y}}, l^{\mathrm{m}}} \sum_{(i,j) \in \{H,L\}^2} [u(c^{\mathrm{y}}(\theta_i)) + \beta u(c^{\mathrm{m}}(\theta_i, \theta_j'))$$

$$+ \beta^2 u(c^{\mathrm{o}}(\theta_i, \theta_j')) - v(l^{\mathrm{y}}(\theta_i))$$

$$- \beta v(l^{\mathrm{m}}(\theta_i, \theta_j'))] \qquad (6.32)$$

s.t. $W(c^{\mathrm{y}}, c^{\mathrm{m}}, c^{\mathrm{o}}, l^{\mathrm{y}}, l^{\mathrm{m}}; \sigma^{\mathrm{TT}})$

$$\geqslant W(c^{\mathrm{y}}, c^{\mathrm{m}}, c^{\mathrm{o}}, l^{\mathrm{y}}, l^{\mathrm{m}}; \sigma) \quad \text{for all } \sigma \text{ in } \Sigma,$$

$$Y = \sum_{i \in \{H,L\}} \frac{l^{\mathrm{y}}(\theta_i)\theta_i}{2} + \sum_{(i,j) \in \{H,:L\}^2} \frac{l^{\mathrm{m}}(\theta_i, \theta_j')\theta_i \theta_j'}{4},$$

$$\sum_{i \in \{H,L\}} \frac{c^{\mathrm{y}}(\theta_i)}{2} + \sum_{(i,j) \in \{H,L\}^2} \frac{c^{\mathrm{m}}(\theta_i, \theta_j')}{4}$$

$$+ \sum_{(i,j) \in \{H,L\}^2} \frac{c^{\mathrm{o}}(\theta_i, \theta_j')}{4} + \delta k^* Y$$

$$= F(k^* Y, Y).$$

In words, the planner's problem maximizes the expected utility of a given agent among all incentive-compatible and feasible allocations, given that the capital–effective labor ratio is k^*.

The planner's problem (6.32) has sixteen controls, one feasibility constraint, and sixty-three incentive constraints. I consider a relaxed problem in which the agent is allowed to use only four different mimicking strategies $\{\sigma^{TT}, \sigma^1, \sigma^2, \sigma^3\}$, where

$$\sigma_1^1(\theta_i) = \theta_i; \quad \sigma_2^1(\theta_L, \theta_j') = \theta_j'; \quad \sigma_2^1(\theta_H, \theta_j') = \theta_L'$$

$$\text{for } (i,j) \in \{H,L\}^2,$$

$$\sigma_1^2(\theta_i) = \theta_i; \quad \sigma_2^2(\theta_L, \theta_j') = \theta_H'; \quad \sigma_2^2(\theta_H, \theta_j') = \theta_j'$$

$$\text{for } (i,j) \in \{H,L\}^2,$$

$$\sigma_1^3(\theta_i) = \theta_L; \quad \sigma_2^3(\theta_L, \theta_j') = \theta_j'; \quad \sigma_2^3(\theta_H, \theta_j') = \theta_H'$$

$$\text{for } (i,j) \in \{H,L\}^2.$$

Under mimicking strategy σ^1, agents who have skill history (θ_H, θ_H) when middle-aged pretend to be low-skilled in that period. Under mimicking strategy σ^2, agents who have skill history (θ_L, θ_H) when middle-aged pretend to be low-skilled in that period. Finally, under mimicking strategy σ^3, agents who are highly skilled when young pretend to be low-skilled in that period, and then pretend to be high-skilled when middle-aged if they are actually low-skilled.

The resulting relaxed problem has sixteen controls, and only four constraints. To solve this problem, I derived analytical formulas for the twenty first-order conditions to this problem. I then computed an approximate solution to these first-order conditions by using the GAUSS routine EQSOLVE. For this scale of problem, this routine is extremely fast (it took 0.02 seconds). The approximation is highly accurate, in the sense that the twenty first-order necessary conditions were all less than 10^{-15} in absolute value.

Finally, to ensure that I actually have a solution to the original planner's problem (6.32), I checked the sixty discarded incentive constraints. They were all satisfied by my computed solution to the relaxed problem.

It might be helpful for readers to know that I tried a different relaxed problem first. In this alternative relaxed problem, I allowed the agent to use three possible mimicking strategies: σ^1, σ^2, and $\sigma^{3'}$, where $\sigma^{3'}$ is defined by

$$\sigma^{3'}(\theta_i) = \theta_L; \qquad \sigma_2^{3'}(\theta_i, \theta_j') = \theta_j'$$
$$\text{for all } (i,j) \in \{H,L\}^2.$$

In this mimicking strategy, agents who are highly skilled in period 1 deviate in that period by acting low-skilled. Unlike in strategy σ^3, they never deviate again.

Surprisingly (at least to me), the solution to this alternative relaxed problem ends up not being incentive-compatible. The solution offers big incentives to a middle-aged person with history (θ_L, θ_H') to ensure that he does not mimic a person with history (θ_L, θ_L'). However, the persistence of skills means that these incentives in middle age have a perverse effect on choices of young agents. Consider a person with skill θ_H when young who pretends to have skill θ_L. The contract is designed so that he loses when young by doing so. However, the big incentives when middle-aged mean that he can recoup this loss by acting as if he has skill $\theta_L \theta_H'$, when his true skill level is $\theta_H \theta_L'$. In other words, the solution to the alternative relaxed problem makes σ_3 a profitable deviation, and so I was led to use my formulation of the relaxed problem (with σ_3 instead of σ_3') instead.

Table 6.1. Optimal quantities in the calibrated model.

	$\psi = 0.1$	$\psi = 0.5$	$\psi = 1$
c_H^y, l_H^y	0.68, 1.01	0.82, 0.94	0.92, 0.80
c_L^y, l_L^y	0.59, 0.92	0.53, 0.63	0.50, 0.40
c_{HH}^m, l_{HH}^m	0.49, 1.12	0.71, 1.47	0.85, 1.80
c_{HL}^m, l_{HL}^m	0.41, 1.05	0.39, 1.20	0.37, 1.40
c_{LH}^m, l_{LH}^m	0.41, 1.02	0.39, 1.02	0.38, 1.01
c_{LL}^m, l_{LL}^m	0.38, 0.96	0.32, 0.81	0.29, 0.66

6.2.4   Optimal Quantities and Optimal Taxes

In this section, I describe the optimal quantities and optimal taxes for this calibrated example. To economize on space, I use subscripts to refer to the agents' realized skills. Hence, c_i^y represents $c^y(\theta_i)$, l_i^y represents $l^y(\theta_i)$, c_{ij}^a represents $c^a(\theta_i, \theta_j)$, and l_{ij}^m represents $l^m(\theta_i, \theta_j)$ for $(i, j) \in \{H, L\}^2$ and $a \in \{m, o\}$.

6.2.4.1   Optimal Quantities

The computed optimal quantities are in table 6.1. I do not tabulate c_{ij}^o explicitly; it equals βc_{ij}^m for all (i, j).

These computed solutions have two interesting properties. First, the gap between $\ln(c_{LH}^m)$ and $\ln(c_{LL}^m)$ is smaller than between $\ln(c_{HL}^m)$ and $\ln(c_{HH}^m)$. Agents who are low-skilled when young are better insured, in terms of consumption, against future skill shocks than are agents who are high-skilled in period 1. Relatedly, the cross-sectional distribution of consumption among middle-aged and old agents is skewed to the right. Second, for $\psi = 0.5$ or $\psi = 1$, the gap between $\ln(l_{LH}^m)$ and $\ln(l_{LL}^m)$ is larger than the gap between $\ln(l_{HL}^m)$ and $\ln(l_{HH}^m)$. Agents who are low-skilled when young face larger amounts of hours risk when middle-aged than do agents who are high-skilled when young.

These two features of the optimal solution are generated by two elements of the model. The first is that skills are persistent, and so it is optimal for low-skilled young agents to work less (on average) when middle-aged than high-skilled young agents. The second is that the disutility of labor is convex. These two ingredients mean that the disutility of middle-aged labor for young high-skilled agents is steeper than for young low-skilled agents. This difference in slope implies that it is optimal for high-skilled young agents to face more consumption risk and less hours risk when middle-aged than do low-skilled young agents.

6.2.4.2 Optimal Capital Income Taxes

Given the computed optimal allocation, we can use the lessons of chapter 4 to translate it into an optimal tax system in which capital income taxes are linear. Recall that in this tax system, the optimal tax on (gross) capital income is set so that agents' *ex post* Euler equations are satisfied. Similarly, in this economy, we can define the optimal capital income tax τ_{ij}^k so that it satisfies

$$\beta u'(c_{ij}^m)(1 - \delta + (1 - \tau_{ij}^k)\delta)/u'(c_i^y) = 1. \qquad (6.33)$$

(Here, I exploit the fact that the marginal product of capital equals δ in the optimal allocation.) We can rewrite this formula (6.33) to get

$$\tau_{ij}^k = \frac{1}{\delta}\left[1 - \frac{\beta^{-1}u'(c_i^y)}{u'(c_{ij}^m)}\right]. \qquad (6.34)$$

I describe these optimal taxes in table 6.2.

Table 6.2. Optimal capital income taxes.

	$\psi = 0.1$	$\psi = 0.5$	$\psi = 1$
τ^k_{HH}	-0.11	-0.33	-0.45
τ^k_{HL}	0.11	0.33	0.45
τ^k_{LH}	-0.038	-0.11	-0.15
τ^k_{LL}	0.038	0.11	0.15

As in chapter 4, the expected capital income tax rate is zero for any young agent. The variance of capital income tax rates, however, differs across young agents. Young low-skilled agents face capital income tax rates that are near zero in absolute value, especially if the elasticity of labor supply ψ is small. In contrast, young high-skilled agents face capital income tax rates that are large in absolute value. These differences in capital income tax rates are a direct reflection of differences in the optimal degree of consumption insurance across the two groups of agents.

6.2.4.3 *Optimal Labor Income Taxes*

There are (at least) two ways to think about optimal labor income taxes in this dynamic setting. The optimal allocation features wedges between agents' consumption–labor marginal rates of substitution and marginal rates of transformation. These wedges can be interpreted as being implicit marginal tax rates on labor

$$\eta^y_i = 1 - \frac{v'(l^y_i)}{w^* \theta_i u'(c^y_i)},$$

Table 6.3. Optimal wedges.

	$\psi = 0.1$	$\psi = 0.5$	$\psi = 1$
H	0	0	0
L	0.071	0.21	0.27
HH	0	0	0
HL	0.094	0.26	0.33
LH	0.13	0.28	0.33
LL	0.10	0.27	0.33

$$\eta_{ij}^{\mathrm{m}} = 1 - \frac{v'(l_{ij}^{\mathrm{m}})}{w^* \theta_i \theta_j' u'(c_{ij}^{\mathrm{m}})}.$$

Here, w^* is the marginal product of effective labor in the optimal allocation ($w^* = (1 - \alpha)k^{*\alpha}$). The resulting values for η are reported in table 6.3.

The wedge is zero for young highly skilled agents (η_H^{y}) or for agents who are highly skilled in both periods (η_{HH}^{m}) of their working lives. This result is another manifestation of the usual "no-distortion-at-the-top" principle. It is more surprising that the wedge is nonzero for high-skilled middle-aged agents if they were low-skilled when young. This positive wedge is generated by the binding double-deviation incentive constraint faced by young agents.

Chapter 4 describes another way to think about optimal labor income taxes. For all (i, j) in $\{H, L\}^2$, define

$$\mathrm{LI}_{ij} = u'(c_{ij}^{\mathrm{o}})^{-1} \beta^{-2} w^* [u'(c_i^{\mathrm{y}}) l_i^{\mathrm{y}} \theta_i + u'(c_{ij}^{\mathrm{m}}) \beta l_{ij}^{\mathrm{m}} \theta_i \theta_j']$$

to be the future value (when old) of the labor income received by an agent who gets skill shocks (θ_i, θ_j') over

Table 6.4.   Optimal future values of
labor earnings and taxes.

	$\psi = 0.1$	$\psi = 0.5$	$\psi = 1$
$\text{LI}_{HH}, \text{TAX}_{HH}$	2.52, 0.96	3.15, 0.91	3.58, 0.88
$\text{LI}_{HL}, \text{TAX}_{HL}$	1.47, 0.18	1.41, 0.18	1.42, 0.25
$\text{LI}_{LH}, \text{TAX}_{LH}$	0.83, -0.45	0.76, -0.47	0.69, -0.50
$\text{LI}_{LL}, \text{TAX}_{LL}$	0.51, -0.69	0.38, -0.63	0.28, -0.63

his lifetime. At the same time, we can define

$$\text{TAX}_{ij} = \text{LI}_{ij} - u'(c_{ij}^o)^{-1}\beta^{-2}[u'(c_i^y)c_i^y + \beta u'(c_{ij}^m)c_{ij}^m$$
$$+ \beta^2 u'(c_{ij}^o)c_{ij}^o]$$

to be the future value of taxes paid by an agent with the same history. Then, we can define a function that maps realizations of LI_{ij} into corresponding realizations of TAX_{ij}. A labor income tax schedule (regardless of its actual timing of tax collections) is optimal if and only if it is consistent with this function from LI_{ij} into TAX_{ij}.

Table 6.4 describes this function from LI_{ij} into TAX_{ij} for various specifications of ψ. The results are relatively intuitive: in order to share skill risk, high-skilled agents are taxed to subsidize low-skilled ones. The absolute levels of taxes are surprisingly unaffected by the level of ψ.

6.3   Summary

This chapter describes methods to solve for optimal allocations in dynamic economies with private information frictions. When agents are infinitely lived, we need to make the optimization problem recursive with respect to a low-dimensional state variable. If skill shocks are i.i.d., and the rate of return on capital is exogenous, then the problem is recursive with respect to a one-dimensional state variable (continuation utility). It is quite practical to compute approximate solutions to these problems, and Albanesi and Sleet (2006) do in fact compute optimal tax systems in a calibrated version of such an economy. The i.i.d. assumption is, however, highly restrictive. We can also make the social planner's problem recursive if skills are Markov. However, the dimension of the summary state variable equals the number of elements of the state space, and the state variable's domain must also be computed. The resulting method is only practical if the state space has a small number of elements (no more than three).

In the next chapter, I discuss possible fixes to the problems associated with the case in which skills are Markov. However, in the short run and possibly even intermediate run, I believe that we should resort to computing solutions to overlapping-generations economies in which agents live for a small number of periods. As the analysis in section 6.2 indicates, these exercises can be quite informative.

References

Albanesi, S., and C. Sleet. 2006. Dynamic optimal taxation with private information. *Review of Economic Studies* 73:1–30.

Battaglini, M., and S. Coate. 2008. Pareto efficient income taxation with stochastic abilities. *Journal of Public Economics* 92:844–68.

Fernandes, A., and C. Phelan. 2000. A recursive formulation for repeated agency with history dependence. *Journal of Economic Theory* 91:223–47.

Heathcote, J., K. Storesletten, and G. Violante. 2007. Consumption and labor supply with partial insurance: an analytical framework. Working Paper, University of Oslo.

Huggett, M., and J. Parra. 2009. How well does the U.S. social insurance system provide social insurance? Working Paper, Georgetown University.

Low, H. 2005. Self-insurance in a life-cycle model of labour supply and savings. *Review of Economic Dynamics* 8: 945–73.

Ordover, K., and E. Phelps. 1979. The concept of optimal taxation in the overlapping-generations model of capital and wealth. *Journal of Public Economics* 12:1–24.

Phelan, C. 2006. Opportunity and social mobility. *Review of Economic Studies* 73:487–505.

Spear, S., and S. Srivastava. 1987. On repeated moral hazard with discounting. *Review of Economic Studies* 54: 599–617.

Zhang, Y. 2009. Dynamic contracting with persistent shocks. *Journal of Economic Theory* 144:635–675.

7

The Way Forward

In the preceding chapters, I have provided a survey of the current state of the new dynamic public finance. Much has been accomplished in a relatively short period, but there is certainly more to be done. In this chapter, I discuss what strike me as promising directions for future research. I focus on tax systems that are more widely applicable, on better solution methods, and on what information we need from the data to implement the new dynamic public finance.

7.1 More Widely Applicable Tax Systems

I show in chapters 4 and 5 that, given any data-generation process for skills, we can design a class of optimal tax systems. We know from chapter 3 that optimal tax systems must deter asset accumulation in some fashion. The tax systems presented in chapters 4 and 5 do so in simple ways: the tax systems in chapter 4 feature linear taxes on asset income, and the tax systems in the intergenerational setup within chapter 5 feature linear taxes on bequests.

The main restriction underlying the analysis in these chapters is that preferences are additively separable between consumptions at different dates and states, and between consumption and leisure. There is a considerable amount of work on asset pricing that suggests that the former assumption is problematic. With this motivation in mind, Grochulski and Kocherlakota (2008) extend the analysis in chapter 4 to preferences that exhibit nonseparabilities (like habit formation) between consumptions at different dates. The resulting tax systems are, as before, linear in asset incomes.

Grochulski and Kocherlakota (2008) do continue to require *weak separability* between consumption sequences and labor sequences. (That is, they require the marginal rate of substitution between consumption at two different dates to be the same, regardless of the agent's chosen sequence of labor inputs.) It is unlikely that even this weaker assumption is plausible. For example, Aguiar and Hurst (2005) document that when people decrease market hours upon retirement, they also decrease their consumptions. This connection between market hours and consumption growth is inconsistent with weak separability of preferences. It would definitely be desirable to be able to construct optimal tax systems in dynamic settings in which preferences are nonseparable between consumption and labor inputs.

In a recent working paper, Werning (2009) tackles this problem with great success. He considers a class of model economies similar to the ones in chapter 3. He starts with an arbitrary incentive-compatible allocation (not necessarily an optimal one), assuming that skills are private information. Definitionally, given such an allocation, no agent of a given skill wants to change his effort choices so as to mimic some other agent's output choices. Werning expands the range of possible choices for agents by allowing them to borrow/lend at a fixed gross interest rate R in addition to their being allowed to alter their effort choices. He then asks the question: how should society design taxes on savings to deter agents from using this extra ability to borrow and lend?

For any incentive-compatible allocation, there are many such tax schedules, but Werning is able to provide a complete characterization of the entire set. This characterization turns out to be particularly interesting when skills evolve according to a Markov process with a continuous transition density. In that case, any incentive-compatible allocation can be supported using a tax schedule that satisfies two properties. First, the tax schedule is differentiable with respect to period t savings, when the derivative is evaluated at agents' equilibrium savings levels. Second, the tax on period t savings does not depend on labor income in period $(t + 1)$. (Note that section 4.3.3 shows that it is impossible to construct an optimal tax schedule that satisfies these two properties when skills have a finite support.)

In this differentiable tax system, the marginal tax rate on savings is equal to the wedge between the interest rate R and the shadow interest rate associated with the allocation. In the special case of preferences that are additively separable between consumption and leisure, we know from our analysis in chapter 3 that shadow interest rates in an optimal allocation are never larger than, and are typically lower than, the interest rate R. Hence, with additively separable preferences, the marginal tax rate on period t savings is typically positive in any optimal tax schedule that is differentiable and independent from period $(t + 1)$ labor income.

Werning's derivation does assume that preferences are additively separable over dates and states. However, he allows preferences to be nonseparable between consumption and leisure. This ability to handle this broader class of preferences makes Werning's construction especially appealing. Werning's construction also suggests that in the context of the new dynamic public finance, it may be better to use processes with continuous densities to model the evolution of the underlying shocks. The next section underscores this message.

7.2   New Solution Methods

Chapter 6 proposed a way of computing optimal taxes in model economies in which skills are Markov. The proposed method is, at best, computationally intensive. It can be implemented if the state space of the Markov chain has only two elements (Fernandes and Phelan 2000), but is probably impractical otherwise.[1] Recent work by Kapicka (2008) and Pavan et al. (2008) suggests that it may be easier to proceed if the set Θ of skills is actually an interval, and the transition density $\pi(\theta_t \mid \theta_{t-1})$ is differentiable with respect to θ_{t-1}.

To understand the basic logic, it is helpful to consider a two-period model with hidden skills. In period 1, agents' skills are drawn from the density π_1, which

---

[1] Fukushima and Waki (2009) generalize the approach in chapter 6 to design a solution method that is practical for a larger class of transition matrices. As of this writing, their method does require that the *rank* of the transition matrix be 3. Such Markov chains are nongeneric, given a state space that has more than three elements. However, Fukushima and Waki argue that it should be possible to use their method to construct approximate solutions for a wide class of Markov chains.

is continuous over an interval $\Theta = [\underline{\theta}, \bar{\theta}]$. The draws are i.i.d. over agents, so that there is no aggregate risk. Then, conditional on θ_1, agents' skills in period 2 are drawn from the density $\pi_2(\theta_2 \mid \theta_1)$. Here, π_2 is continuous with respect to θ_2 (over Θ) and differentiable with respect to θ_1. Again, conditional on θ_1, the draws are i.i.d. over agents. Agents have a momentary utility function of the form $u(c, y/\theta)$ such that both utility and marginal utility are nonnegative and bounded from above.

Suppose (c, y) is an allocation in this setting. Define

$$W(\theta_1, \hat{\theta}_1)$$

$$= \int_{\Theta} u\left(c_2(\hat{\theta}_1, \theta_2), \frac{y_2(\hat{\theta}_1, \theta_2)}{\theta_2}\right) \pi_2(\theta_2 \mid \theta_1) \, d\theta_2 \quad (7.1)$$

to be the agent's period 2 (*ex ante*) continuation utility. If the agent acts as if his skill realization is $\hat{\theta}_1$, then he gets the continuation utility function $W(\cdot, \hat{\theta}_1)$, as a function of his true type θ_1. Thus, W is the analog of the continuation utility vector that we used in section 6.1.2. The allocation (c, y) is incentive-compatible if and only if

$$u\left(c_1(\theta_1), \frac{y_1(\theta_1)}{\theta_1}\right) + \beta W(\theta_1, \theta_1)$$

$$\geqslant u\left(c_1(\hat{\theta}_1), \frac{y_1(\hat{\theta}_1)}{\theta_1}\right) + \beta W(\theta_1, \hat{\theta}_1)$$

$$\text{for all } \theta_1, \hat{\theta}_1,$$

$$u\left(c_2(\theta_1, \theta_2), \frac{y_2(\theta_1, \theta_2)}{\theta_2}\right)$$

$$\geqslant u\left(c_2(\theta_1, \hat{\theta}_2), \frac{y_2(\theta_1, \hat{\theta}_2)}{\theta_2}\right)$$

$$\text{for all } \theta_1, \theta_2, \hat{\theta}_2 \text{ in } \Theta.$$

These inequalities suggest that, to verify incentive-compatibility, we need to know the entire continuation utility function W. From a computational point of view, keeping track of this much information in the planner's problem would be impossible.

However, it is possible to create a *relaxed problem* that has a simpler recursive structure. The key to doing so is that the transition density π_2 is differentiable with respect to θ_1. Suppose (c, y) is incentive-compatible. Define

$$R(\theta_1, \hat{\theta}_1; c, y) = u(c_1(\hat{\theta}_1), y_1(\hat{\theta}_1)/\theta_1) + \beta W(\theta_1, \hat{\theta}_1)$$
$$(7.2)$$

to be the utility that a type θ_1 agent receives from pretending to have skill $\hat{\theta}_1$, and define

$$R^*(\theta_1; c, y) = R(\theta_1, \theta_1; c, y) \qquad (7.3)$$

to be the utility that a type θ_1 agent gets from not mimicking any other type. The assumption that π_2 is differentiable with respect to θ_1 implies that W and R are both differentiable with respect to θ_1. For now, suppose (c_1, y_1, W) are differentiable with respect to $\hat{\theta}_1$. (This strong restriction on the incentive-compatible allocation is not necessary. In the technical notes to this chapter, I generate the same results under the assumption that the allocation is continuous with respect to $\hat{\theta}_1$.)

Since (c, y) is incentive-compatible, the partial derivative $R_2(\theta_1, \theta_1; c, y) = 0$ for all θ_1. Hence

$$R^{*\prime}(\theta_1; c, y) = R_1(\theta_1, \theta_1; c, y) + R_2(\theta_1, \theta_1; c, y)$$
$$= R_1(\theta_1, \theta_1; c, y). \qquad (7.4)$$

It follows from the fundamental theorem of calculus that

$$R^*(\theta_1; c, y) = \int_{\underline{\theta}}^{\theta_1} R_1(\varepsilon, \varepsilon; c, y)\, d\varepsilon + R^*(\underline{\theta}; c, y), \quad (7.5)$$

which can be rewritten as

$$u(c_1(\theta_1), y_1(\theta_1)/\theta_1) + \beta W(\theta_1, \theta_1)$$

$$= \int_{\underline{\theta}}^{\theta_1} \left[-u_y\left(c_1(\varepsilon), \frac{y_1(\varepsilon)}{\varepsilon}\right) \frac{y_1(\varepsilon)}{\varepsilon^2} + \beta W_1(\varepsilon, \varepsilon) \right] d\varepsilon$$

$$+ u(c_1(\underline{\theta}), y_1(\underline{\theta})/\underline{\theta}) + \beta W(\underline{\theta}, \underline{\theta}). \tag{7.6}$$

Here, W_1 is the partial derivative of W with respect to its first argument. Checking this necessary condition (7.6) does not require us to know the entire continuation utility function W. Instead, we need only know the level and partial derivative of W at all points at which its arguments are the same. Thus, making sure that (c, y) satisfies local incentive-compatibility, as opposed to global incentive-compatibility, greatly reduces the amount of information that we need to carry forward from one period to the next. Intuitively, to check first-order conditions, we do not need to know all of W. We only need to know how W changes with respect to infinitesimal changes in θ_1 to make sure that agents do not want to mimic another type.

This argument suggests the following approach to solving for optimal allocations. Given a planner's problem, replace the incentive-compatibility constraints with the first-order conditions (7.6). The above paragraph indicates that this relaxed problem has a relatively simply recursive structure (with two state variables instead of a continuum). It is therefore possible to compute its solution numerically (as Kapicka (2008) does).

The resulting allocation solves the relaxed problem. We still need to check if this solution lies in the constraint set of the original problem. We do so by verifying if the putative solution is in fact incentive-compatible. In the technical notes, I show that any element (c, y) of the relaxed problem constraint set is incentive-compatible if it satisfies a particular *endogenous* single-crossing condition (the partial derivative $R_1(\theta_1, \hat{\theta}_1; c, y)$ is nondecreasing in $\hat{\theta}_1$).

7.3 Inputs from the Data

This book characterizes optimal tax systems in dynamic economies. The characterizations are robust (they apply for a wide class of preferences and virtually all data-generation processes for skills). Nonetheless, they are only partial and (largely) qualitative in nature. Going forward, it will be desirable to develop much more complete and quantitative descriptions of optimal tax systems.

We can gain an understanding of how this might work by reading Saez's (2001) classic paper about optimal taxation in static economies. Saez rewrites Mirrlees's (1971) formulas in terms of estimable quantities from the data. The resulting optimal tax formulas depend on the nature of the social welfare function (in terms of how it weights people with different skills). More interestingly, Saez's reconstructed formulas show that, to design the optimal tax schedule, an analyst needs to be able to measure the compensated elasticity of labor supply, the uncompensated elasticity of labor supply, and the cross-sectional density of earnings. (Saez's formulas allow for heterogeneity in the various elasticities, so that the term "the" compensated elasticity is misleading.) By plugging in estimates for these quantities, Saez is able to provide a characterization of the optimal labor income tax schedule.

Of course, Saez's analysis is limited by its static nature. He is forced to ignore the interaction between asset accumulation and labor supply that I have stressed in this book (see chapter 3). Perhaps even more importantly, his approach dispenses with dynamic labor supply issues. Over the course of a lifetime, people make choices that influence their labor productivities at future dates. To properly construct an optimal labor income tax schedule, one needs to take into account the response of these human capital accumulation decisions to changes in taxes.

The new dynamic public finance needs to become quantitative by taking into account the dynamic incentive issues that Saez ignores. The requisite extensions will be nontrivial in nature. To begin with, Saez proceeds by mapping estimates of elasticities into optimal tax formulas. In a dynamic setting, in which agents cannot fully insure against idiosyncratic risk, this approach is considerably less fruitful. There are now a host of relevant elasticities. (How does an agent's period s labor supply and human capital accumulation decisions respond to a change in the wages that he anticipates t years from now, for any s, t?) It is impossible to imagine having sufficient data to estimate these elasticities in a fully flexible fashion. Instead, we should proceed by estimating an appropriate specification for momentary utility functions and discount factors. Functional form restrictions on preferences (of the kind often imposed by macroeconomists) will translate directly into useful restrictions across the various elasticities.

Once we have specified preferences, we need to model the evolution of wages over time. (I do not mean to suggest that it will be desirable to estimate preferences and wages separately; joint estimation might well be preferable.) Estimating this law of motion is challenging. In particular, we face the usual (and important) problem of how to sort out persistent shocks from age/cohort effects.

Finally, I have assumed that agents cannot influence the evolution of skills. More realistically, people differ in their abilities to translate current time into human capital (that is, future wages).[2] In dynamic settings, this form of heterogeneity could play a critical role in shaping optimal taxes. For example, I would conjecture that a desirable tax system would feature higher marginal tax rates on *young* high-income agents as opposed to *old* high-income agents. This kind of age dependence would be useful in generating higher levels of human capital accumulation.[3]

7.4 Summary

Throughout most of this book, I have imposed the restriction that skills evolve according to processes with finite support. In this chapter, I argue that we can make progress by assuming instead that skills evolve according to transitions with continuous densities. Under this assumption, Werning suggests a way to design optimal taxes that works even when preferences are not additively separable between consumption and leisure. We may also be able to design

---

[2] Kapicka (2006) analyzes an optimal tax problem with this kind of heterogeneity. Yazici (2009) addresses optimal taxation in the presence of parental investment into their children's human capital.

[3] Grochulski and Piskorski (2006) study a dynamic optimal tax problem, given that agents have different abilities to translate *consumption* into human capital, and that these consumption investments are unobservable to tax authorities.

tractable solution methods for models in which skills are persistent.

The ultimate goal is to generate *quantitative* results of optimal tax schedules in dynamic economies. This analysis will almost inevitably be grounded in large-scale computational work. It will need to accomplish two related objectives. First, it has to provide computational algorithms that map features of preferences, wage evolution, and human capital accumulation technologies into optimal tax schedules. Second, it has to provide ways to measure these inputs from microeconomic evidence. My hope and expectation is that this two-part agenda will lead to the qualitative lessons of this book being supplanted by more precise quantitative ones in the relatively near future.

7.5 Technical Notes

In this section, I first justify (7.5), assuming that (c, y, W) is continuous with respect to $\hat{\theta}_1$. The argument is based on the proof of theorem 2 in Kapicka (2008). I then show that (c, y) is incentive-compatible if it satisfies an appropriate single-crossing condition. This latter argument is based on the proof of theorem 3 in Kapicka (2008).

As in the text, define

$$R(\theta_1, \hat{\theta}_1) = u(c_1(\hat{\theta}_1), y_1(\hat{\theta}_1)/\theta_1) + \beta W(\theta_1, \hat{\theta}_1),$$
$$(7.7)$$

$$R^*(\theta_1) = u(c_1(\theta_1), y_1(\theta_1)/\theta_1) + \beta W(\theta_1, \theta_1).$$
$$(7.8)$$

By the definition of incentive-compatibility, we know that

$$R(\theta_1 + \eta, \theta_1) - R^*(\theta_1 + \eta) \leqslant 0.$$

Hence, for any $\bar{\theta} > \theta_1 > \theta_0 > \underline{\theta}$,

$$
\int_{\theta_0}^{\theta_1} [R(\varepsilon + \eta, \varepsilon) - R(\varepsilon, \varepsilon)] \, d\varepsilon
$$

$$
= \int_{\theta_0}^{\theta_1} [R(\varepsilon + \eta, \varepsilon) - R(\varepsilon + \eta, \varepsilon + \eta)] \, d\varepsilon
$$

$$
+ \int_{\theta_0}^{\theta_1} [R(\varepsilon + \eta, \varepsilon + \eta) - R(\varepsilon, \varepsilon)] \, d\varepsilon
$$

$$
\leqslant \int_{\theta_0}^{\theta_1} [R^*(\varepsilon + \eta) - R^*(\varepsilon)] \, d\varepsilon
$$

$$
= \int_{\theta_0 + \eta}^{\theta_1 + \eta} R^*(\varepsilon) \, d\varepsilon - \int_{\theta_0}^{\theta_1} R^*(\varepsilon) \, d\varepsilon
$$

$$
= \int_{\theta_1}^{\theta_1 + \eta} R^*(\varepsilon) \, d\varepsilon - \int_{\theta_0}^{\theta_0 + \eta} R^*(\varepsilon) \, d\varepsilon
$$

$$
= \int_{0}^{\eta} [R^*(\theta_1 + \tilde{\eta}) - R^*(\theta_0 + \tilde{\eta})] \, d\tilde{\eta}.
$$

Multiply through by η^{-1} and take limits as η converges to zero. We obtain

$$
\lim_{\eta \to 0_-} \eta^{-1} \int_{0}^{\eta} [R^*(\theta_1 + \tilde{\eta}) - R^*(\theta_0 + \tilde{\eta})] \, d\tilde{\eta}
$$

$$
\leqslant \int_{\theta_0}^{\theta_1} R_1(\varepsilon, \varepsilon) \, d\varepsilon
$$

$$
\leqslant \lim_{\eta \to 0_+} \eta^{-1} \int_{0}^{\eta} [R^*(\theta_1 + \tilde{\eta}) - R^*(\theta_0 + \tilde{\eta})] \, d\tilde{\eta}.
$$

By the fundamental theorem of calculus, and because R^* is continuous, the two limits converge to $R^*(\theta_1) - R^*(\theta_0)$. Taking the limit of θ_0 to $\underline{\theta}$ generates the restriction (7.5).

Next, suppose (c, y) satisfies (7.6) and the partial derivative $R_1(\theta_1, \hat{\theta}_1)$ is nondecreasing in $\hat{\theta}_1$. If $\theta_1 > \hat{\theta}_1$, then

$$R(\theta_1, \theta_1) - R(\hat{\theta}_1, \hat{\theta}_1) = \int_{\hat{\theta}_1}^{\theta_1} R_1(\varepsilon, \varepsilon) \, \mathrm{d}\varepsilon$$

$$\geqslant \int_{\hat{\theta}_1}^{\theta_1} R_1(\varepsilon, \hat{\theta}_1) \, \mathrm{d}\varepsilon$$

$$= R(\theta_1, \hat{\theta}_1) - R(\hat{\theta}_1, \hat{\theta}_1)$$

and so $R(\theta_1, \hat{\theta}_1) \leqslant R(\theta_1, \theta_1)$. If $\theta_1 < \hat{\theta}_1$, then

$$R(\hat{\theta}_1, \hat{\theta}_1) - R(\theta_1, \theta_1) = \int_{\theta_1}^{\hat{\theta}_1} R_1(\varepsilon, \varepsilon) \, \mathrm{d}\varepsilon$$

$$\leqslant \int_{\theta_1}^{\hat{\theta}_1} R_1(\varepsilon, \hat{\theta}_1) \, \mathrm{d}\varepsilon$$

$$= R(\hat{\theta}_1, \hat{\theta}_1) - R(\theta_1, \hat{\theta}_1),$$

which again implies $R(\theta_1, \theta_1) \geqslant R(\theta_1, \hat{\theta}_1)$.

References

Aguiar, M., and E. Hurst. 2005. Consumption vs expenditure. *Journal of Political Economy* 113:919–48.

Fernandes, A., and C. Phelan. 2000. A recursive formulation for repeated agency with history dependence. *Journal of Economic Theory* 91:223–47.

Fukushima, K., and Y. Waki. 2009. Computing dynamic optimal mechanisms when private shocks are persistent. Working Paper, University of Minnesota.

Grochulski, B., and N. Kocherlakota. 2008. Nonseparable preferences and optimal social security systems. Working Paper, University of Minnesota.

Grochulski, B., and T. Piskorski. 2006. Risky human capital and deferred capital income taxation. Working Paper, Federal Reserve Bank of Richmond.

Kapicka, M. 2006. Optimal income taxation with human capital accumulation and limited record keeping. *Review of Economic Dynamics* 9:612–39.

———. 2008. Efficient allocations in dynamic private information economies with persistent shocks: a first-order approach. Working Paper, University of California-Santa Barbara.

Mirrlees, J. 1971. An exploration in the theory of optimum income taxation. *Review of Economic Studies* 38:175–208.

Pavan, A., I. Segal, and J. Toikka. 2008. Dynamic mechanism design: incentive compatibility, profit maximization and information disclosure. Working Paper, Northwestern University.

Saez, E. 2001. Using elasticities to derive optimal income tax rates. *Review of Economic Studies* 68:205–29.

Werning, I. 2009. Nonlinear capital taxation. Working Paper, MIT.

Yazici, H. 2009. Efficient investment in children and implications for policy. Working Paper, University of Minnesota.

Index